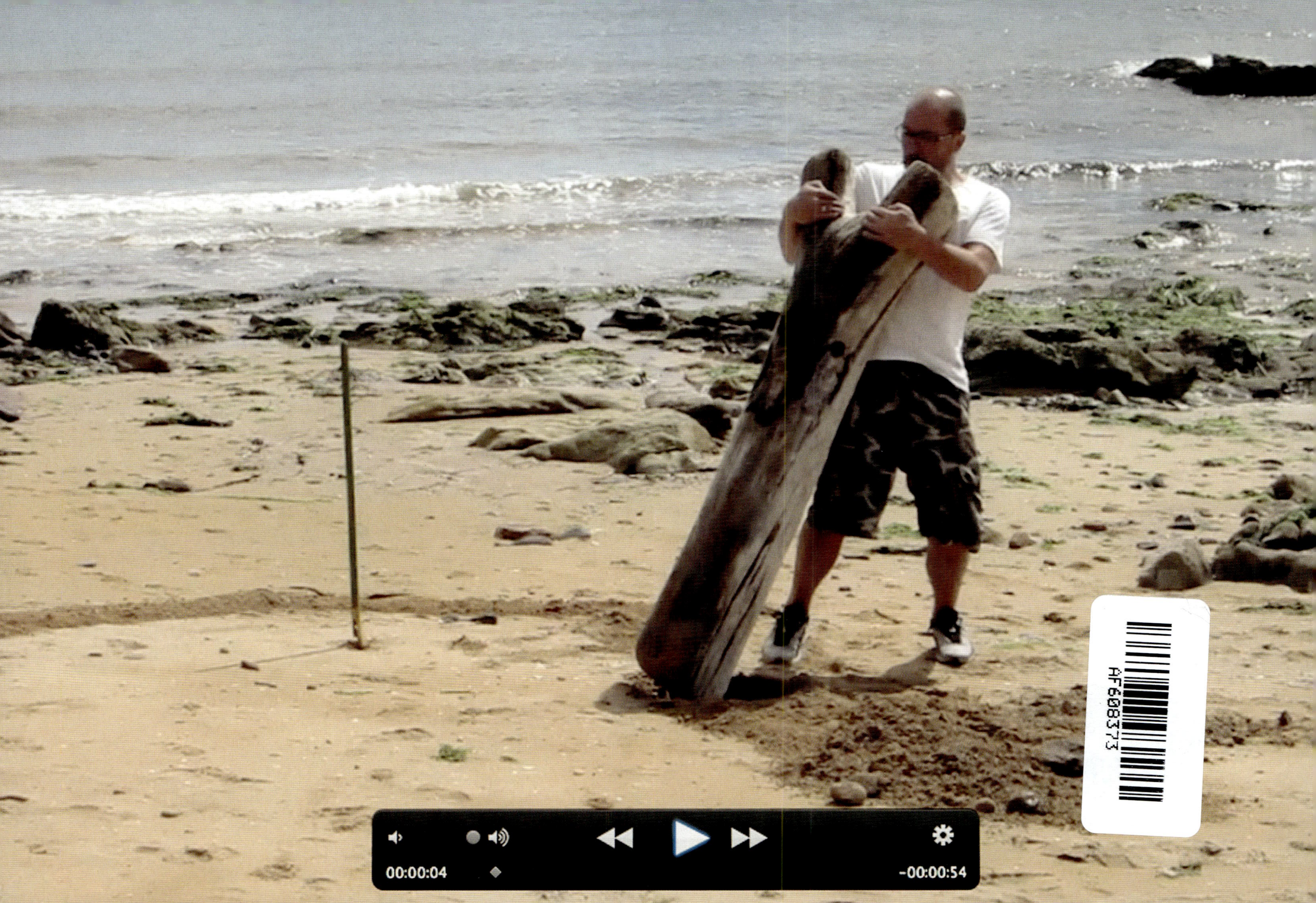
00:00:04
-00:00:54

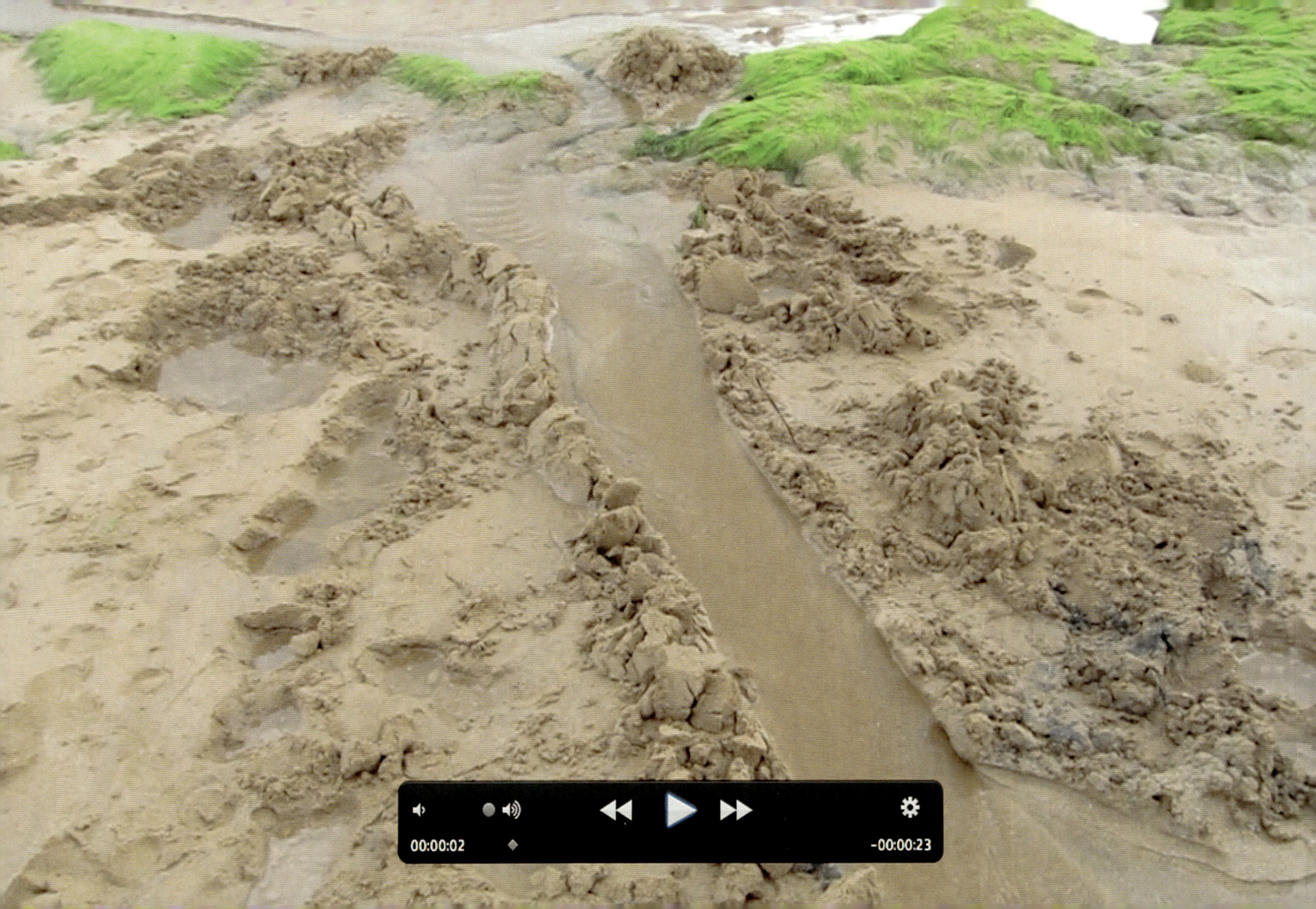
00:00:02
-00:00:23

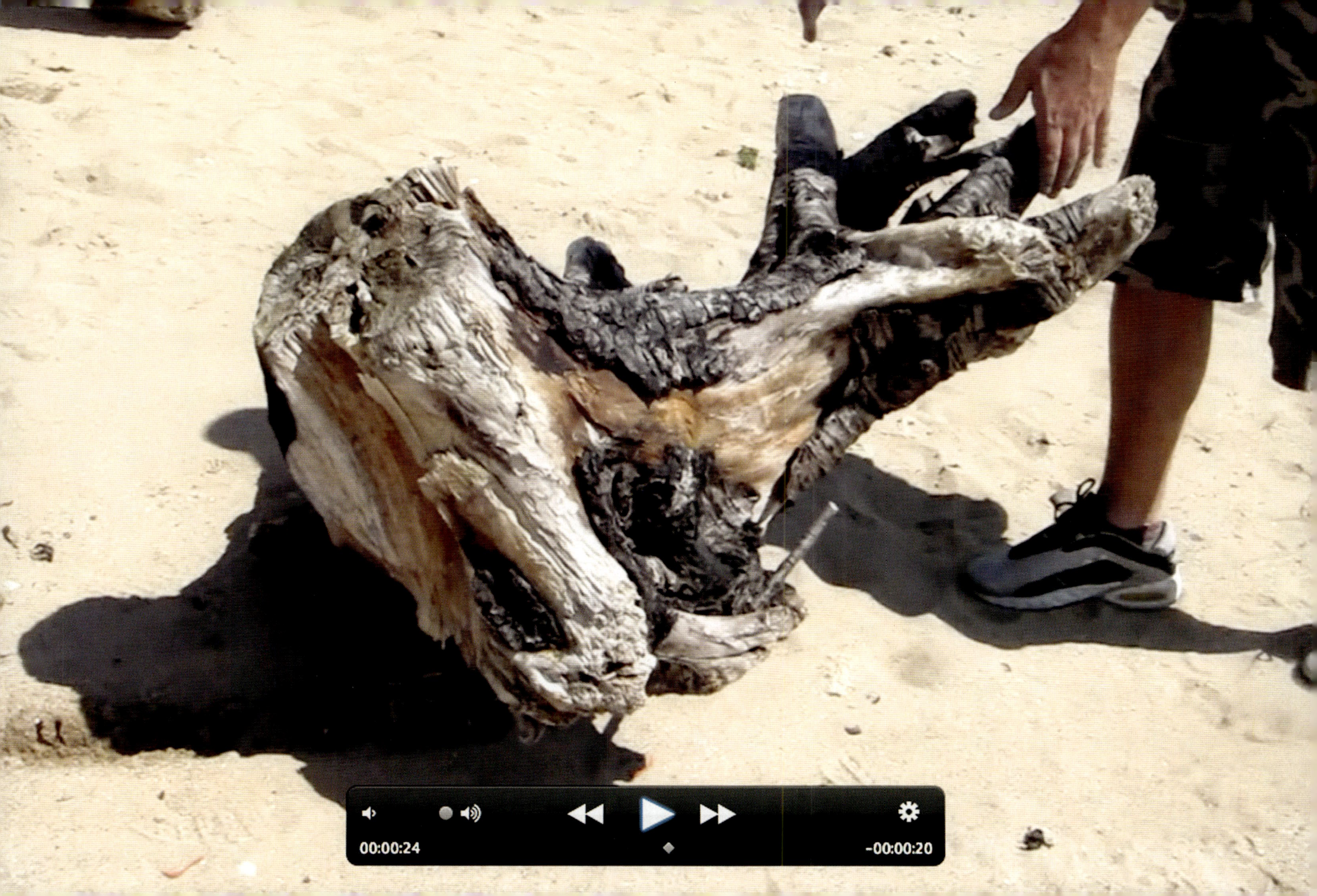
00:00:24
-00:00:20

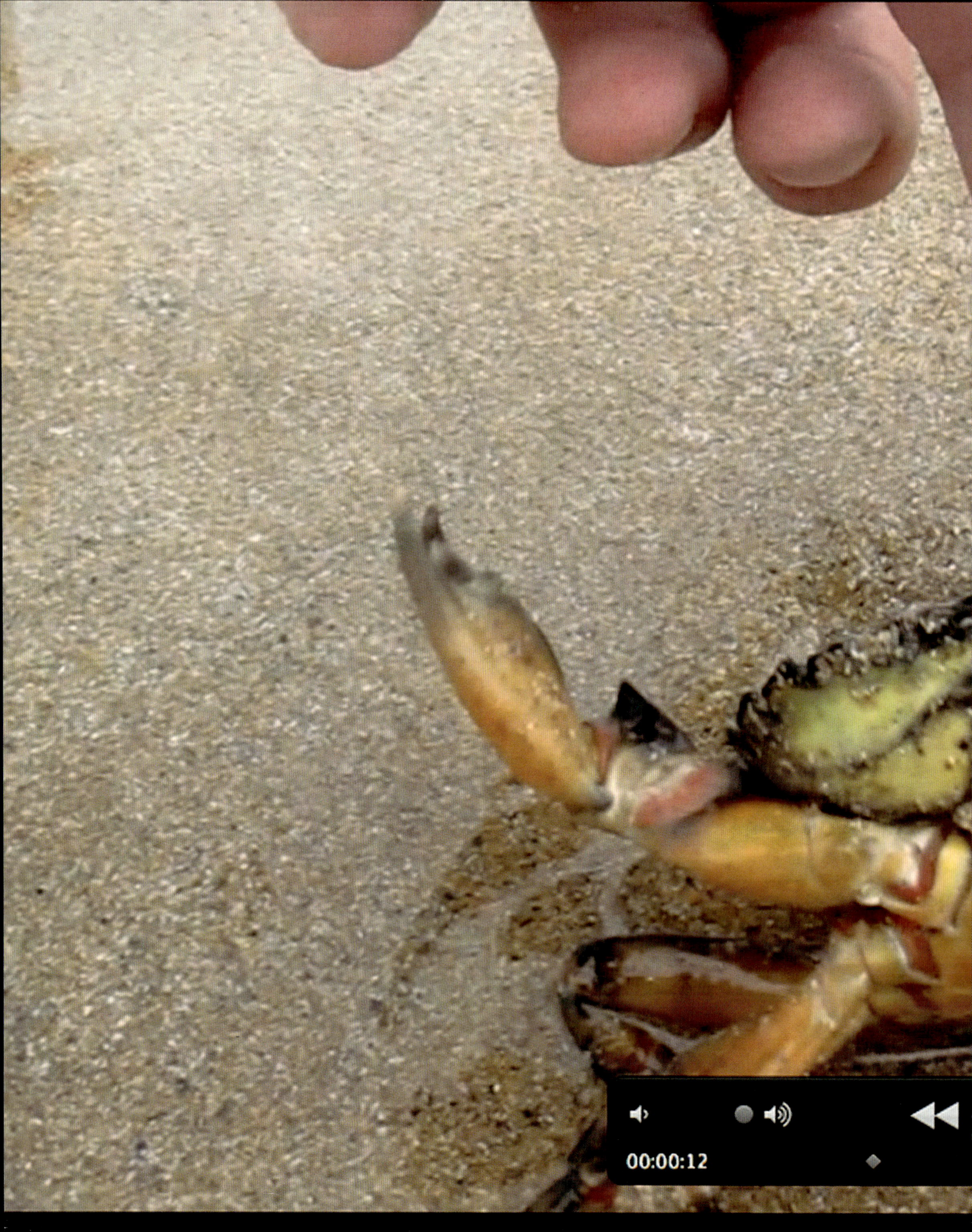
00:00:12

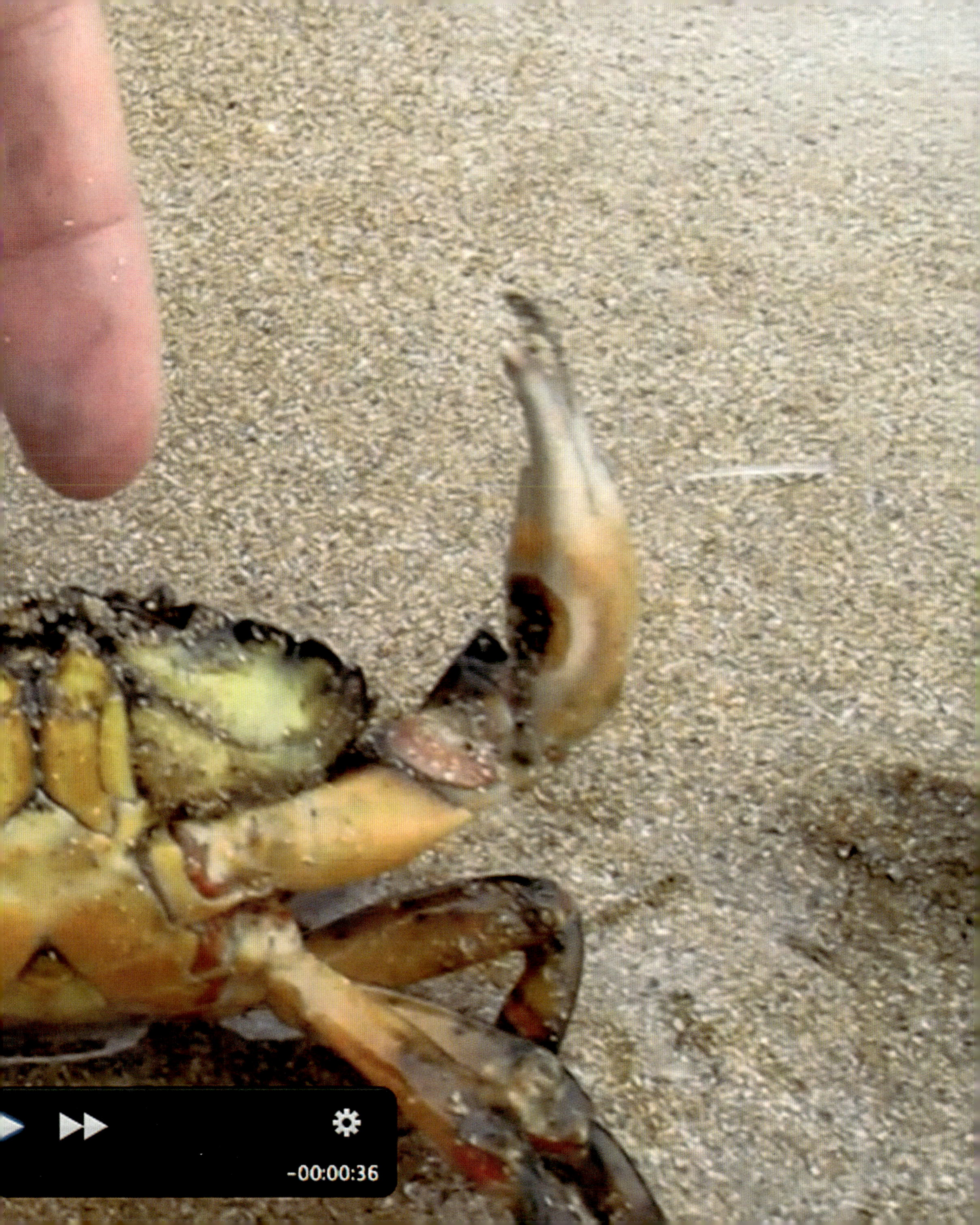
-00:00:36

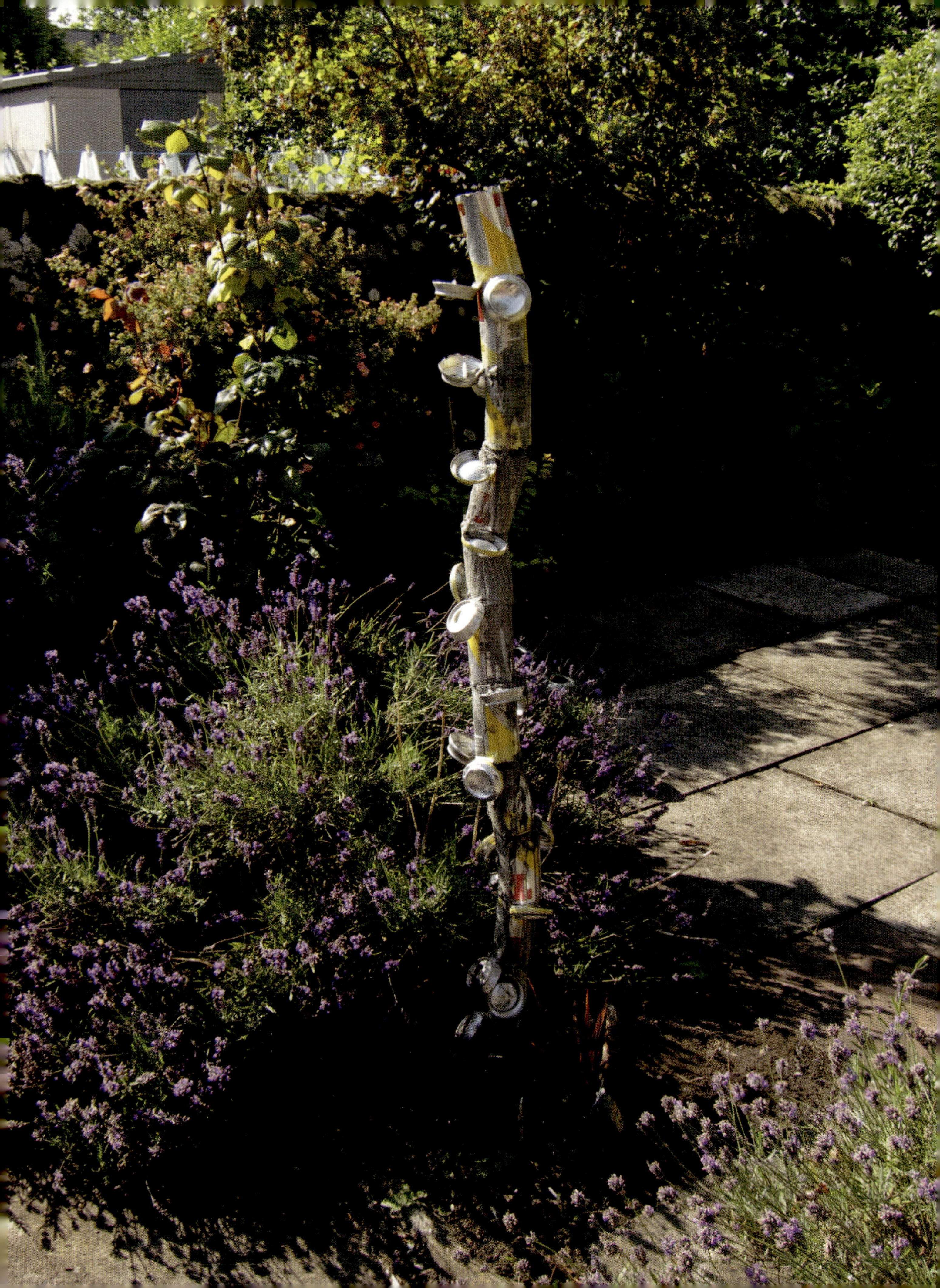

ESTATE OF

KRONOS

by Victor Boullet

Some titles that this publication
has suffered under:

Self Residency
Uranus
The Decadent life of Mr Boullet
What do I care for the twaddle I said yesterday
Soft Mahogany Neck
Neo Conservatism
Flesh Machine
Adidas Monger
Sunday Painter
Land Art Man

I hereby present:
He is an Idiot (.com)
/ all design he did has done for this printed thing /
Please support this Cairo based designer with work
as life has been hard for him and his family.

An index for this publication can be found online
Halls of Justice Painted Green (.com)
...

Victor Boullet is represented by
Anna Franck inc (.com)
campari@annafranckinc.com

Paris / Cairo / Kjelsås / Elie / Anstruther / West Bay
Easter Island / San Francisco / London
Liverpool

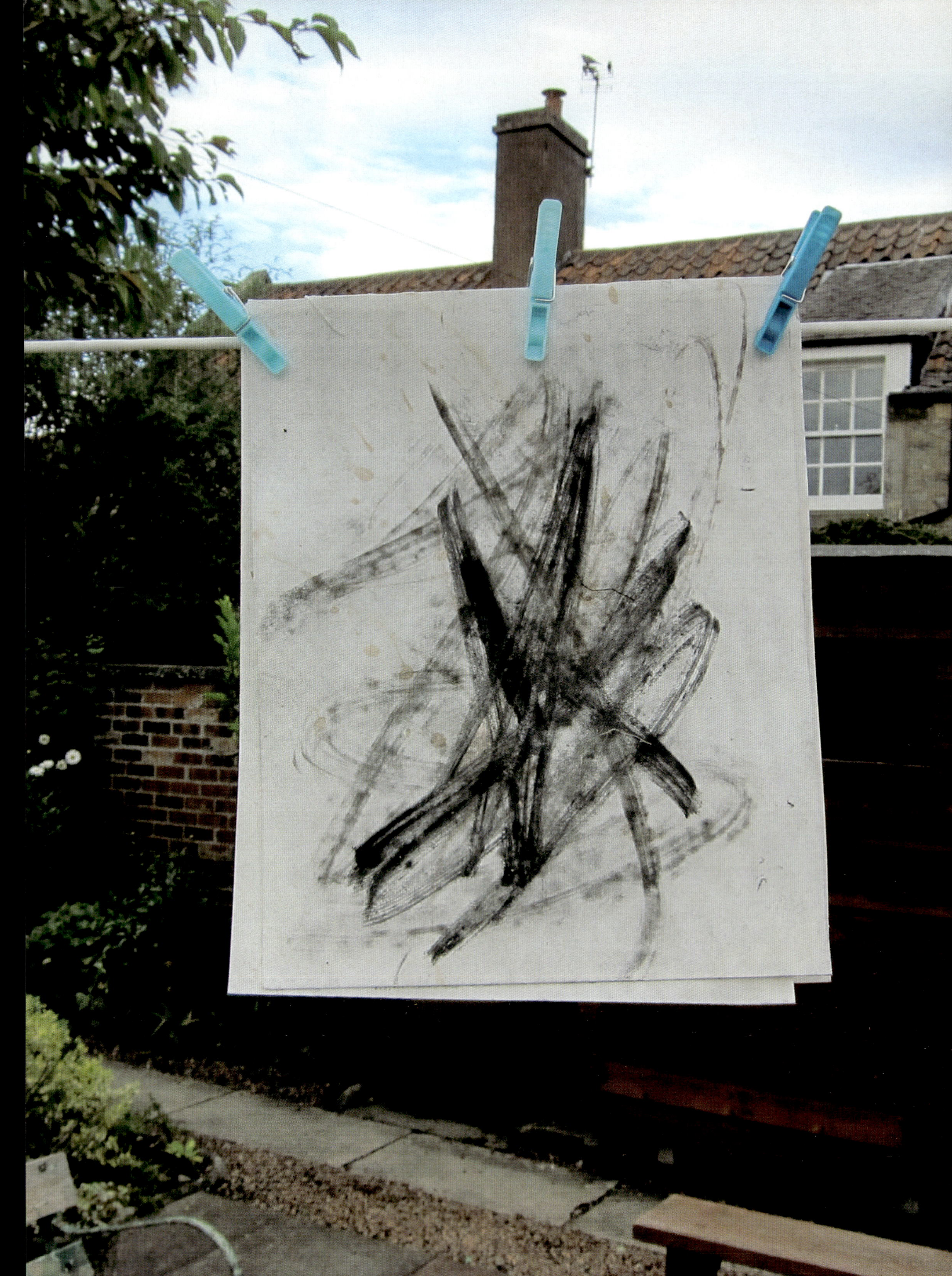

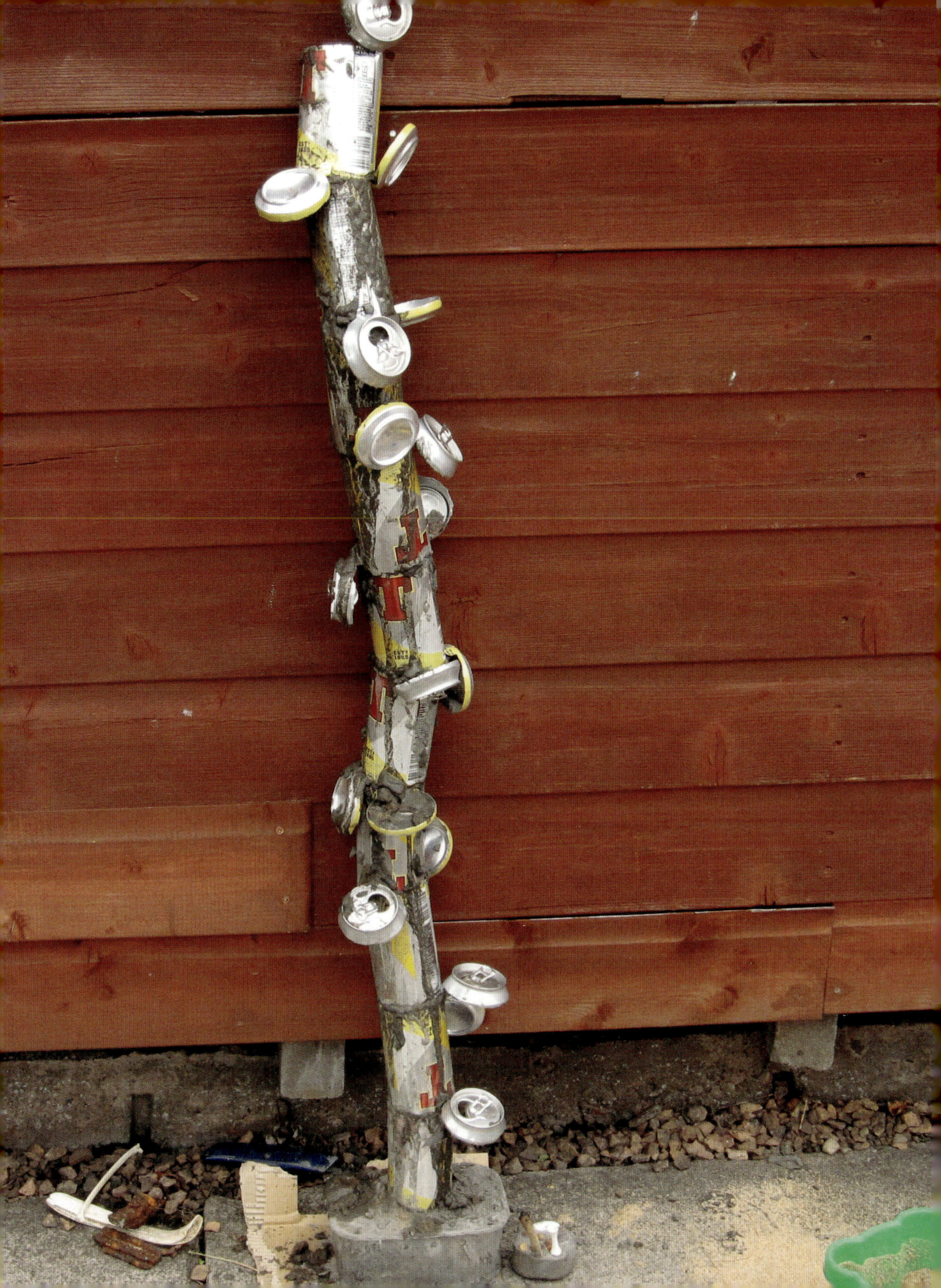

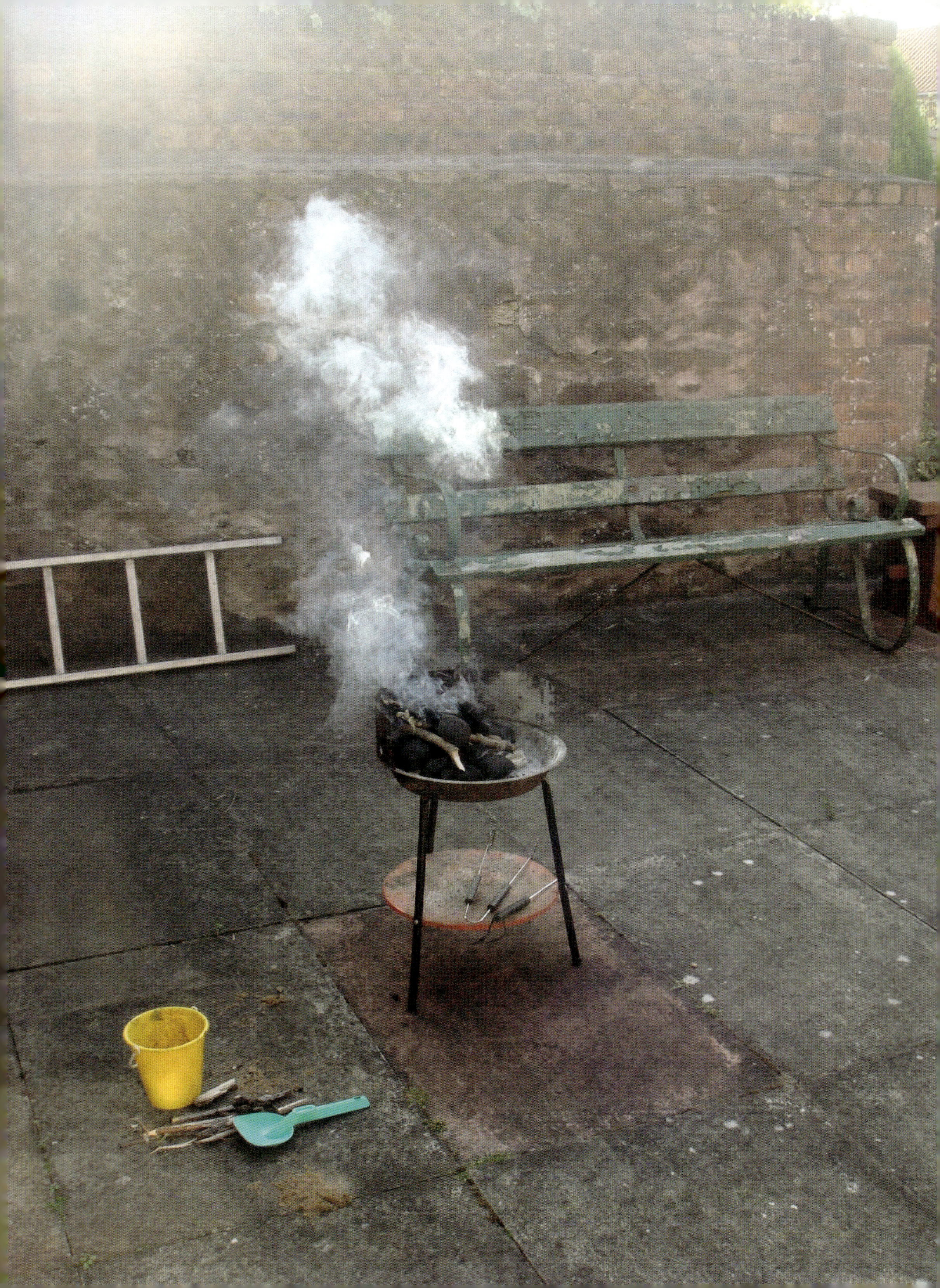

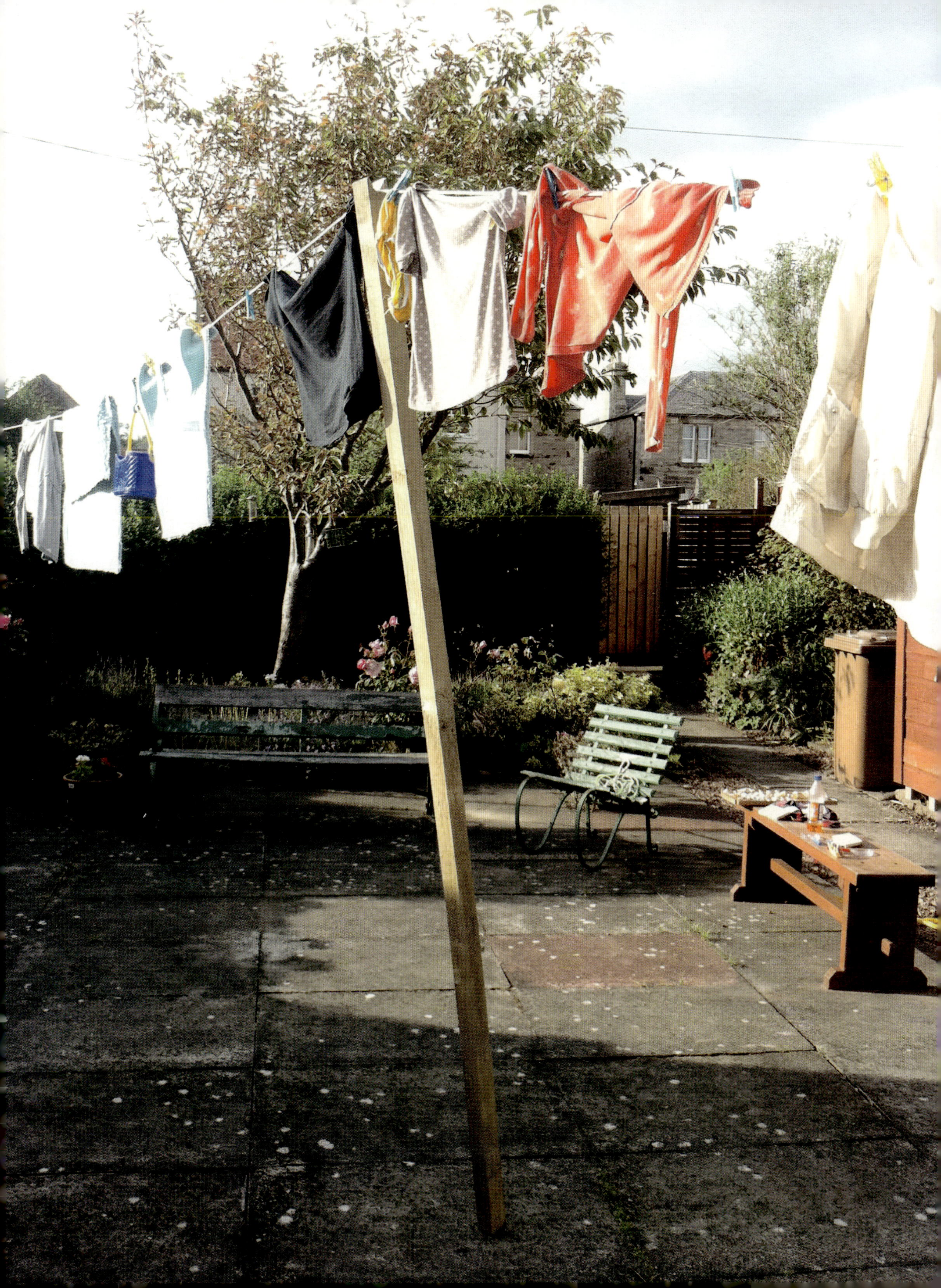

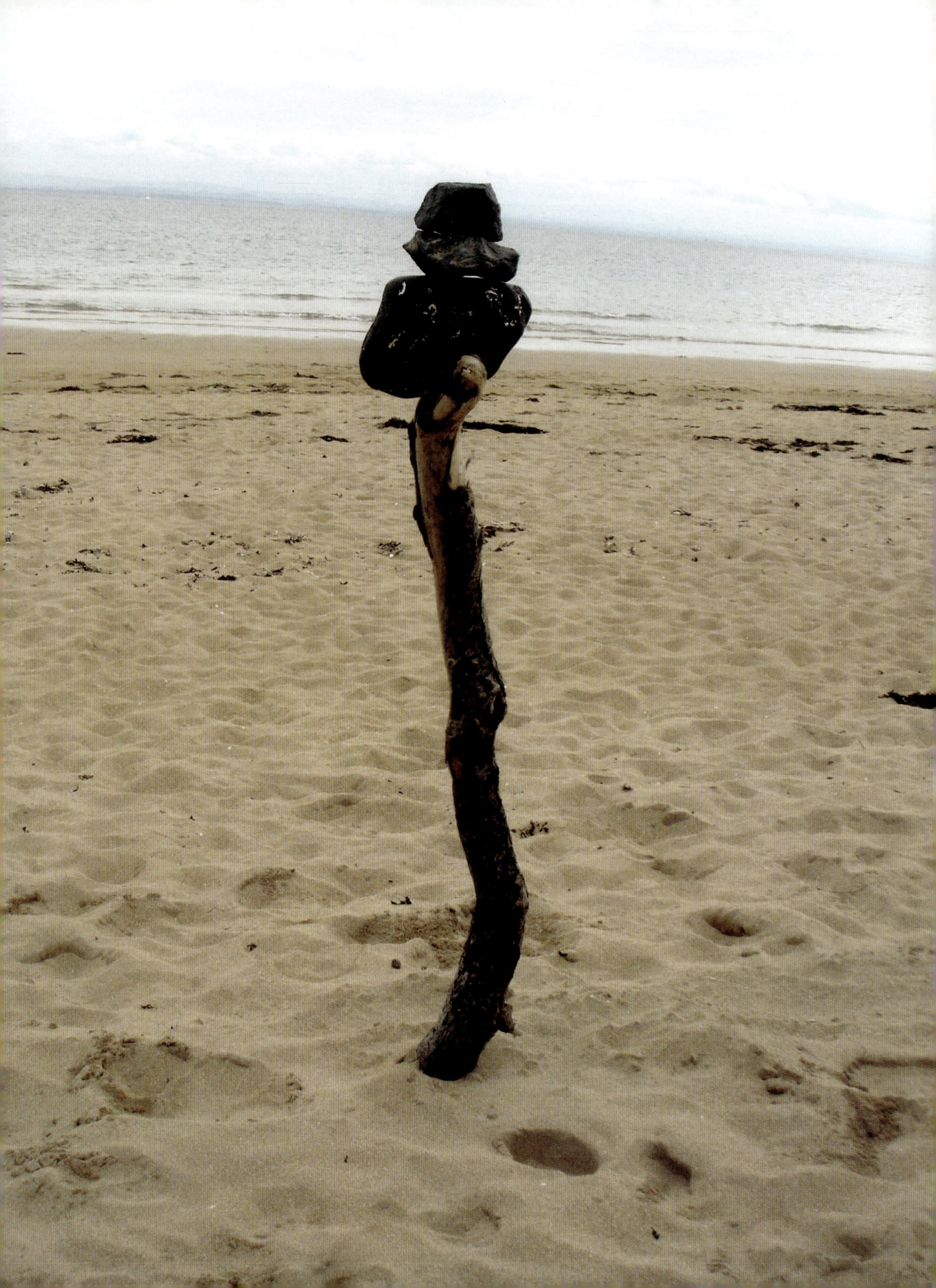

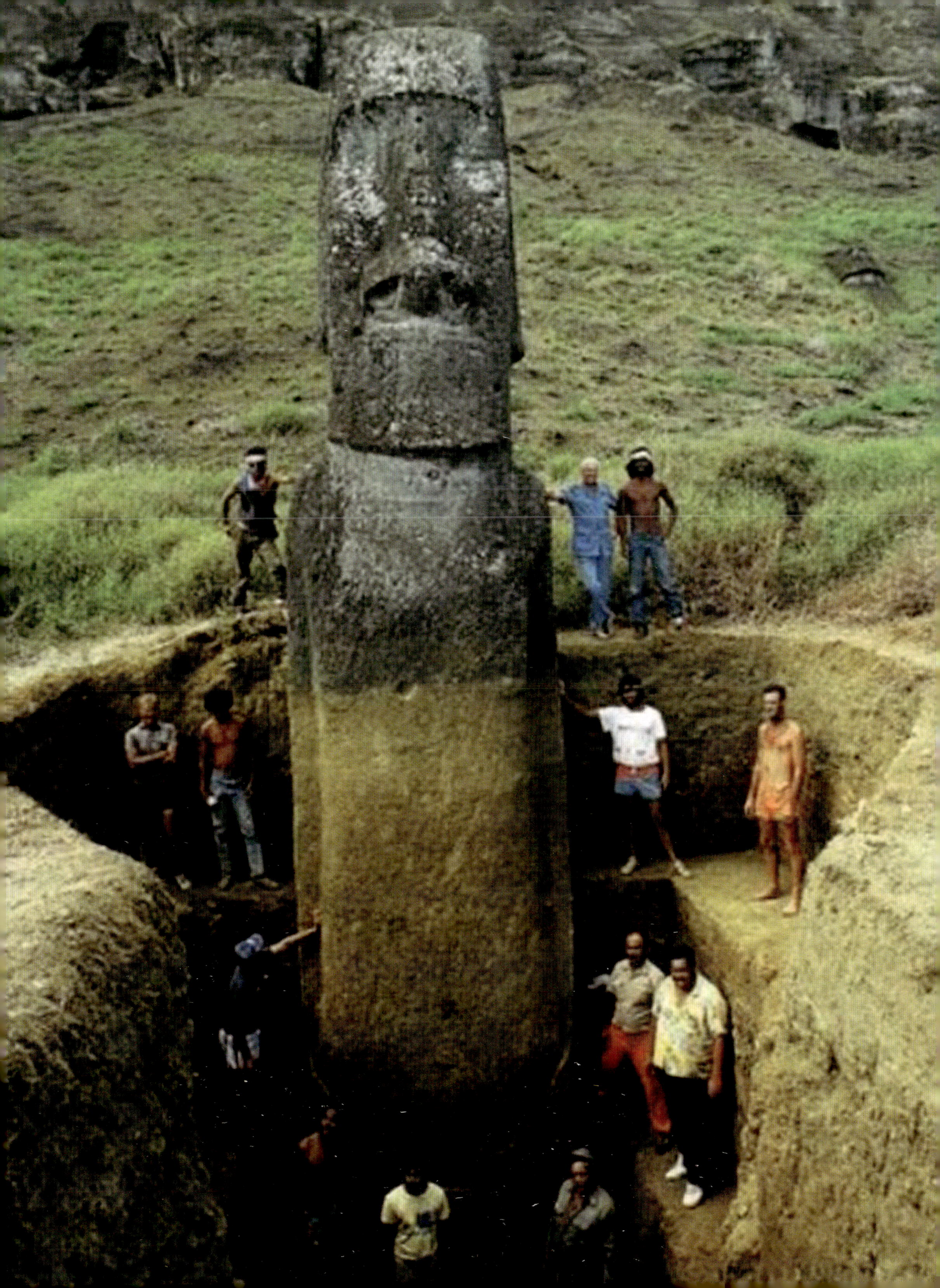

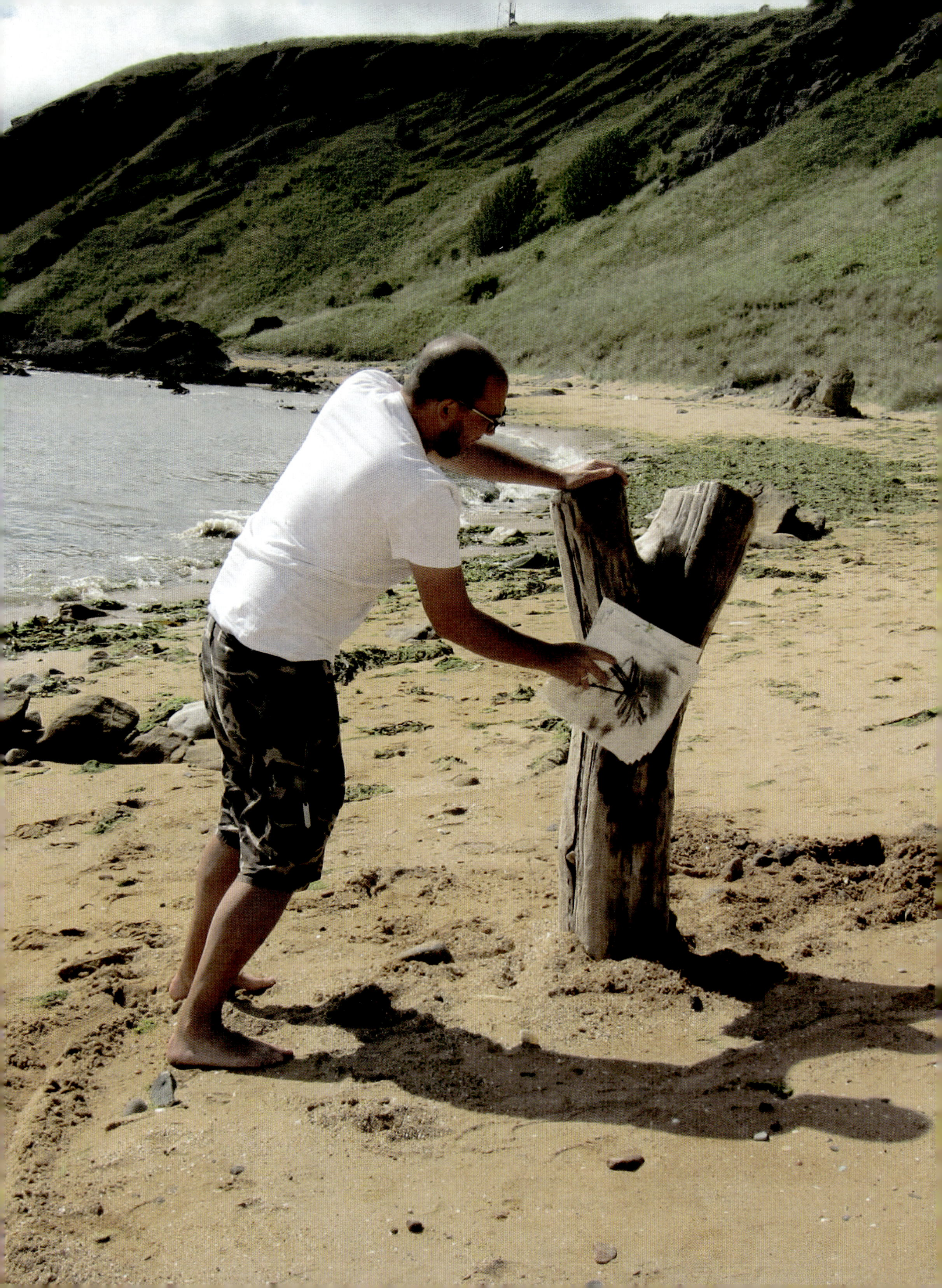

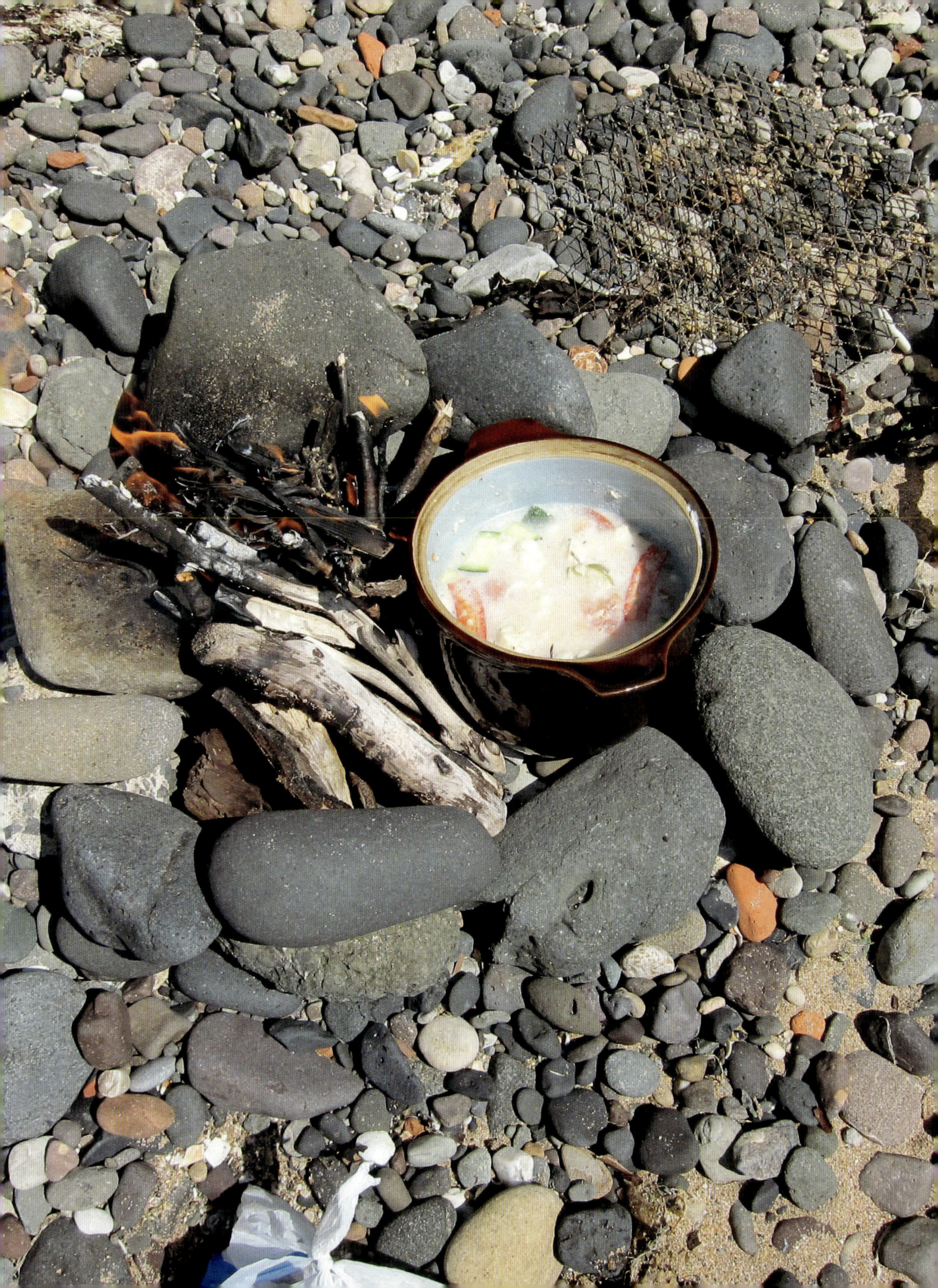

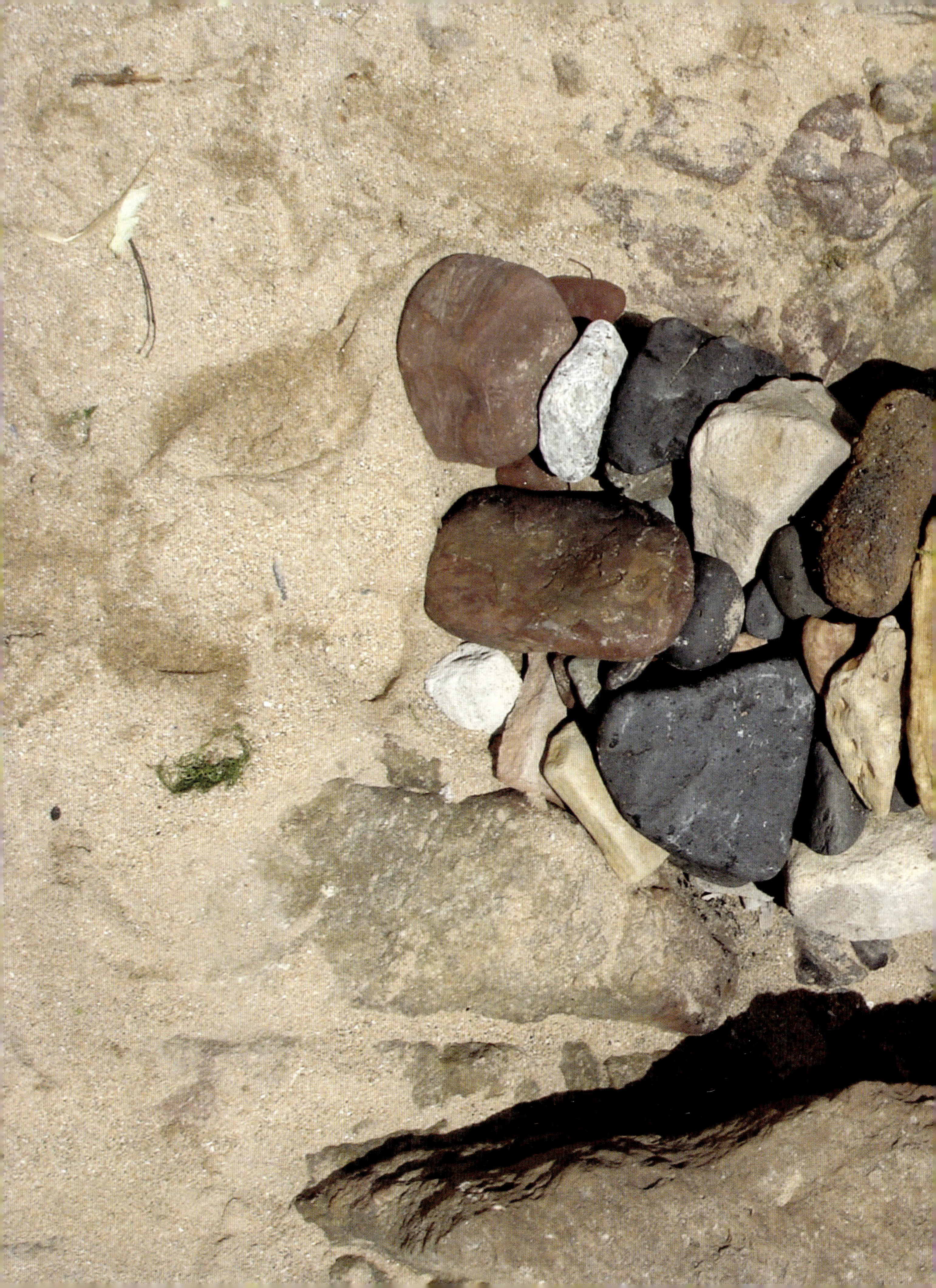

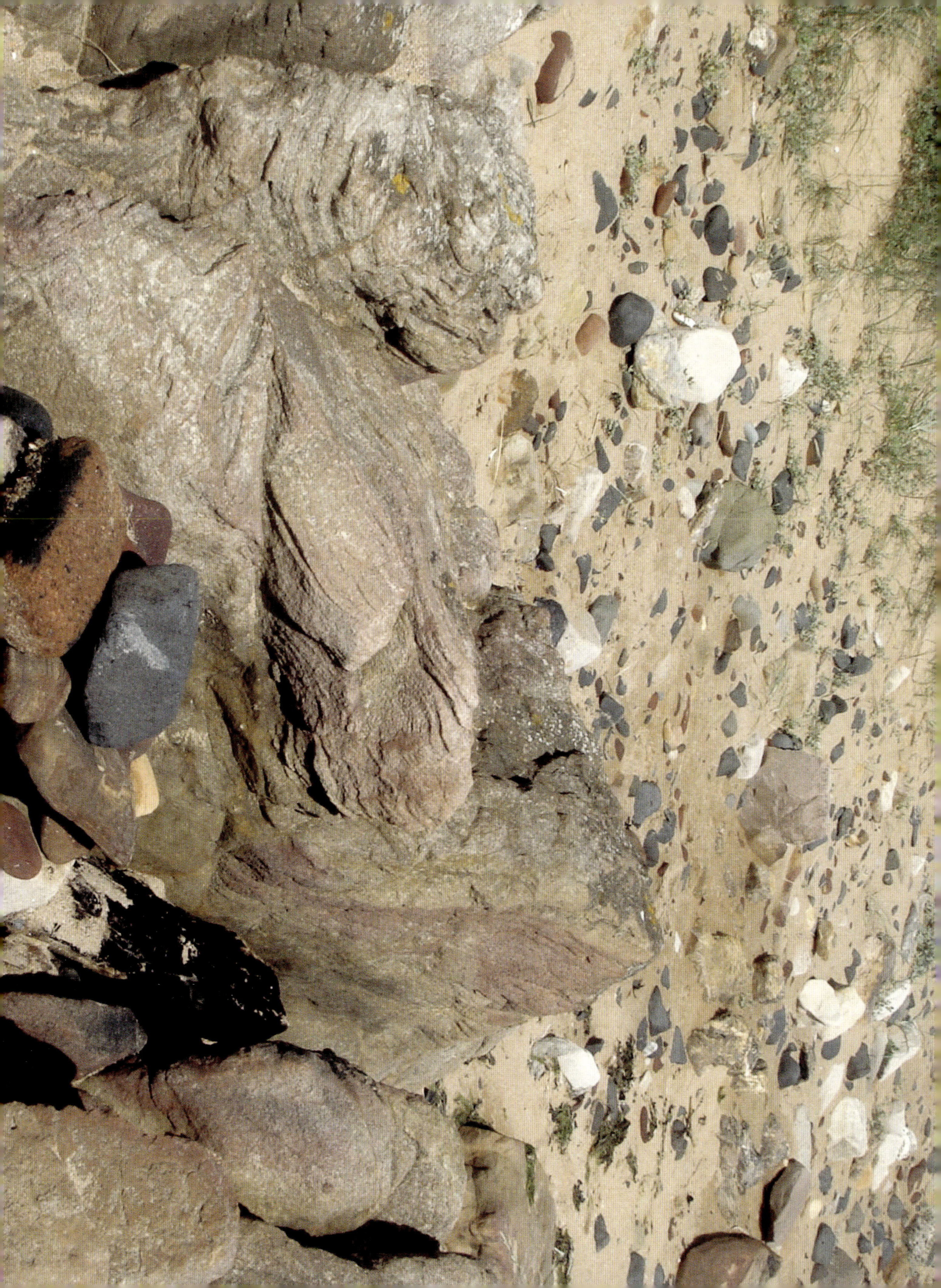

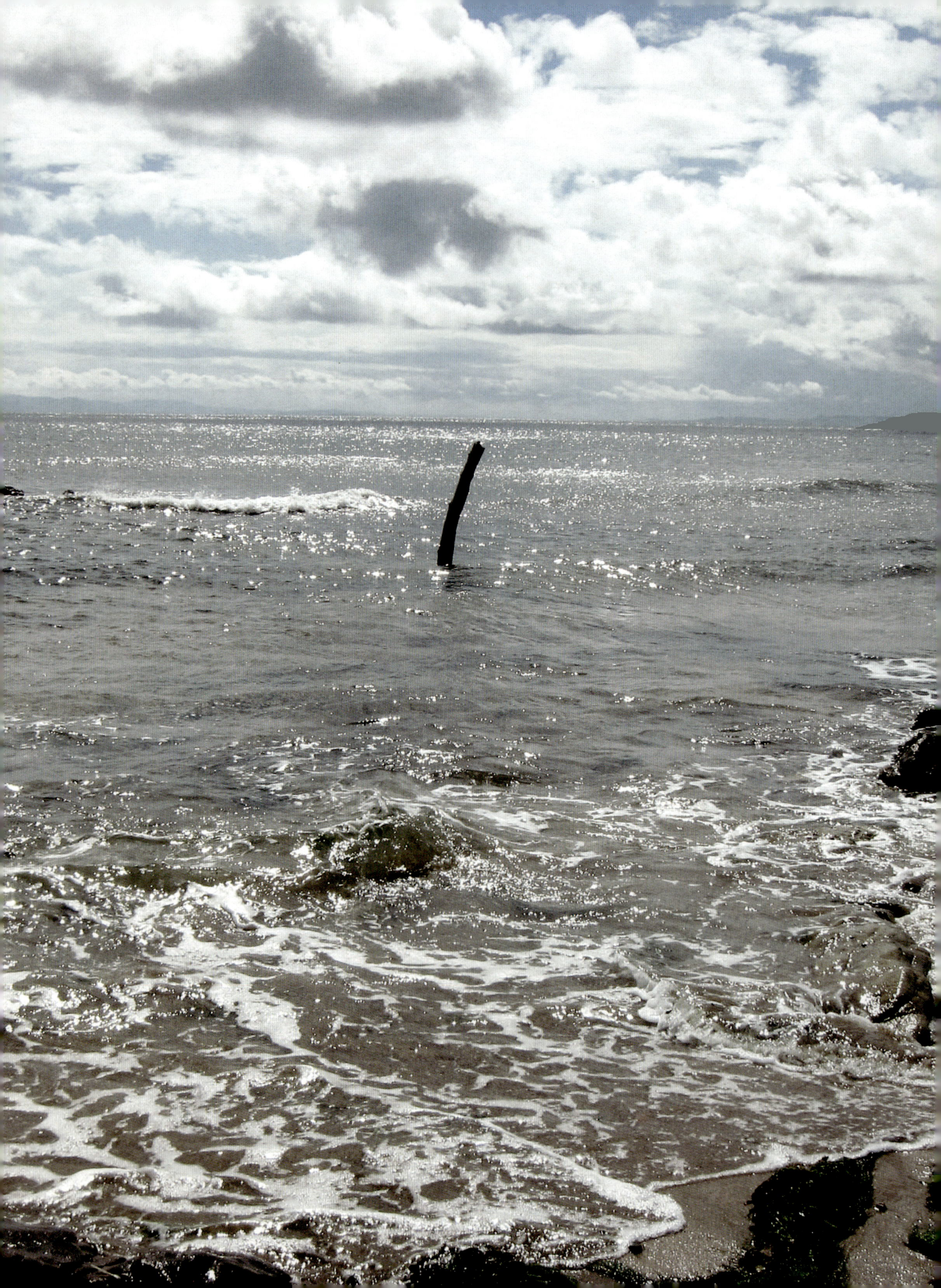

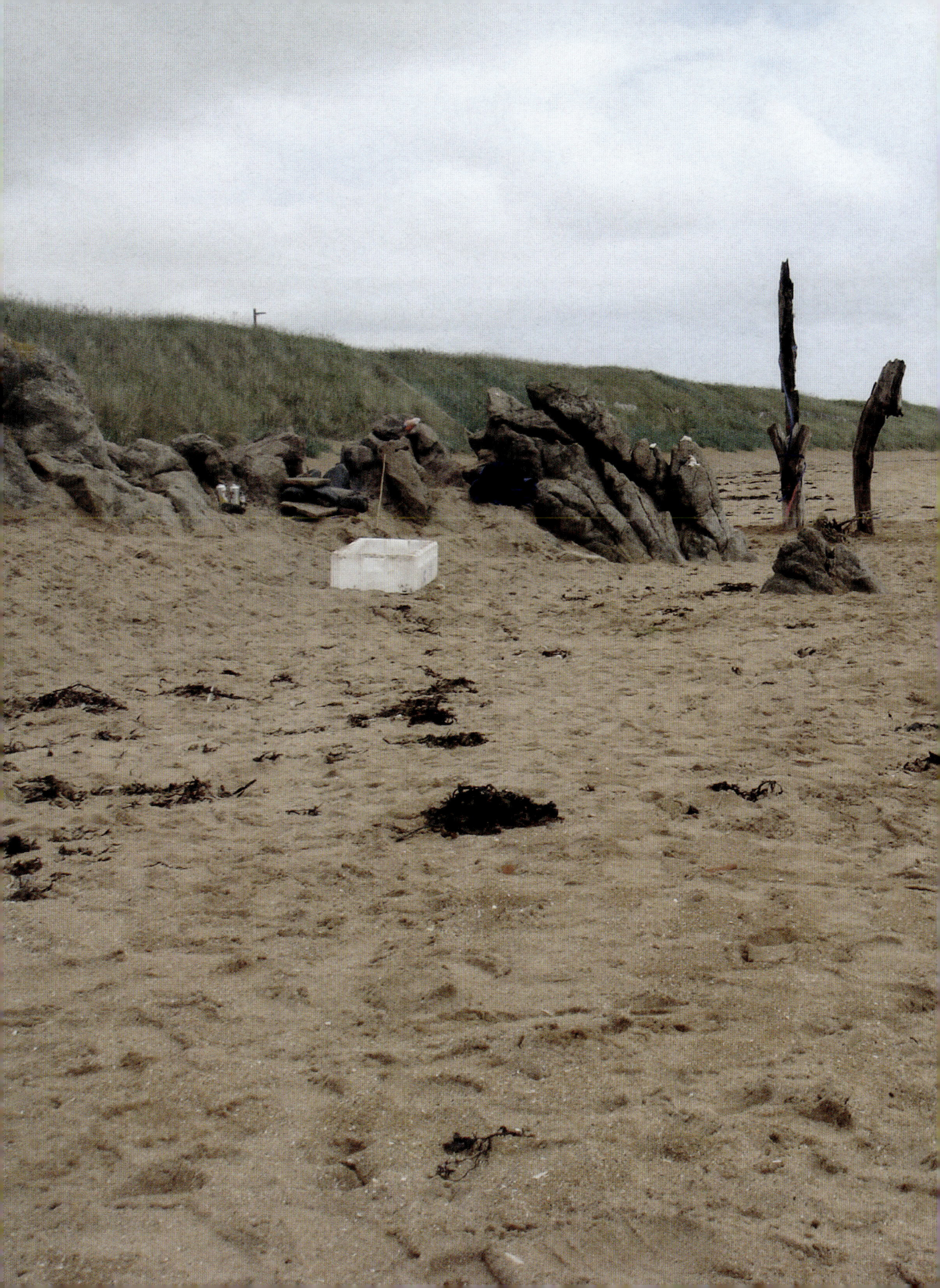

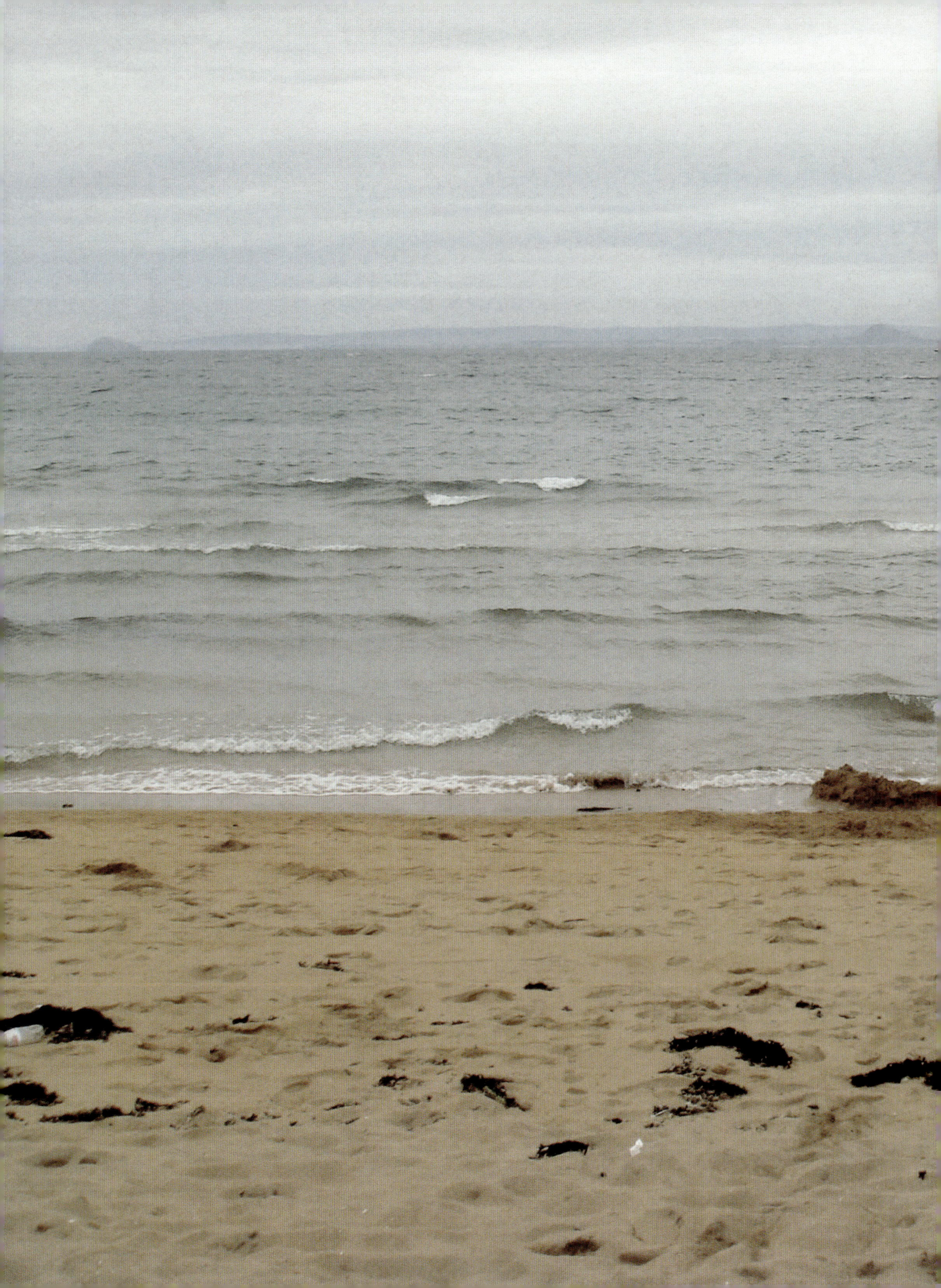

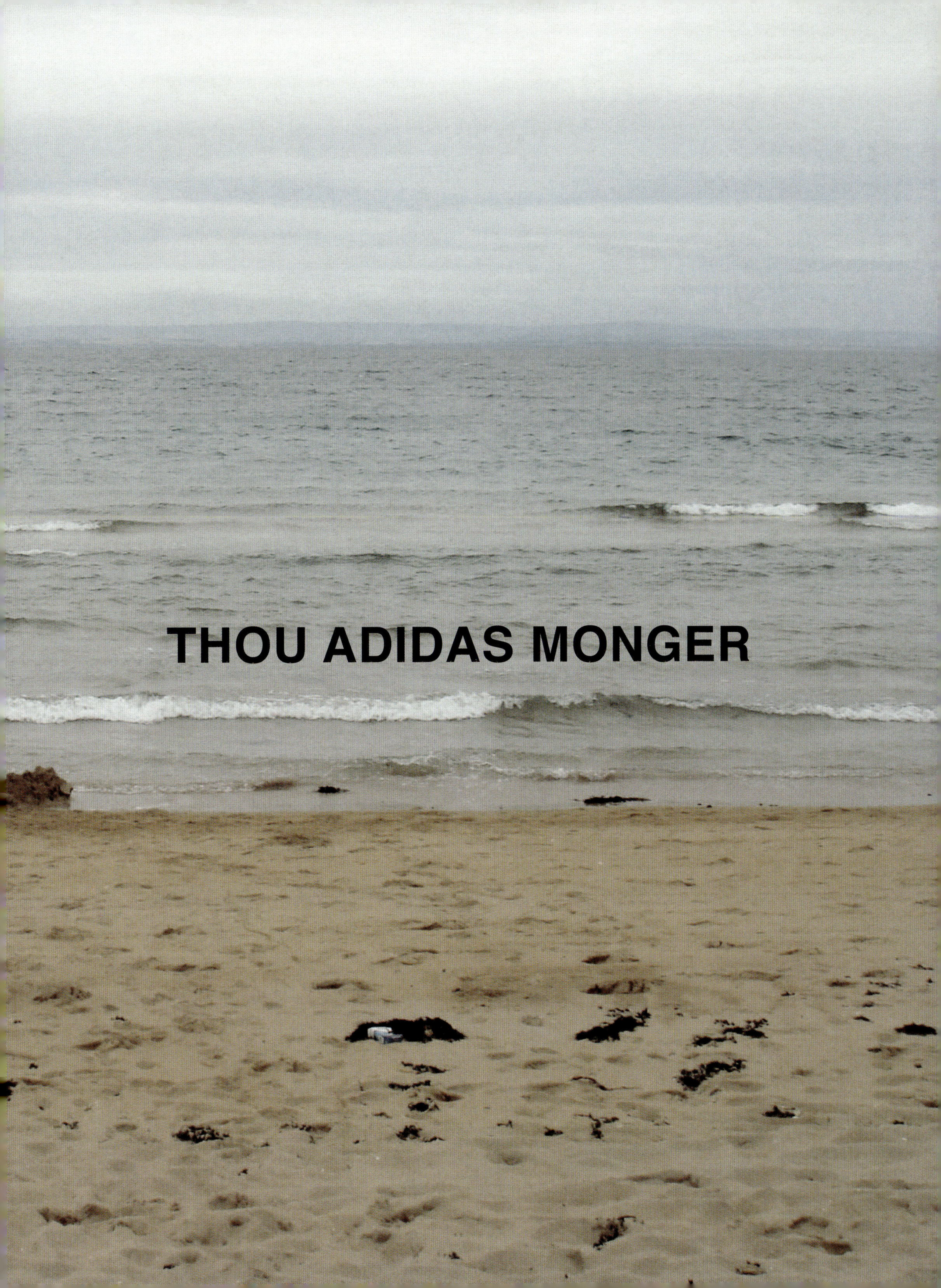

THOU ADIDAS MONGER

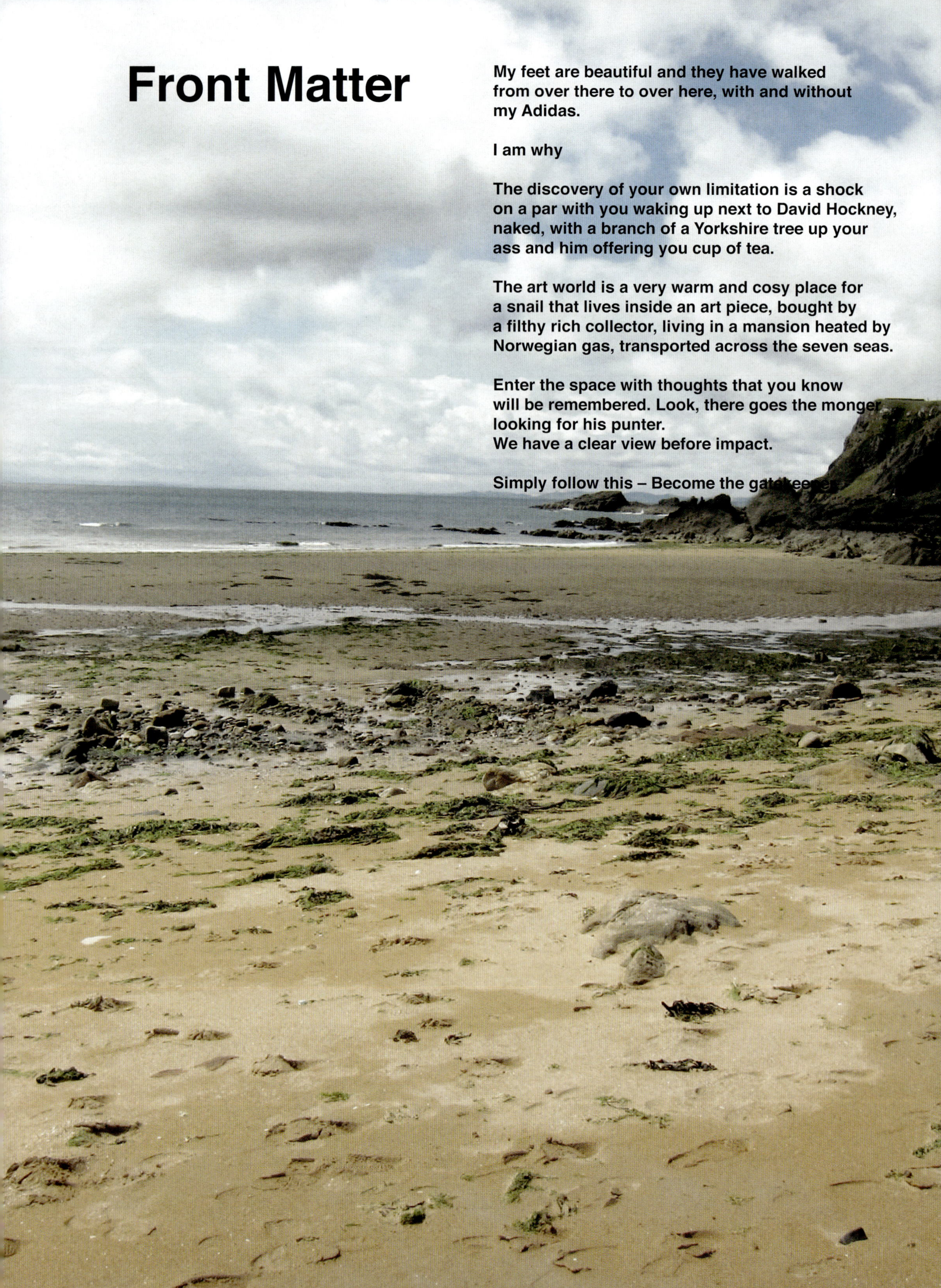

Front Matter

My feet are beautiful and they have walked from over there to over here, with and without my Adidas.

I am why

The discovery of your own limitation is a shock on a par with you waking up next to David Hockney, naked, with a branch of a Yorkshire tree up your ass and him offering you cup of tea.

The art world is a very warm and cosy place for a snail that lives inside an art piece, bought by a filthy rich collector, living in a mansion heated by Norwegian gas, transported across the seven seas.

Enter the space with thoughts that you know will be remembered. Look, there goes the monger looking for his punter.
We have a clear view before impact.

Simply follow this – Become the gatekeeper

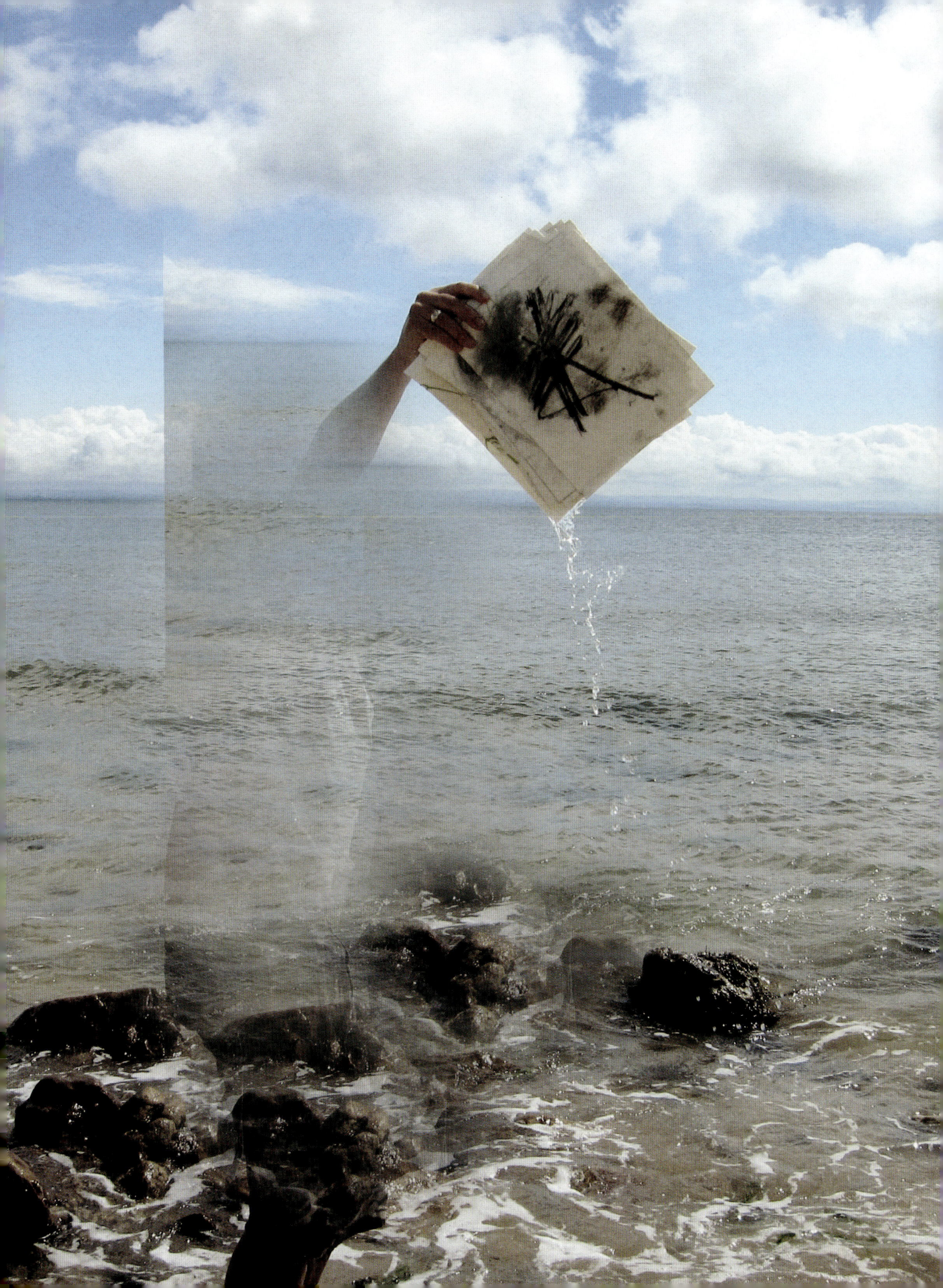

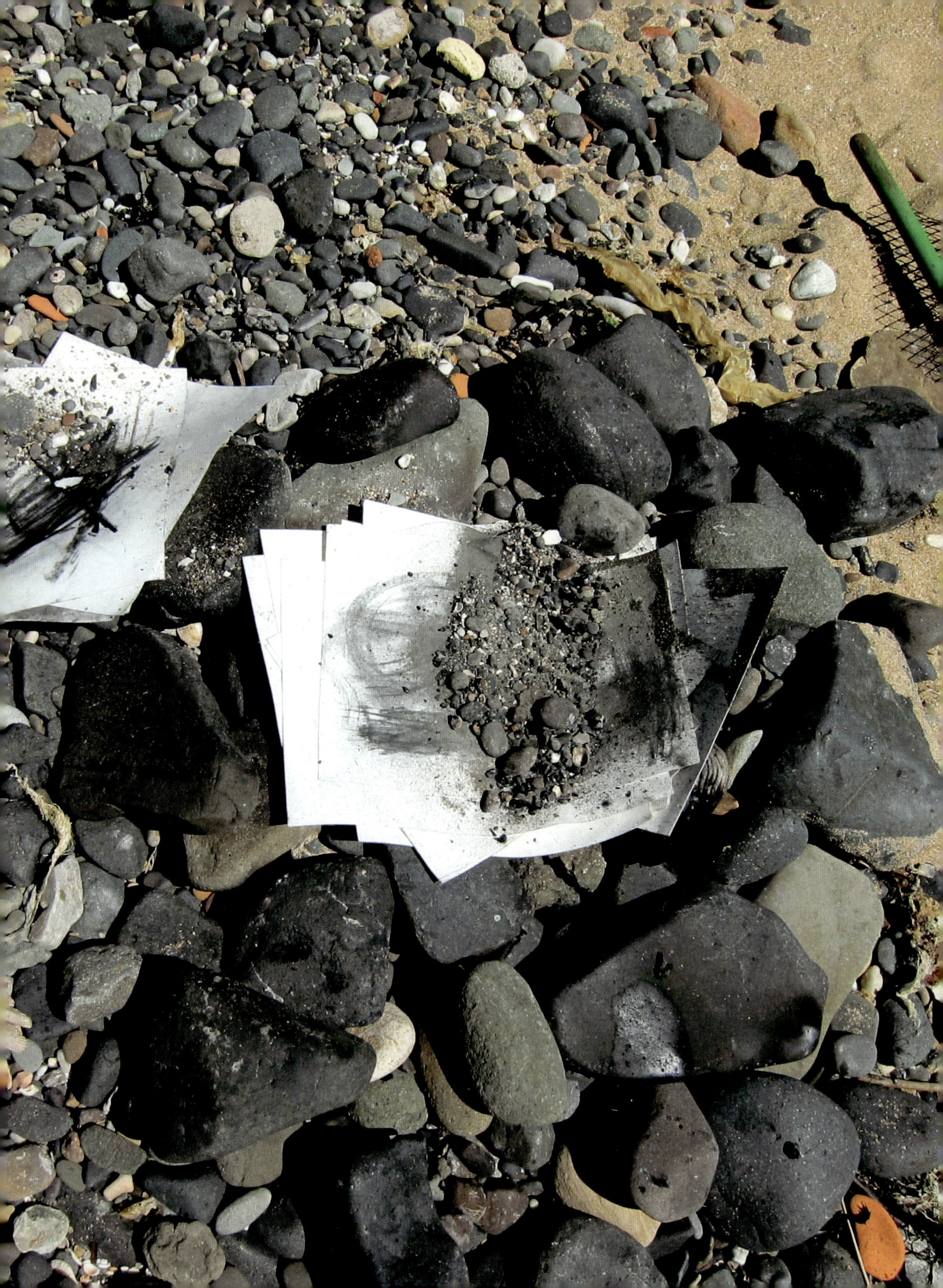

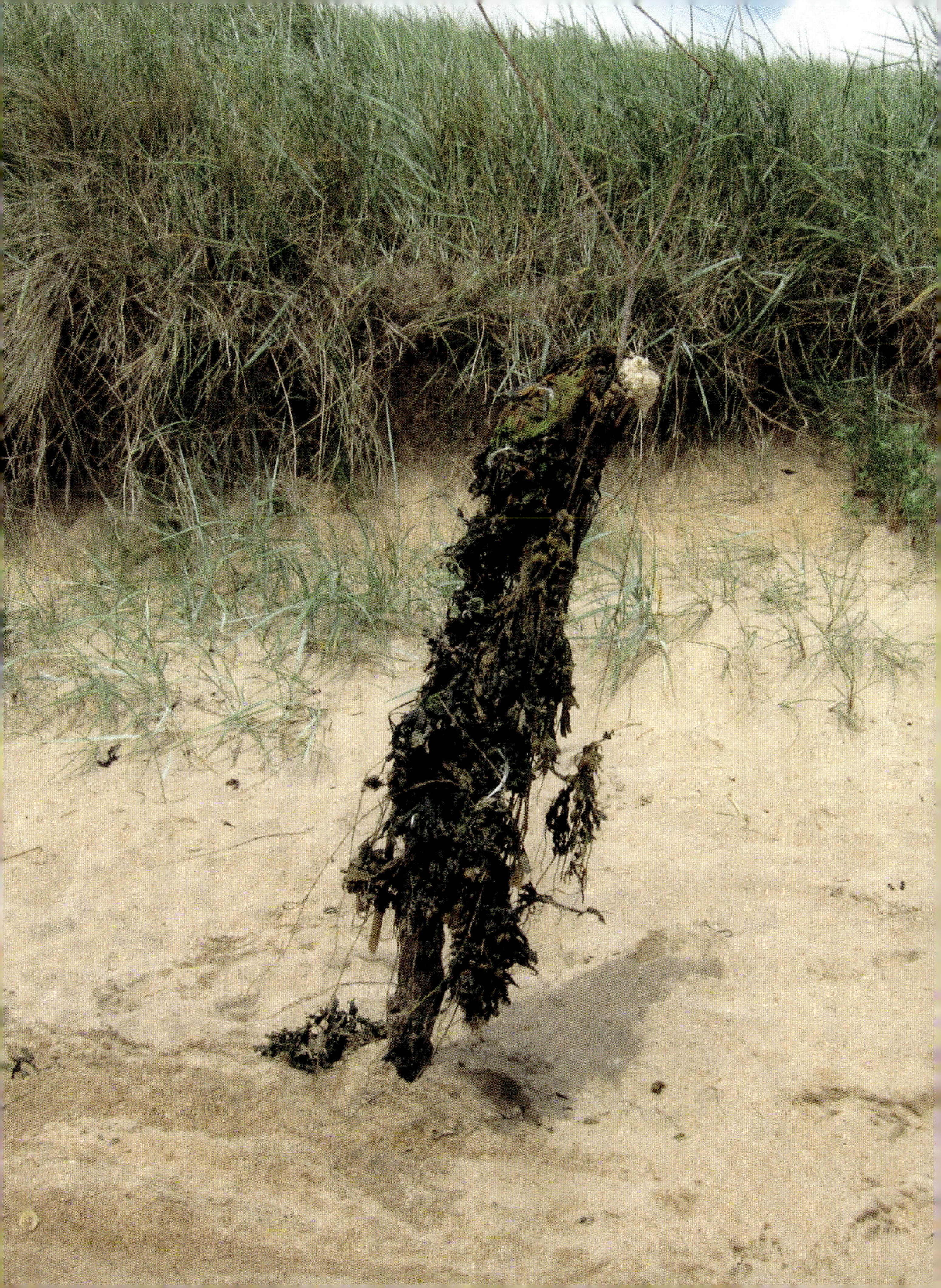

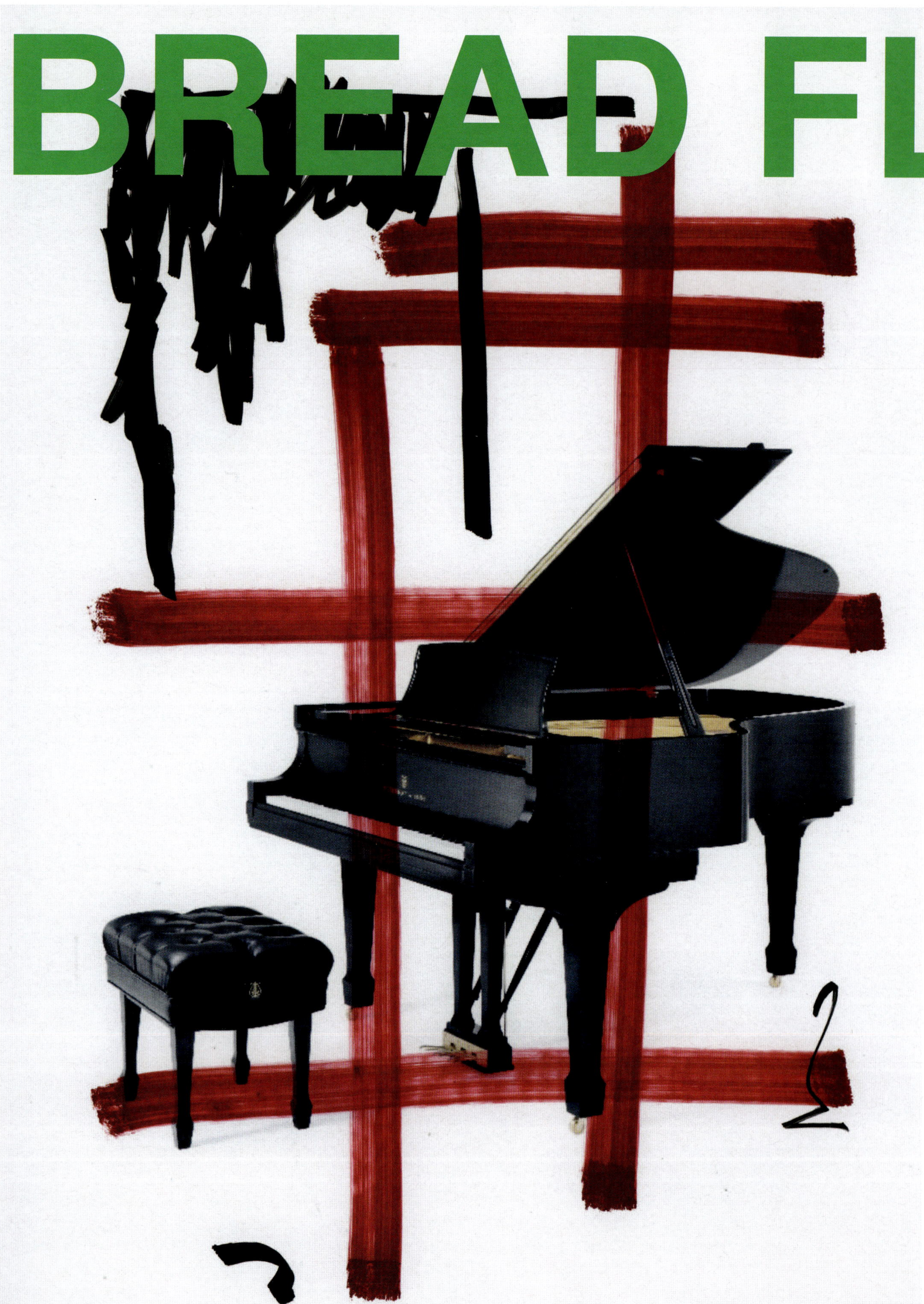
BREAD FL

OUR

BATHING

SUIT

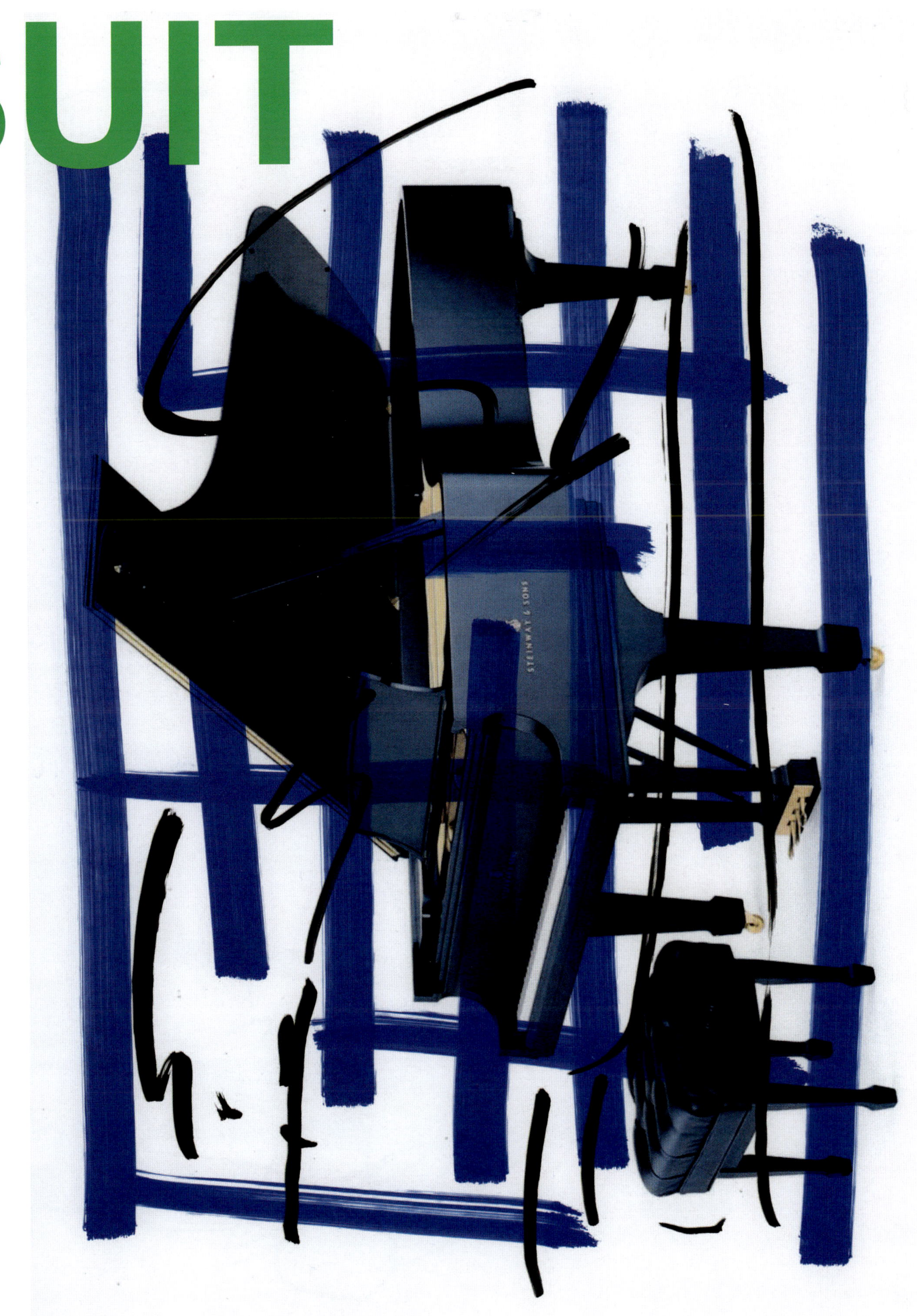

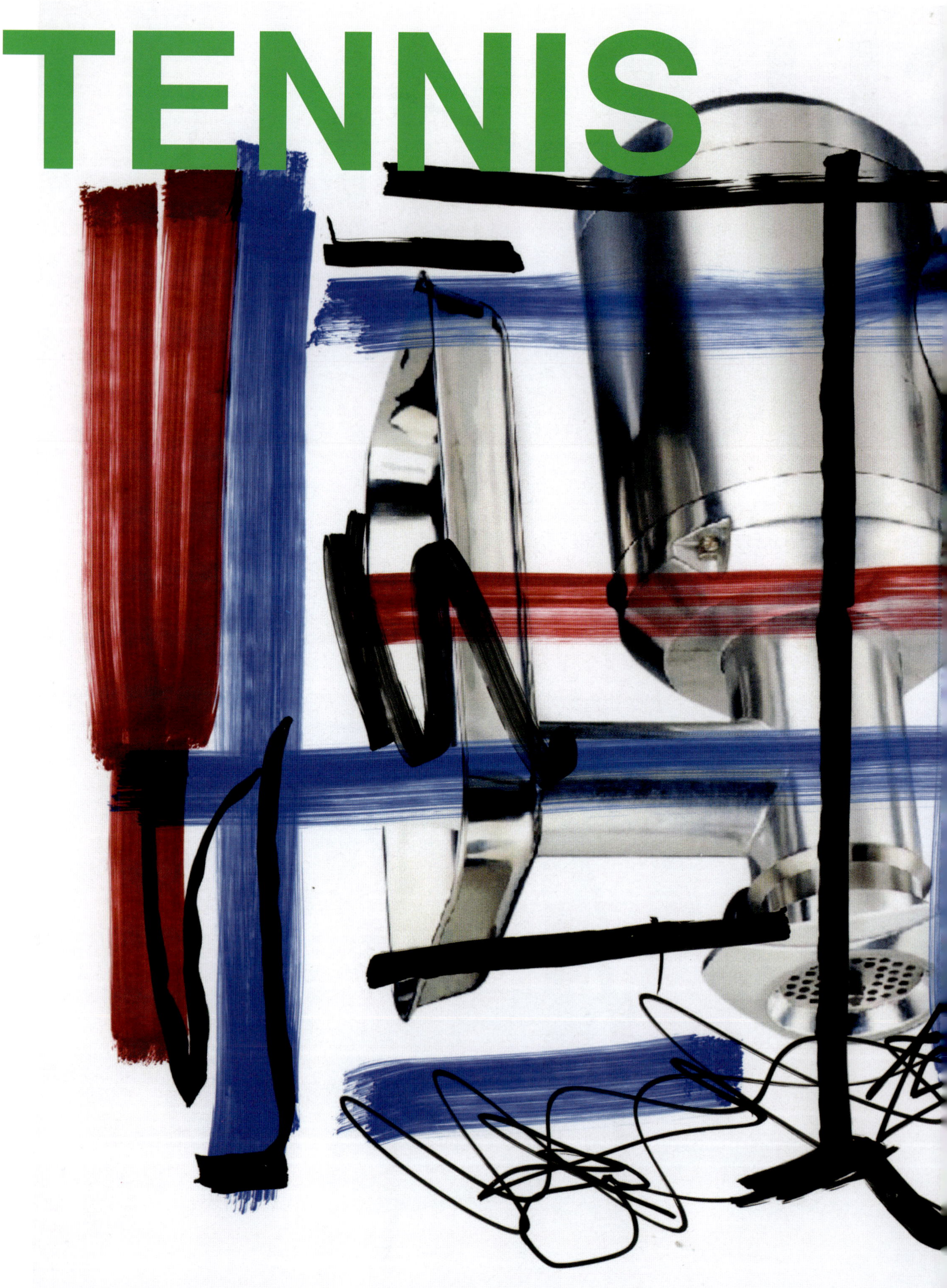
TENNIS

ANO

CHLORINE

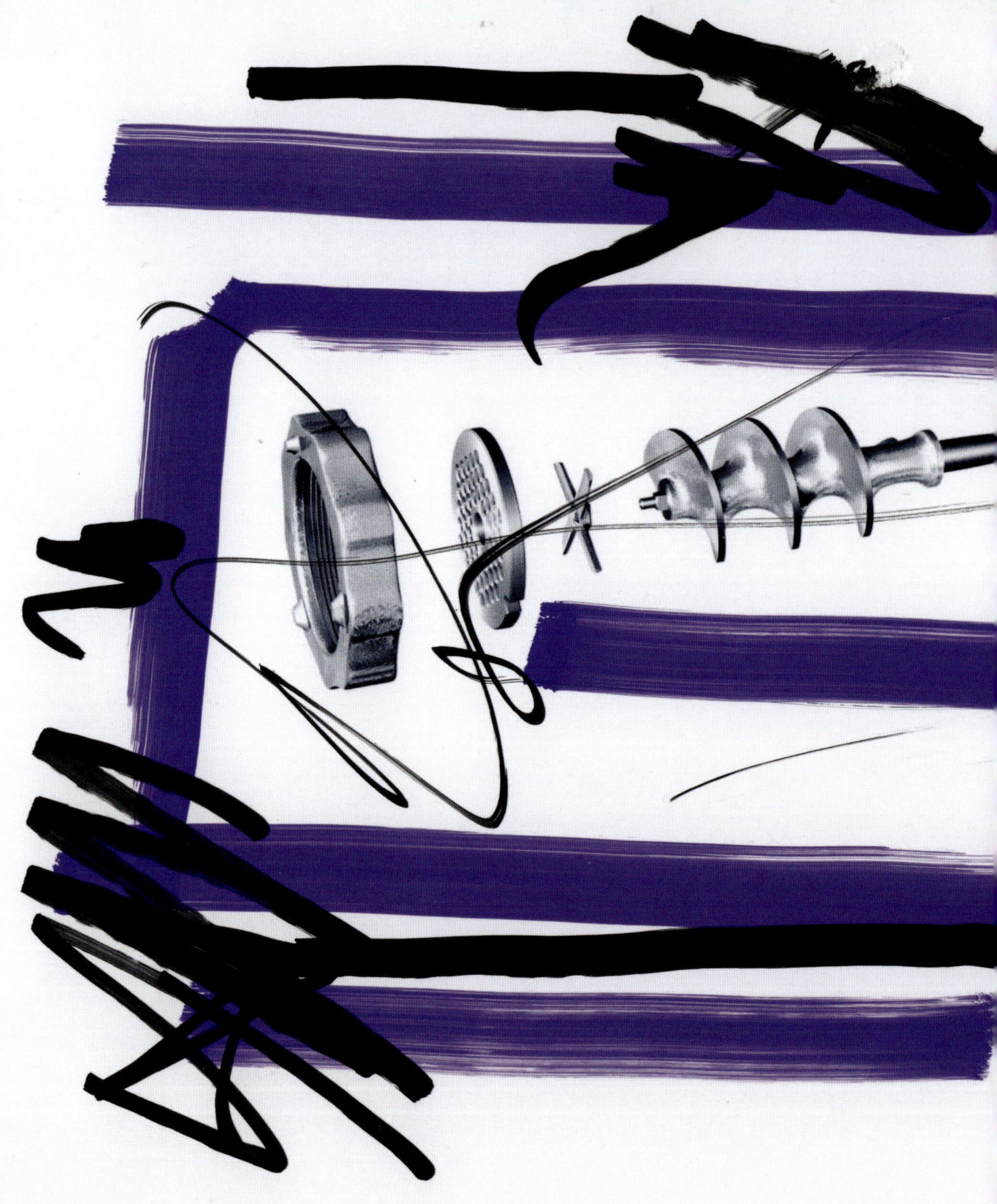

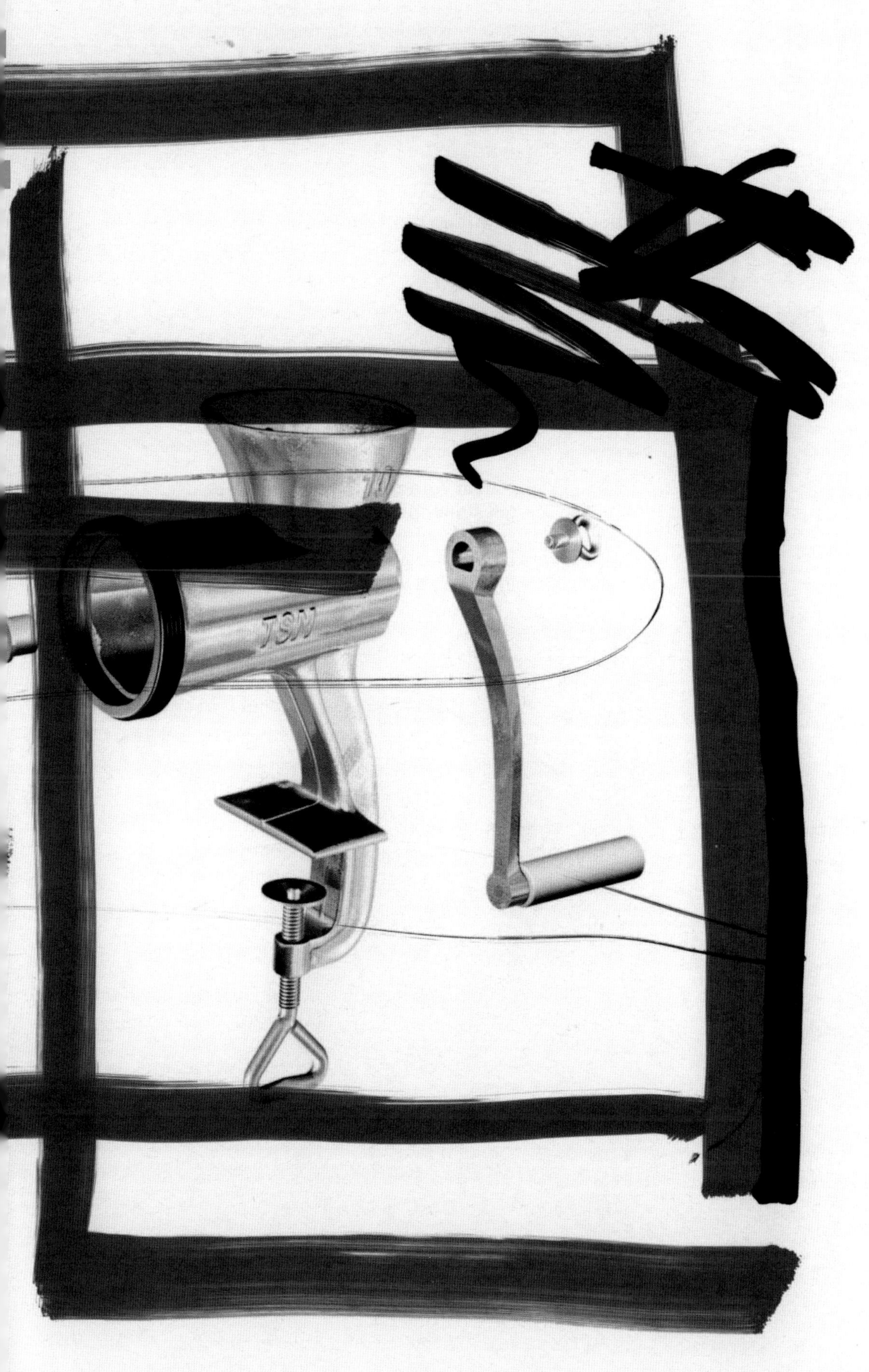

Chapter 1 — Vanity Killed the Cat

Notions of fuck entering the lower part
of my body, fuck travels through my pale and
rotting corpse at the speed of light.
Inside my blue face, I need nothing and then
I eat everything that moves in front of the self,
the great big I.

This is where I was not born.
This is where I will not die.
This is just a geographical root clogging up my view.

Seek

Pride has always been in the way of excellent work,
if excellent work even exists in my part of the universe.
I will approach my work with my dead hands,
I will present work made with a lifeless brain and no
eyes.

I am a man with a brut mahogany neck.
The neck snapped, the intense smell of dark self
was the only hint that harvest time
was entering my id.
Closing in on its next weak, muddy,
prey I discover the harrow leaning against
my history.
Then lowering the iron plough into
the conceptual sorrow.
Ripping the soil to pieces, folding it over onto itself.
Soil to soil and the concept is accepted.

My head falls back, no longer connected
to my body, only the flesh between the two
machines holds [illegible]her.
At last I am the [illegible]at bears nothing.
I stand still in m[illegible] but only for a few
[illegible]rating secon[illegible]

Failing body tum[illegible]

The feeling of defeat is a burden like the heaviest
metal known to man, it pushes you deep down into
the soil. Your own soil.
And you might not recover from its immense
totalitarian pressure of hate. Your pride is torn
apart, crushed to smithereens.

Searching

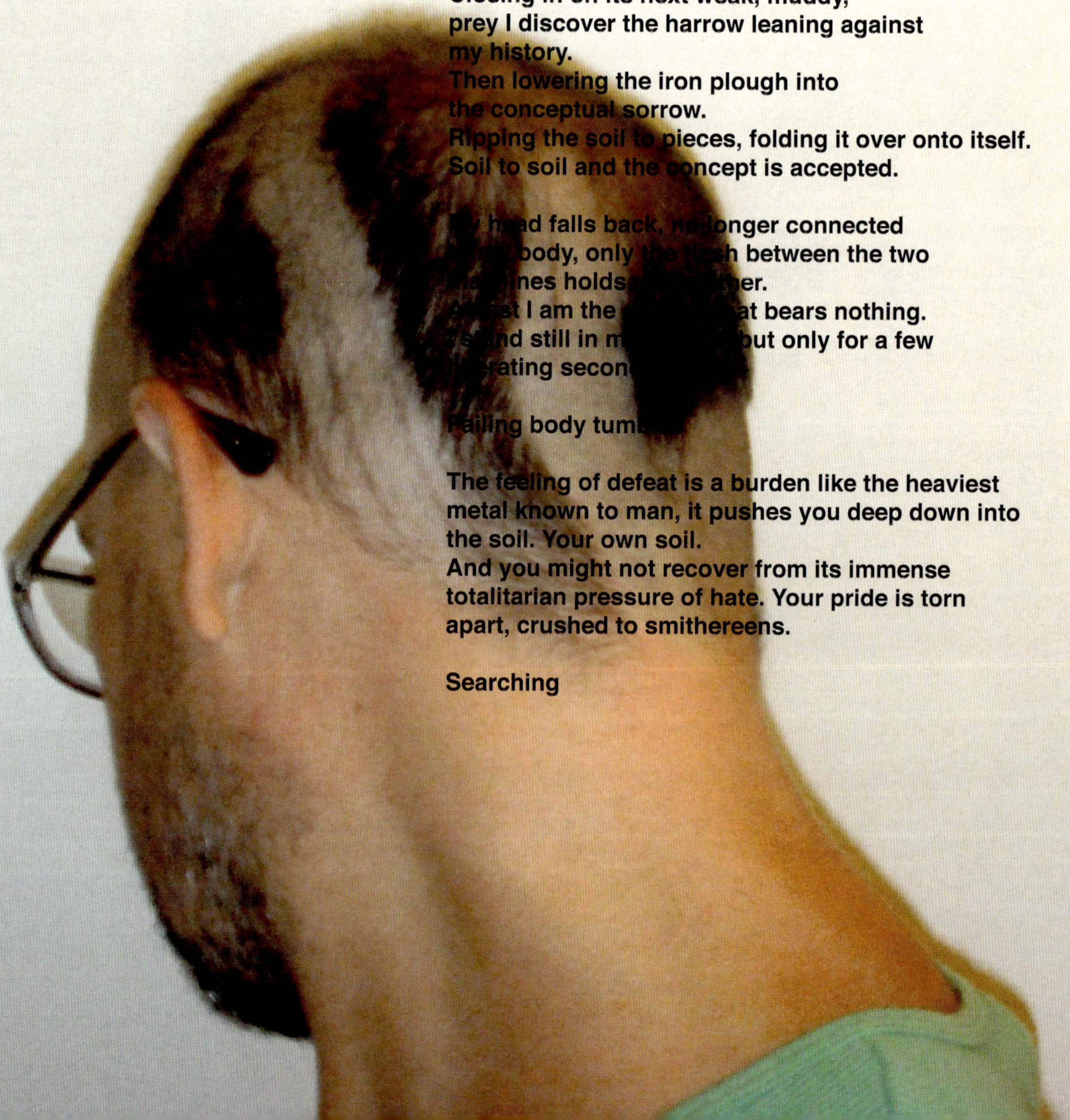

I am defeated, I can't breathe, suffocating. I need air, I try desperately to open my wedged windpipe, to suck some needed air down into my lungs so that my brain and I will not to fade to black. The question is not the beautiful air that is so needed, it is how the hell did I get here, again, into this position of banality and irritation?

Covered with flesh, meat that I own.
I suck and lick the spine clean in hope of a vague taste of heritage.

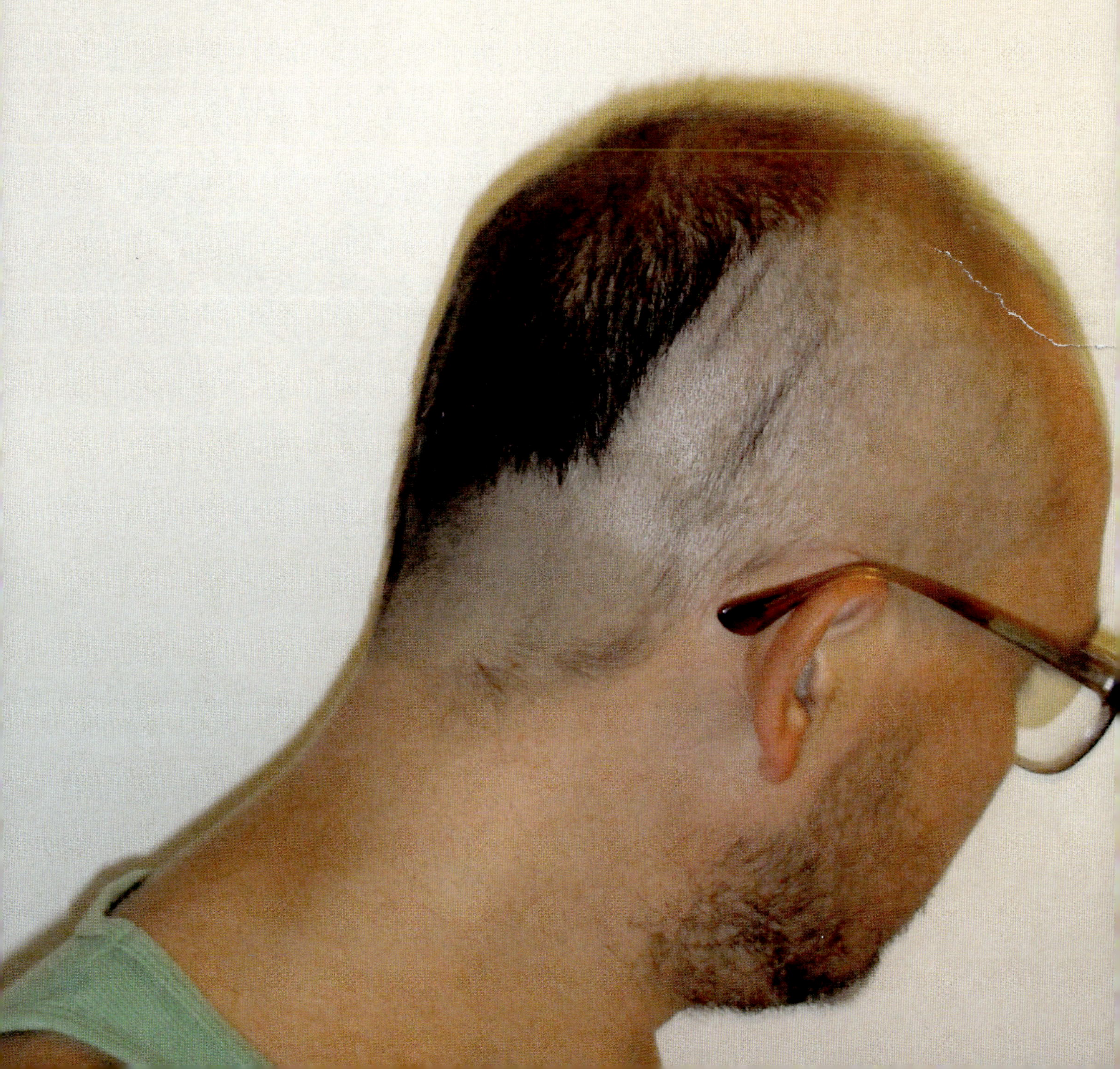

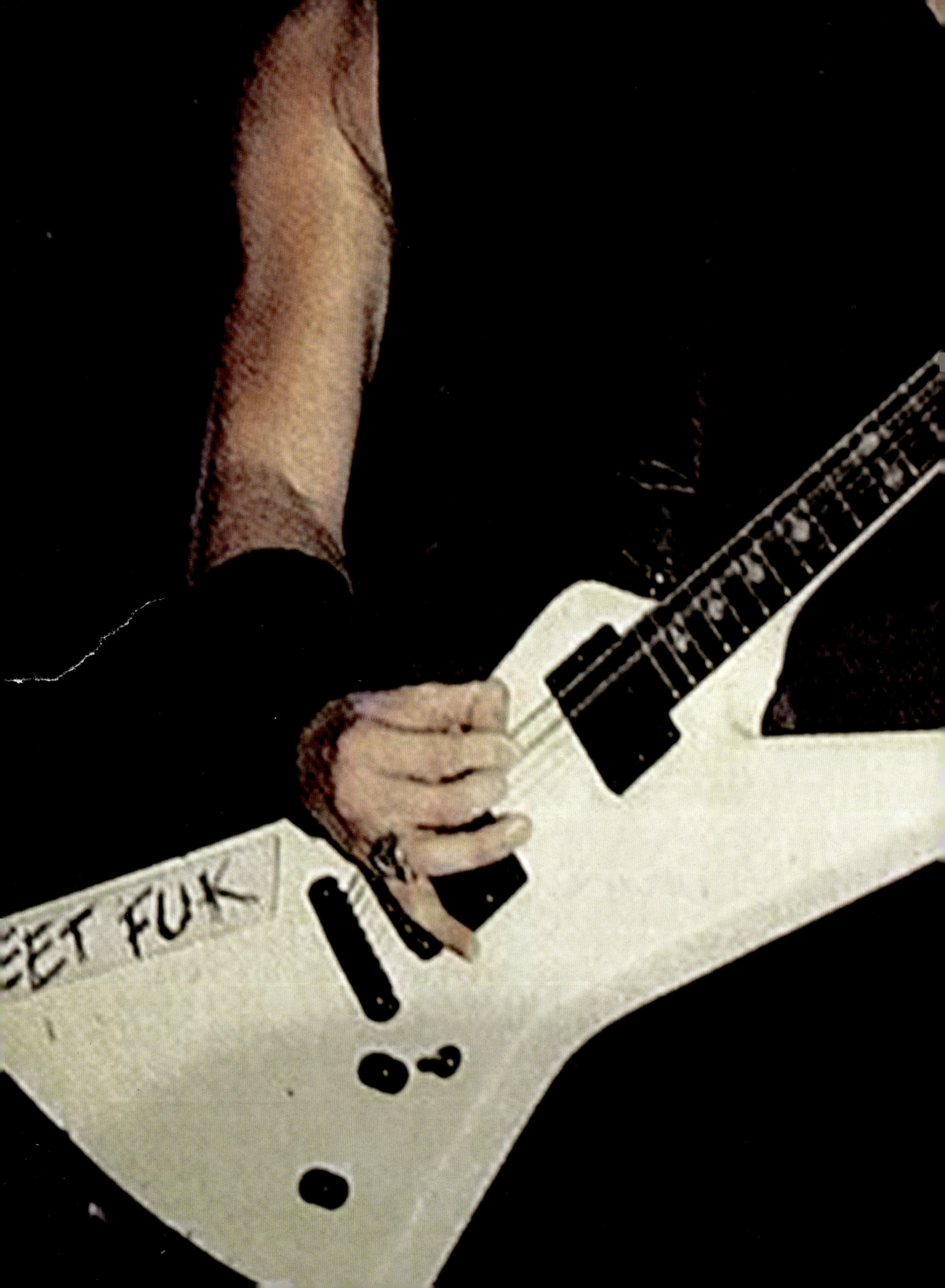
EET FUK

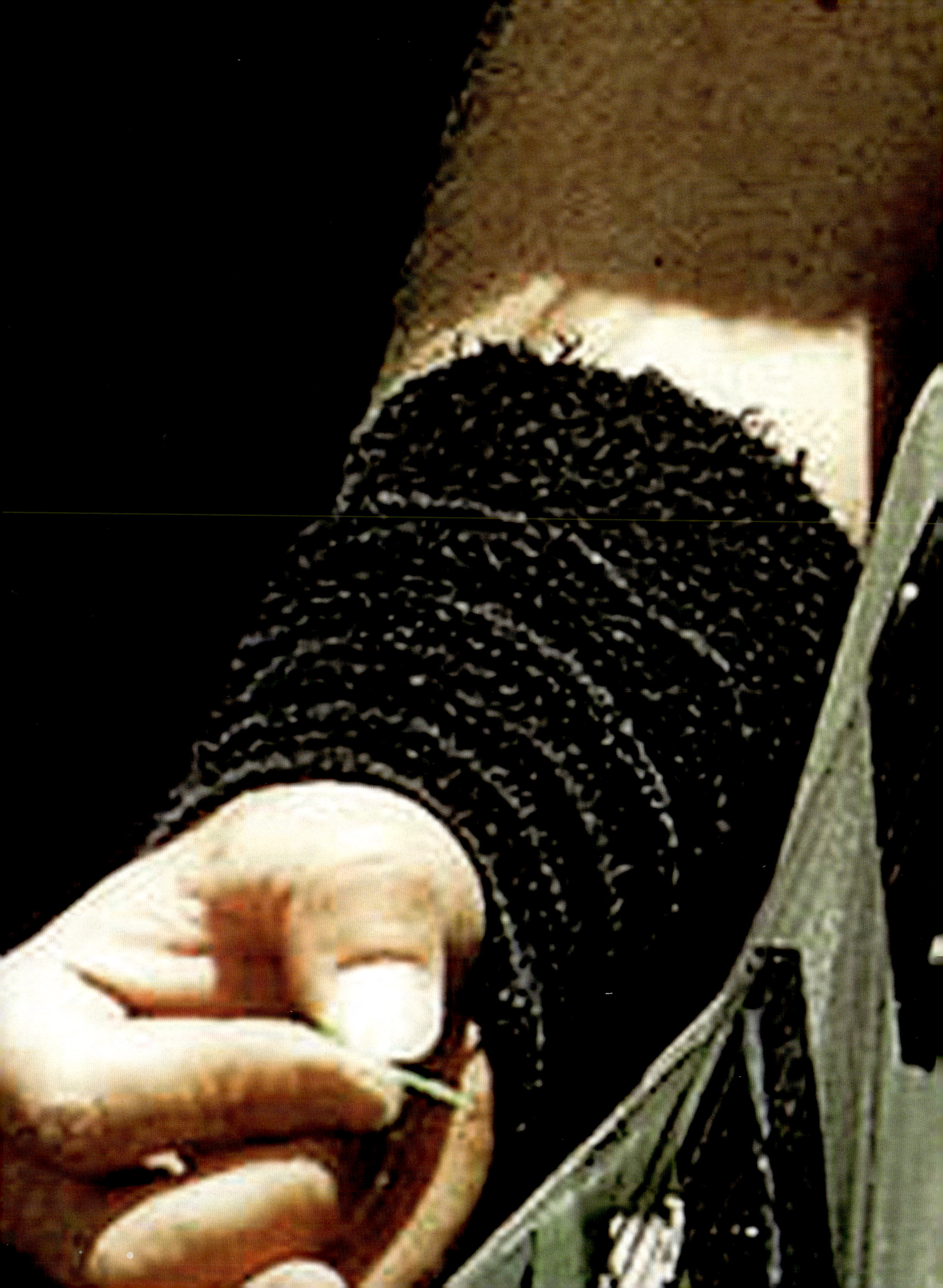

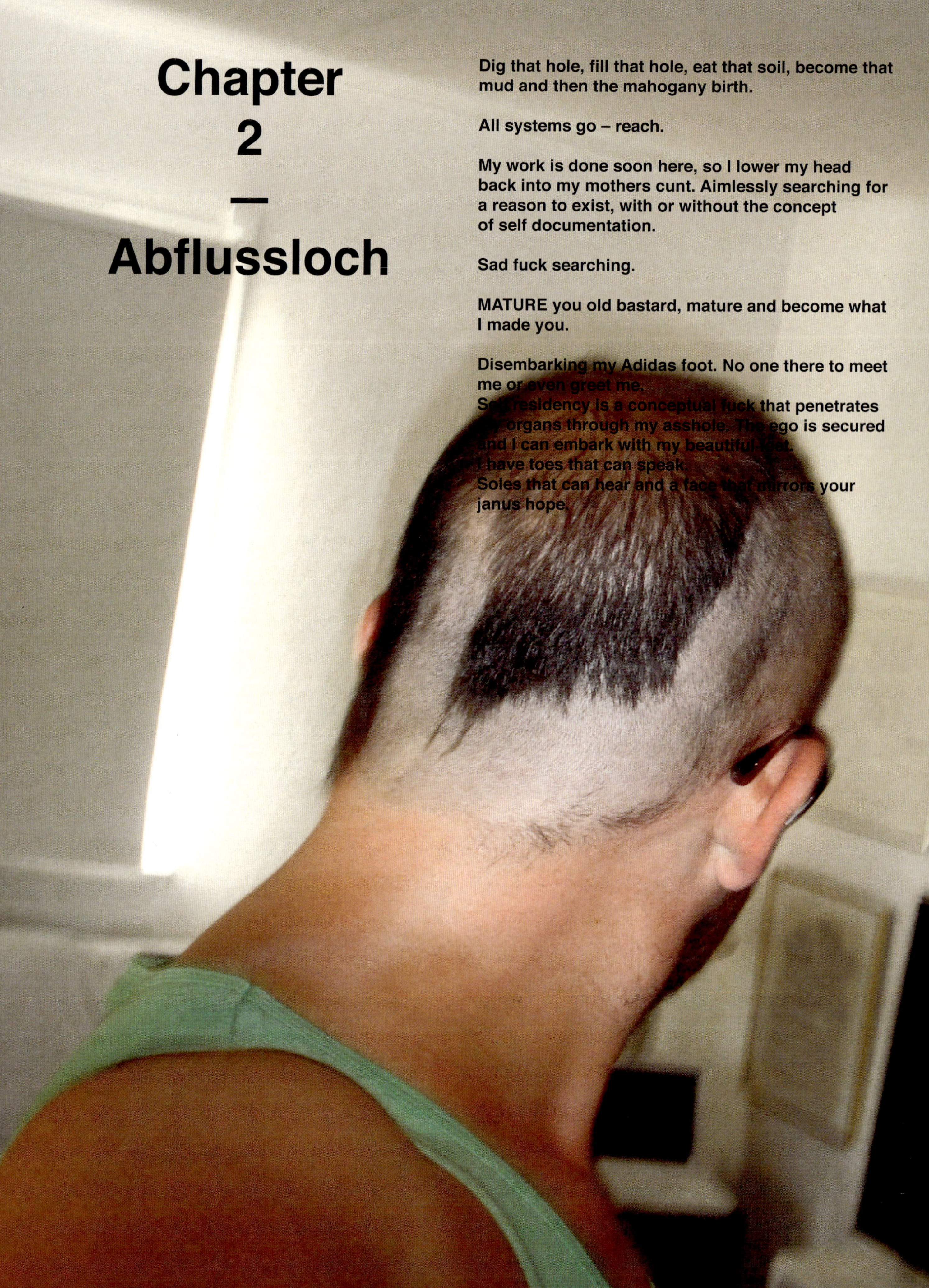

Chapter 2 — Abflussloch

Dig that hole, fill that hole, eat that soil, become that mud and then the mahogany birth.

All systems go – reach.

My work is done soon here, so I lower my head back into my mothers cunt. Aimlessly searching for a reason to exist, with or without the concept of self documentation.

Sad fuck searching.

MATURE you old bastard, mature and become what I made you.

Disembarking my Adidas foot. No one there to meet me or even greet me.
Self residency is a conceptual fuck that penetrates my organs through my asshole. The ego is secured and I can embark with my beautiful feet.
I have toes that can speak.
Soles that can hear and a face that mirrors your janus hope.

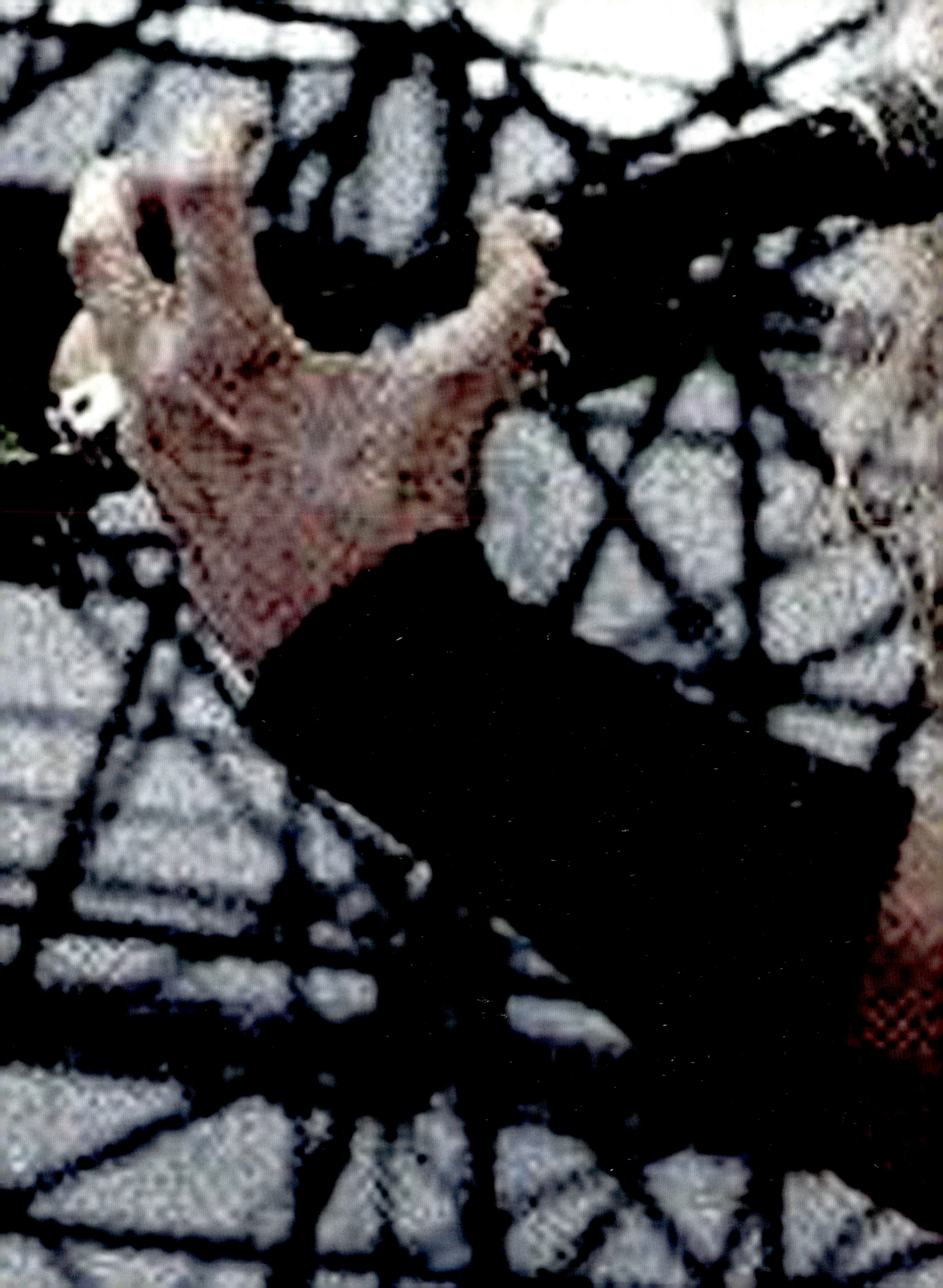

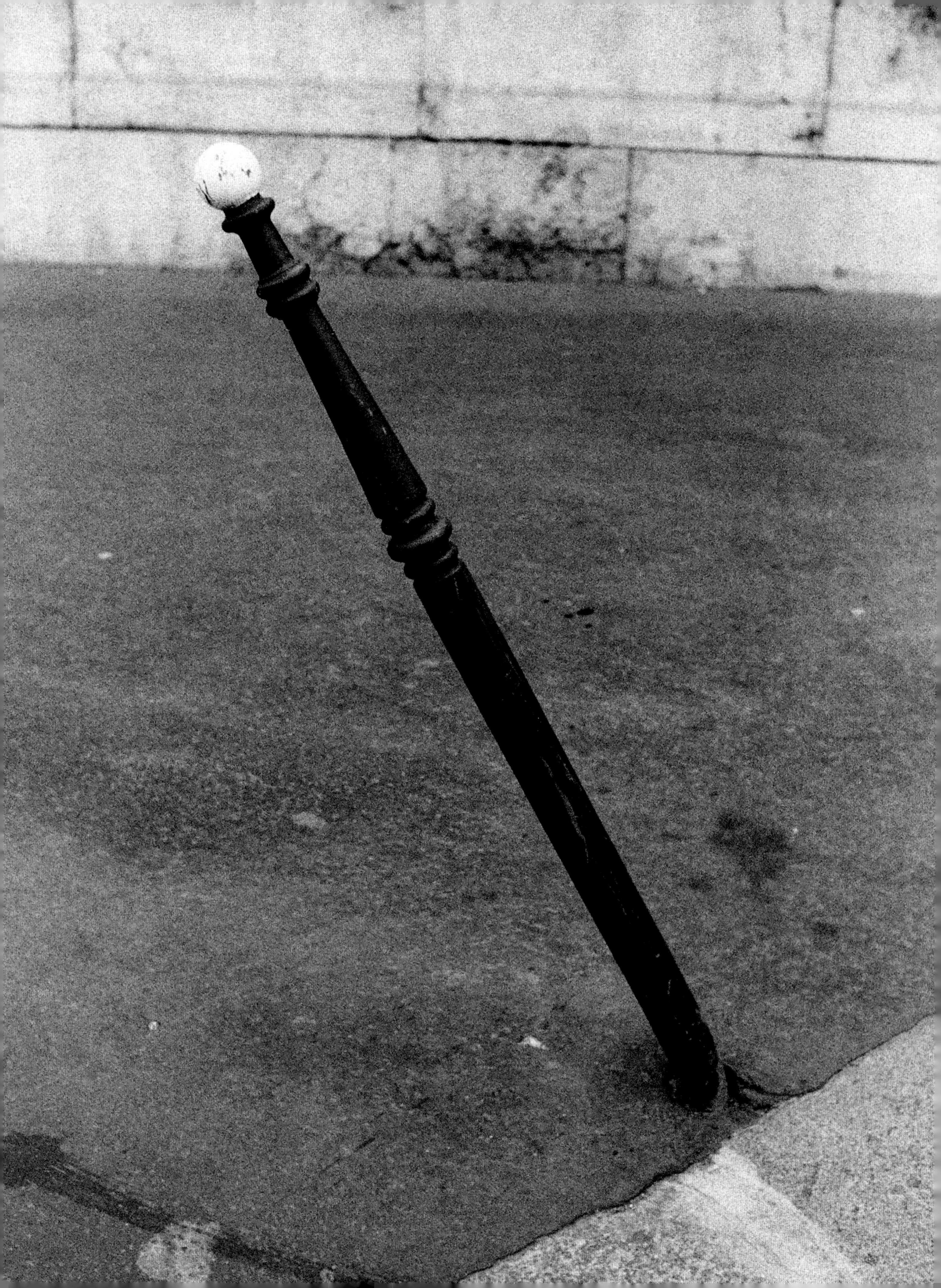

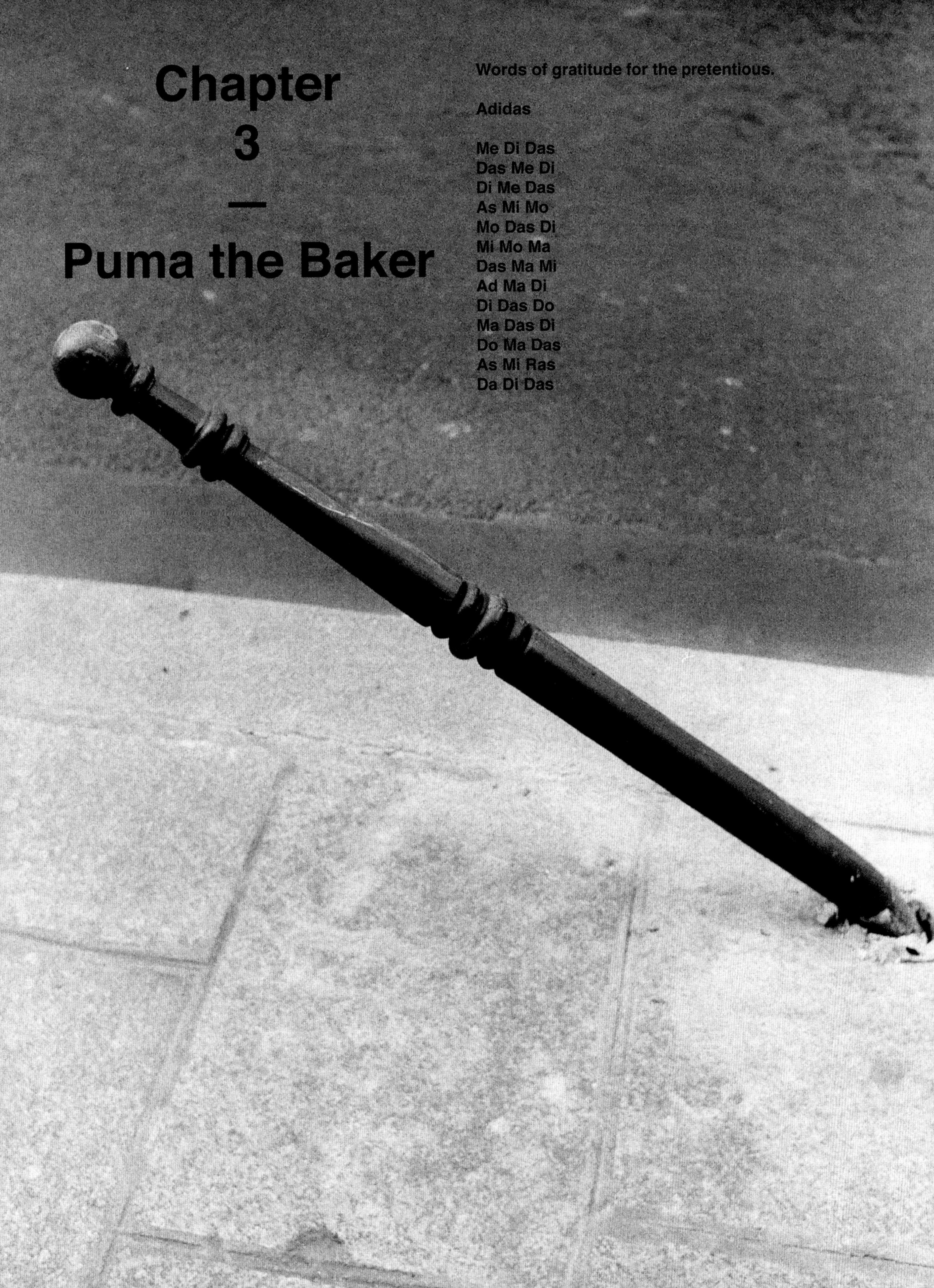

Chapter 3 — Puma the Baker

Words of gratitude for the pretentious.

Adidas

**Me Di Das
Das Me Di
Di Me Das
As Mi Mo
Mo Das Di
Mi Mo Ma
Das Ma Mi
Ad Ma Di
Di Das Do
Ma Das Di
Do Ma Das
As Mi Ras
Da Di Das**

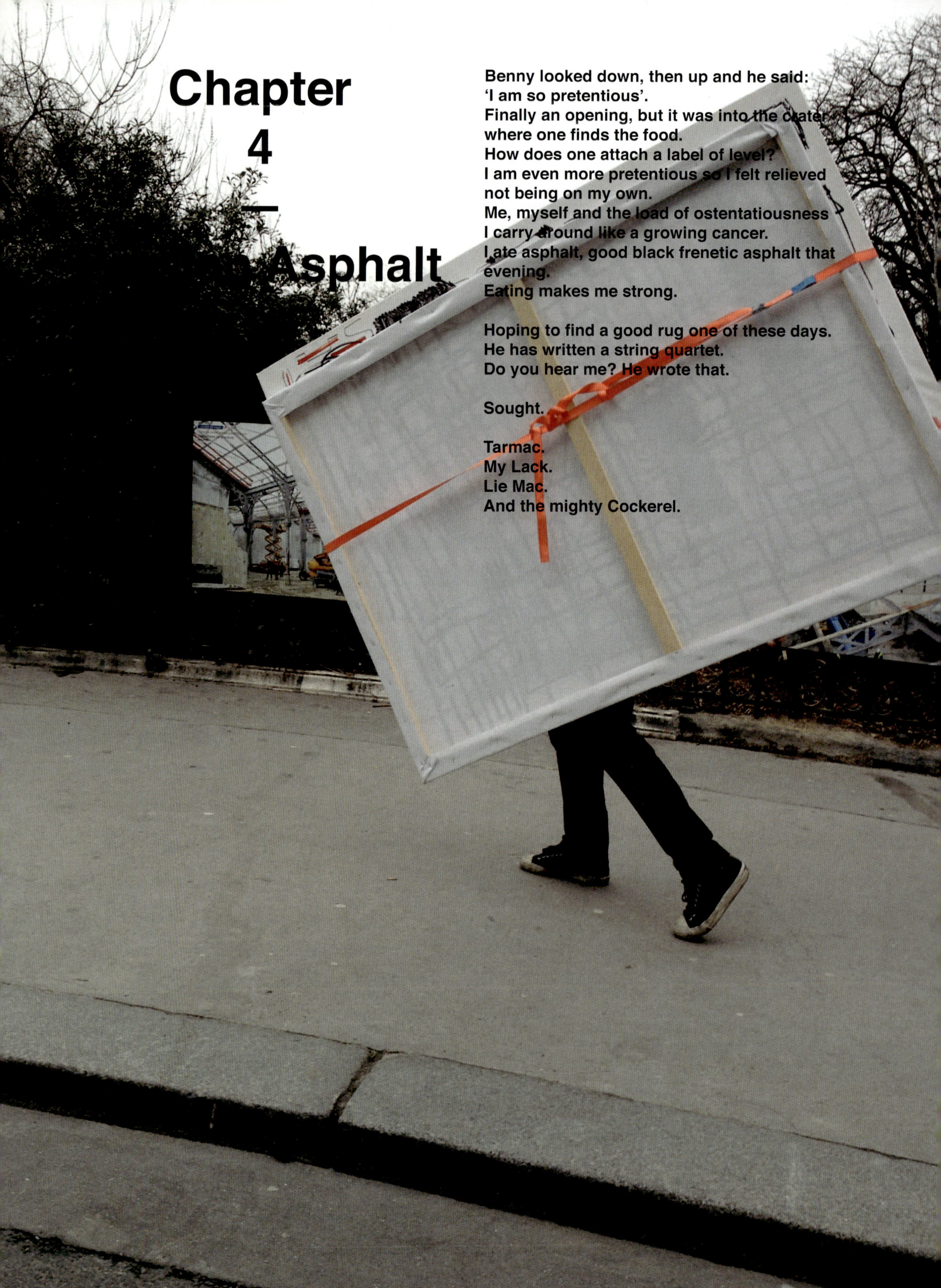

Chapter 4 — Asphalt

Benny looked down, then up and he said:
'I am so pretentious'.
Finally an opening, but it was into the crater
where one finds the food.
How does one attach a label of level?
I am even more pretentious so I felt relieved
not being on my own.
Me, myself and the load of ostentatiousness
I carry around like a growing cancer.
I ate asphalt, good black frenetic asphalt that
evening.
Eating makes me strong.

Hoping to find a good rug one of these days.
He has written a string quartet.
Do you hear me? He wrote that.

Sought.

Tarmac.
My Lack.
Lie Mac.
And the mighty Cockerel.

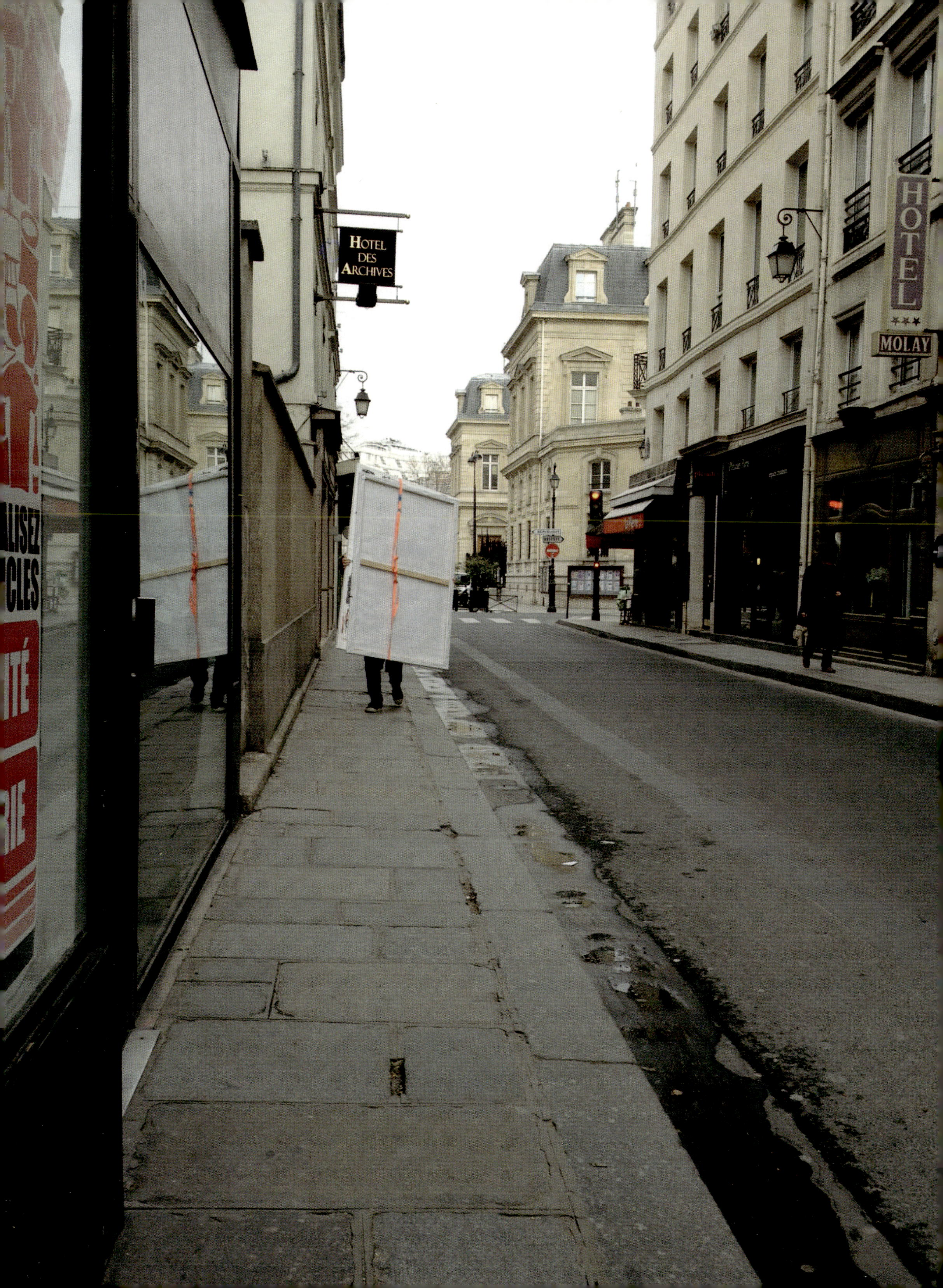

HOTEL DES ARCHIVES
HOTEL
MOLAY

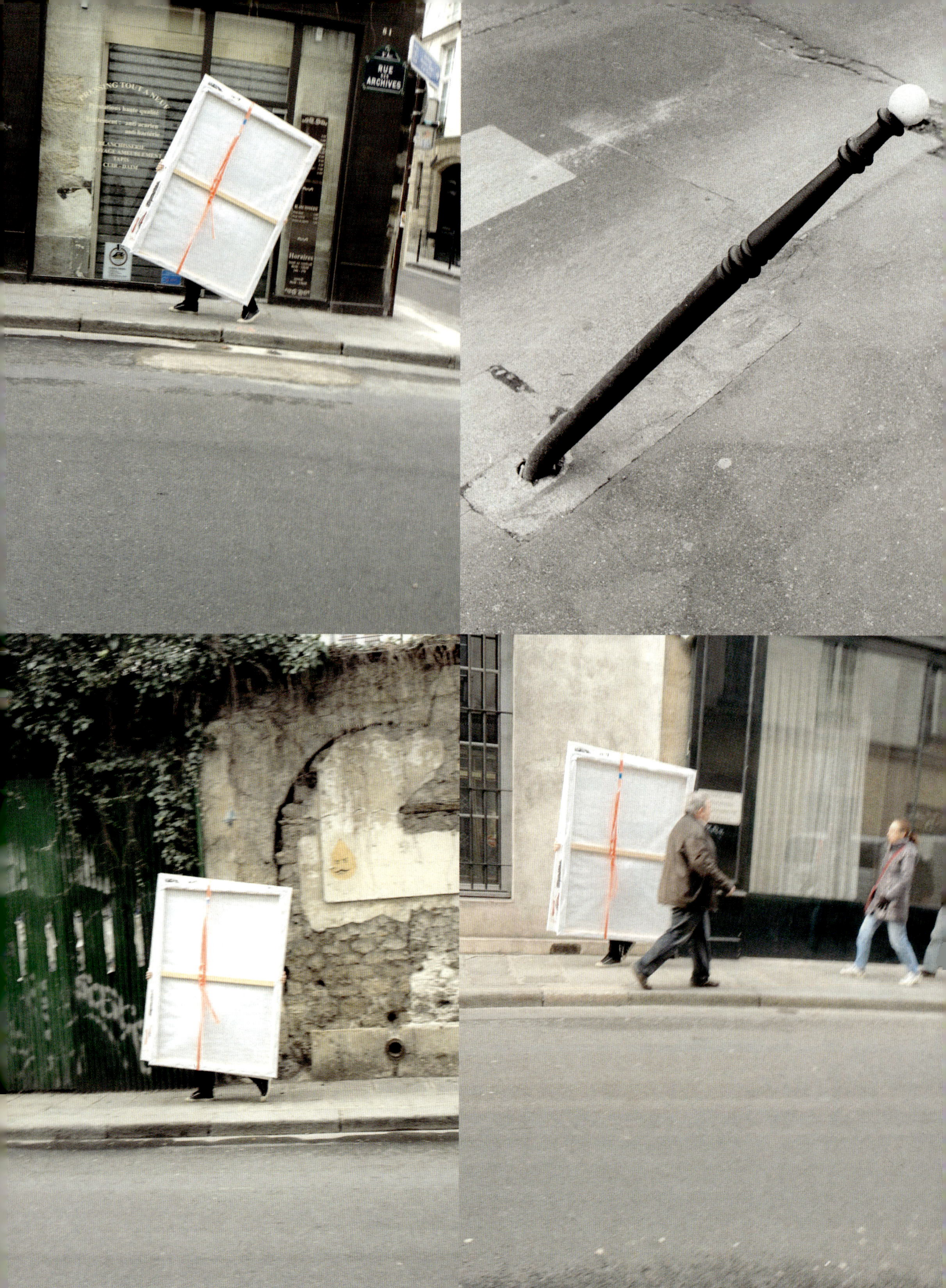
PRESSING TOUT A NEUF
BLANCHISSERIE
RUE
ARCHIVES
Horaires

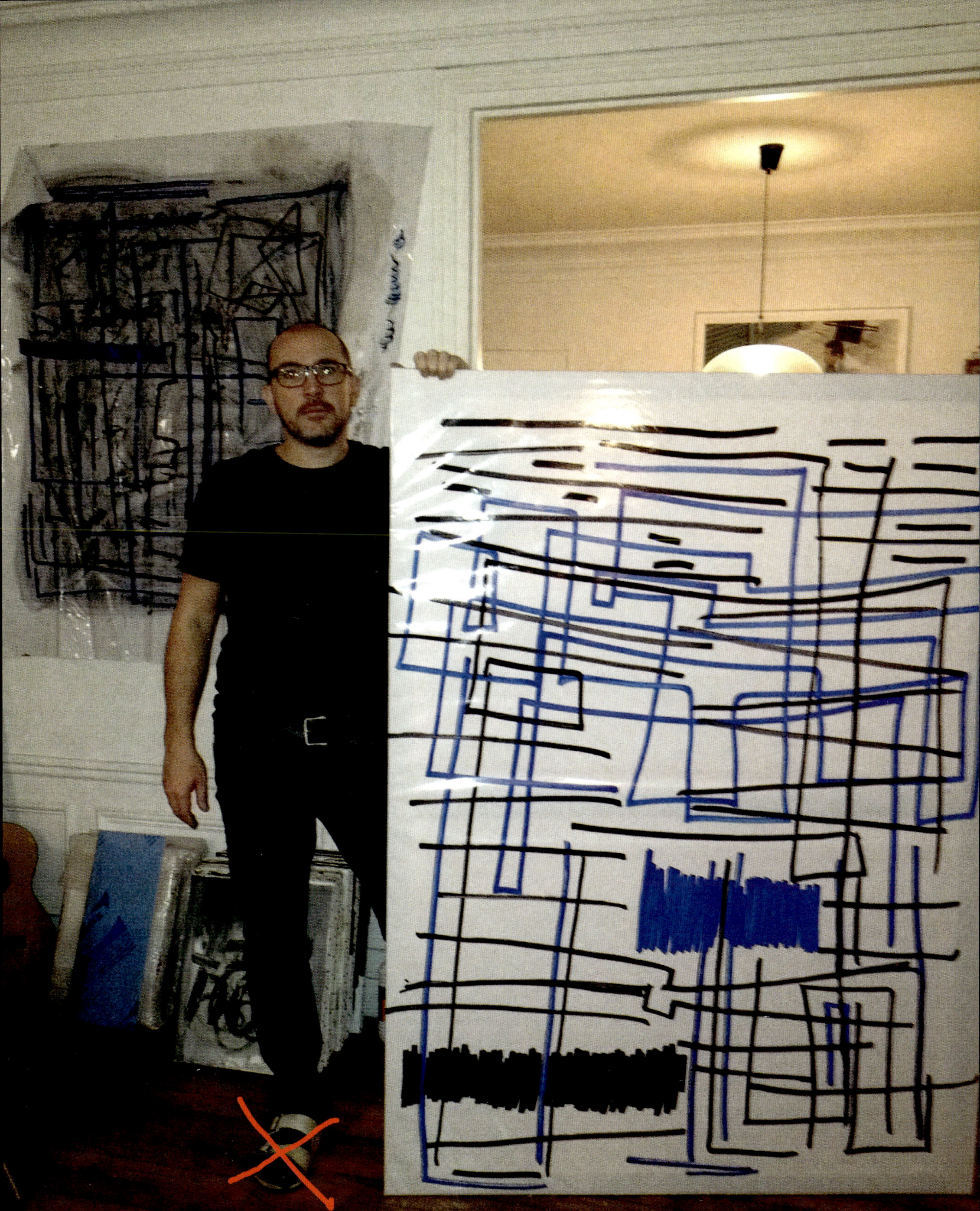

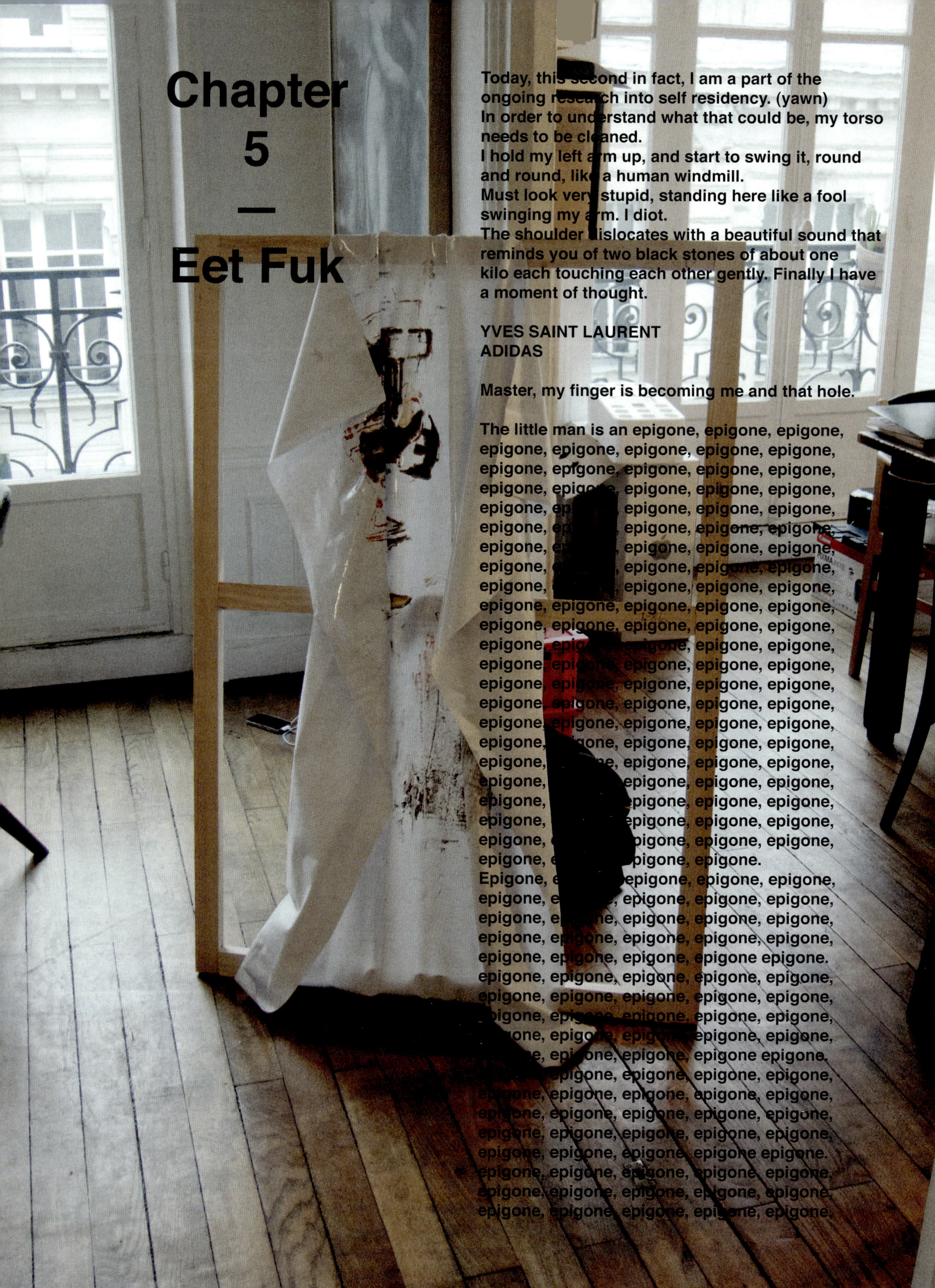

Chapter 5 — Eet Fuk

Today, this second in fact, I am a part of the ongoing research into self residency. (yawn)
In order to understand what that could be, my torso needs to be cleaned.
I hold my left arm up, and start to swing it, round and round, like a human windmill.
Must look very stupid, standing here like a fool swinging my arm. I diot.
The shoulder dislocates with a beautiful sound that reminds you of two black stones of about one kilo each touching each other gently. Finally I have a moment of thought.

YVES SAINT LAURENT
ADIDAS

Master, my finger is becoming me and that hole.

The little man is an epigone, epigone, epigone,
epigone, epigone, epigone, epigone, epigone,
epigone, epigone, epigone, epigone, epigone,
epigone, epigone, epigone, epigone, epigone,
epigone, epigone, epigone, epigone, epigone,
epigone, epigone, epigone, epigone, epigone,
epigone, epigone, epigone, epigone, epigone,
epigone, epigone, epigone, epigone, epigone,
epigone, epigone, epigone, epigone, epigone,
epigone, epigone, epigone, epigone, epigone,
epigone, epigone, epigone, epigone, epigone,
epigone, epigone, epigone, epigone, epigone,
epigone, epigone, epigone, epigone, epigone,
epigone, epigone, epigone, epigone, epigone,
epigone, epigone, epigone, epigone, epigone,
epigone, epigone, epigone, epigone, epigone,
epigone, epigone, epigone, epigone, epigone,
epigone, epigone, epigone, epigone, epigone,
epigone, epigone, epigone, epigone, epigone,
epigone, epigone, epigone, epigone, epigone,
epigone, epigone, epigone, epigone, epigone,
epigone, epigone, epigone, epigone, epigone,
epigone, epigone, epigone, epigone.
Epigone, epigone, epigone, epigone, epigone,
epigone, epigone, epigone, epigone, epigone,
epigone, epigone, epigone, epigone, epigone,
epigone, epigone, epigone, epigone, epigone,
epigone, epigone, epigone, epigone epigone.
epigone, epigone, epigone, epigone, epigone,
epigone, epigone, epigone, epigone, epigone,
epigone, epigone, epigone, epigone, epigone,
epigone, epigone, epigone, epigone, epigone,
epigone, epigone, epigone, epigone epigone.
epigone, epigone, epigone, epigone, epigone,
epigone, epigone, epigone, epigone, epigone,
epigone, epigone, epigone, epigone, epigone,
epigone, epigone, epigone, epigone, epigone,
epigone, epigone, epigone, epigone epigone.
epigone, epigone, epigone, epigone, epigone,
epigone, epigone, epigone, epigone, epigone,
epigone, epigone, epigone, epigone, epigone.

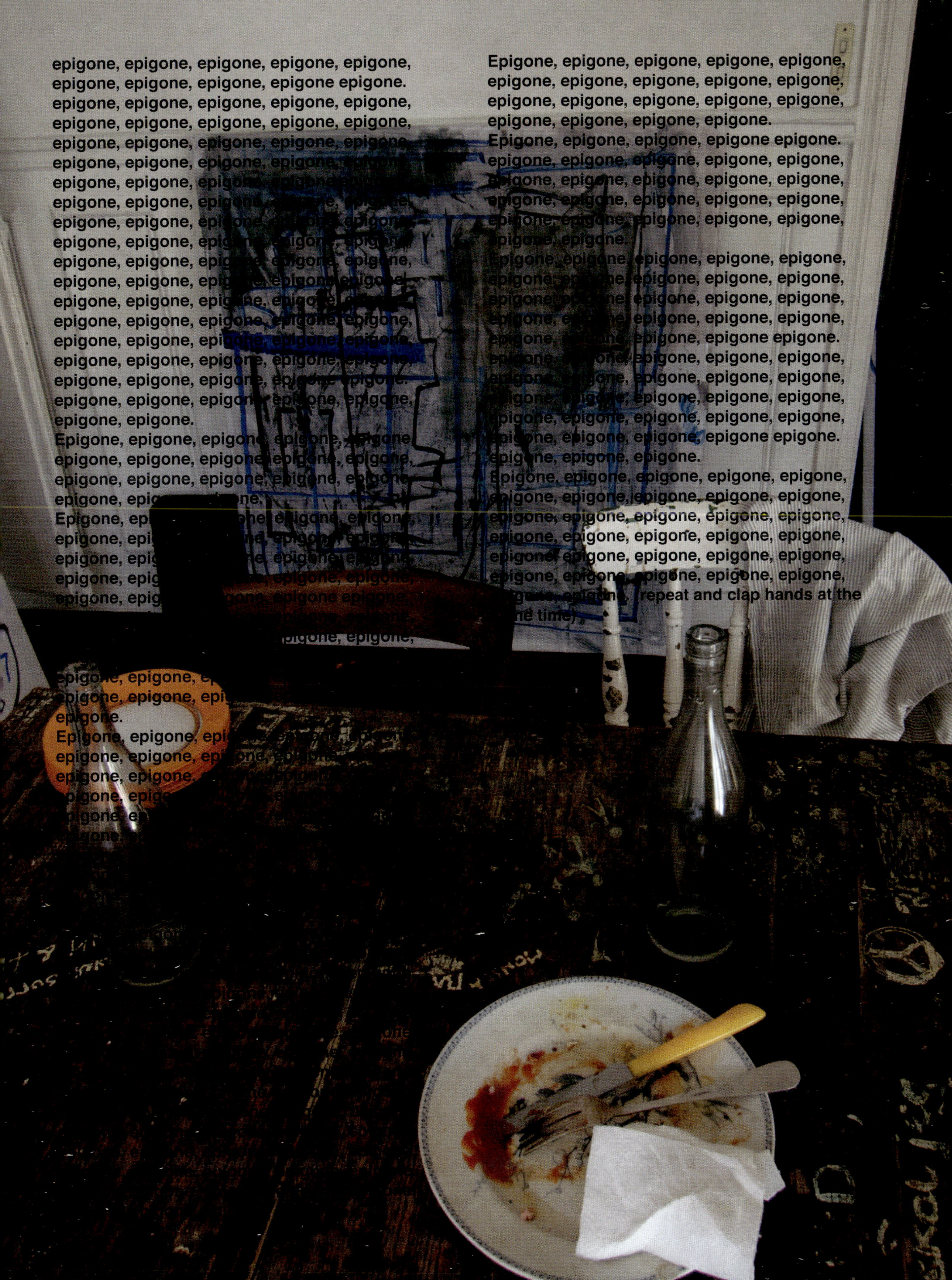
epigone, epigone, epigone, epigone, epigone,
epigone, epigone, epigone, epigone epigone.
epigone, epigone, epigone, epigone, epigone,
epigone, epigone, epigone, epigone, epigone,
epigone, epigone, epigone, epigone, epigone,
epigone, epigone, epigone, epigone, epigone,
epigone, epigone, epigone, epigone, epigone,
epigone, epigone, epigone, epigone, epigone,
epigone, epigone, epigone, epigone, epigone,
epigone, epigone, epigone, epigone, epigone,
epigone, epigone, epigone, epigone, epigone,
epigone, epigone, epigone, epigone, epigone,
epigone, epigone, epigone, epigone, epigone,
epigone, epigone, epigone, epigone, epigone,
epigone, epigone, epigone, epigone, epigone,
epigone, epigone, epigone, epigone, epigone,
epigone, epigone, epigone, epigone, epigone.
epigone, epigone, epigone, epigone, epigone,
epigone, epigone.
Epigone, epigone, epigone, epigone, epigone,
epigone, epigone, epigone, epigone, epigone,
epigone, epigone, epigone, epigone, epigone,
epigone, epig ne,
Epigone, ep epigone, epigone,
epigone, epi epigone, epigone,
epigone, epi epigone, epigone,
epigone, epi epigone, epigone,
epigone, epi epigone epigone.
epigone, epigone,
epigone, epigone,
epigone, epigone,
epigone.
Epigone, epigone,
epigone, epigone,
epigone, epigone,
Epigone, epigone, epigone, epigone, epigone,
epigone, epigone, epigone, epigone, epigone,
epigone, epigone, epigone, epigone, epigone,
epigone, epigone, epigone, epigone.
Epigone, epigone, epigone, epigone epigone.
epigone, epigone, epigone, epigone, epigone,
epigone, epigone, epigone, epigone, epigone,
epigone, epigone, epigone, epigone, epigone,
epigone, epigone, epigone, epigone, epigone,
epigone, epigone.
Epigone, epigone, epigone, epigone, epigone,
epigone, epigone, epigone, epigone, epigone,
epigone, epigone, epigone, epigone, epigone,
epigone, epigone, epigone, epigone, epigone,
epigone, epigone, epigone, epigone epigone.
epigone, epigone, epigone, epigone, epigone,
epigone, epigone, epigone, epigone, epigone,
epigone, epigone, epigone, epigone, epigone,
epigone, epigone, epigone, epigone, epigone,
epigone, epigone, epigone, epigone epigone.
epigone, epigone, epigone.
Epigone, epigone, epigone, epigone, epigone,
epigone, epigone, epigone, epigone, epigone,
epigone, epigone, epigone, epigone, epigone,
epigone, epigone, epigone, epigone, epigone,
epigone, epigone, epigone, epigone, epigone,
epigone, epigone, epigone, epigone, epigone,
epigone, epigone. (repeat and clap hands at the
ne time).

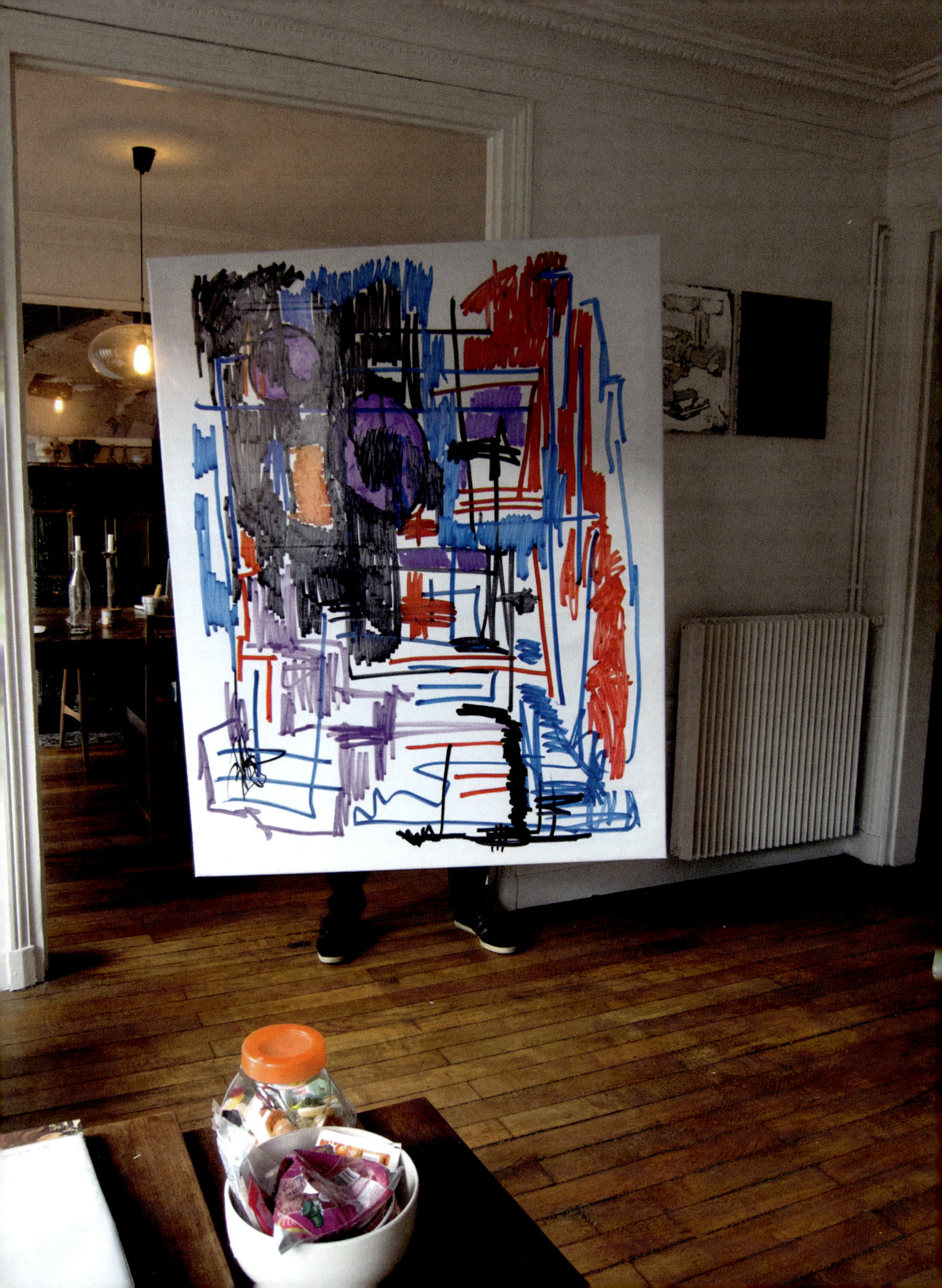

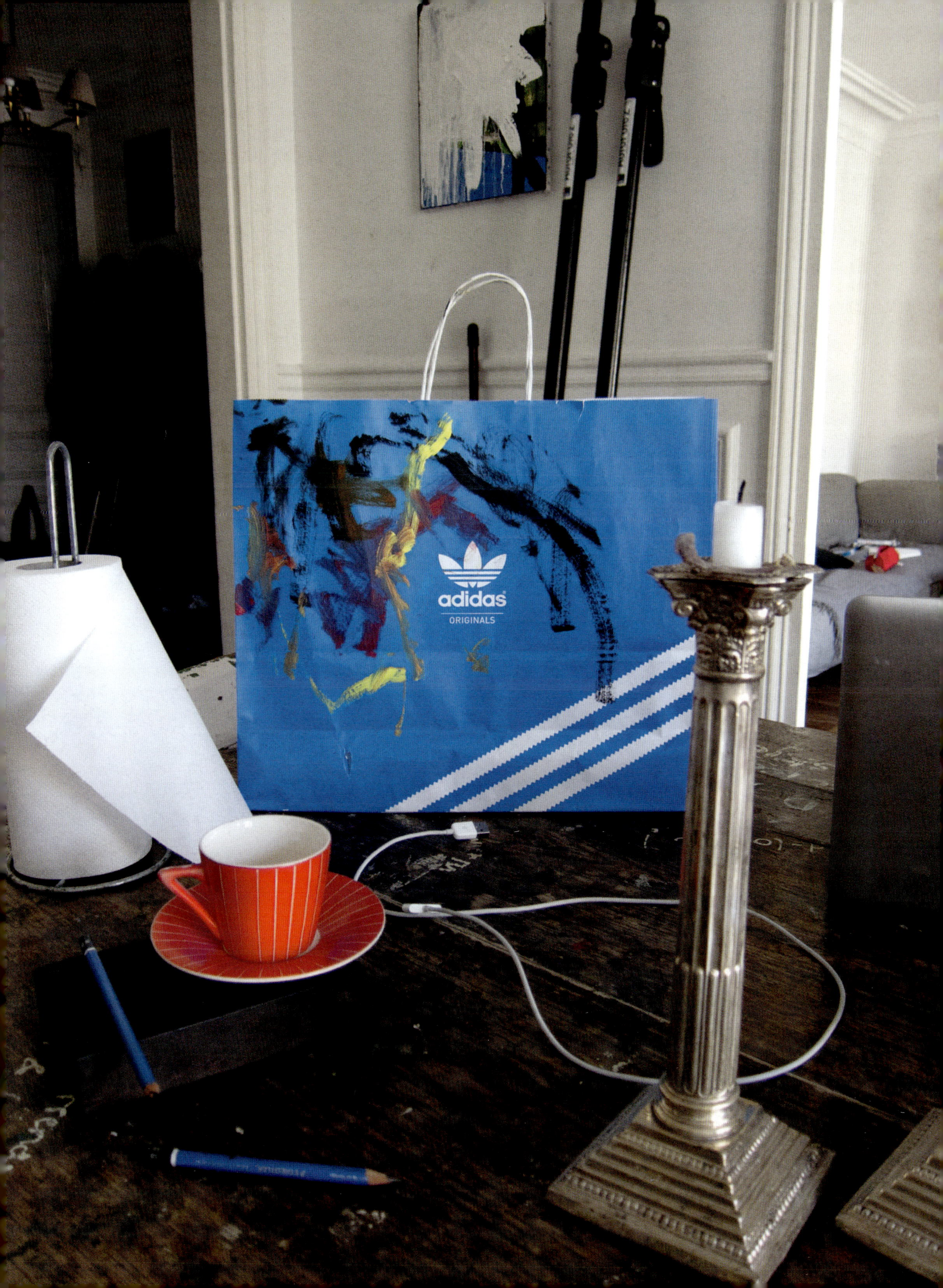
adidas
ORIGINALS

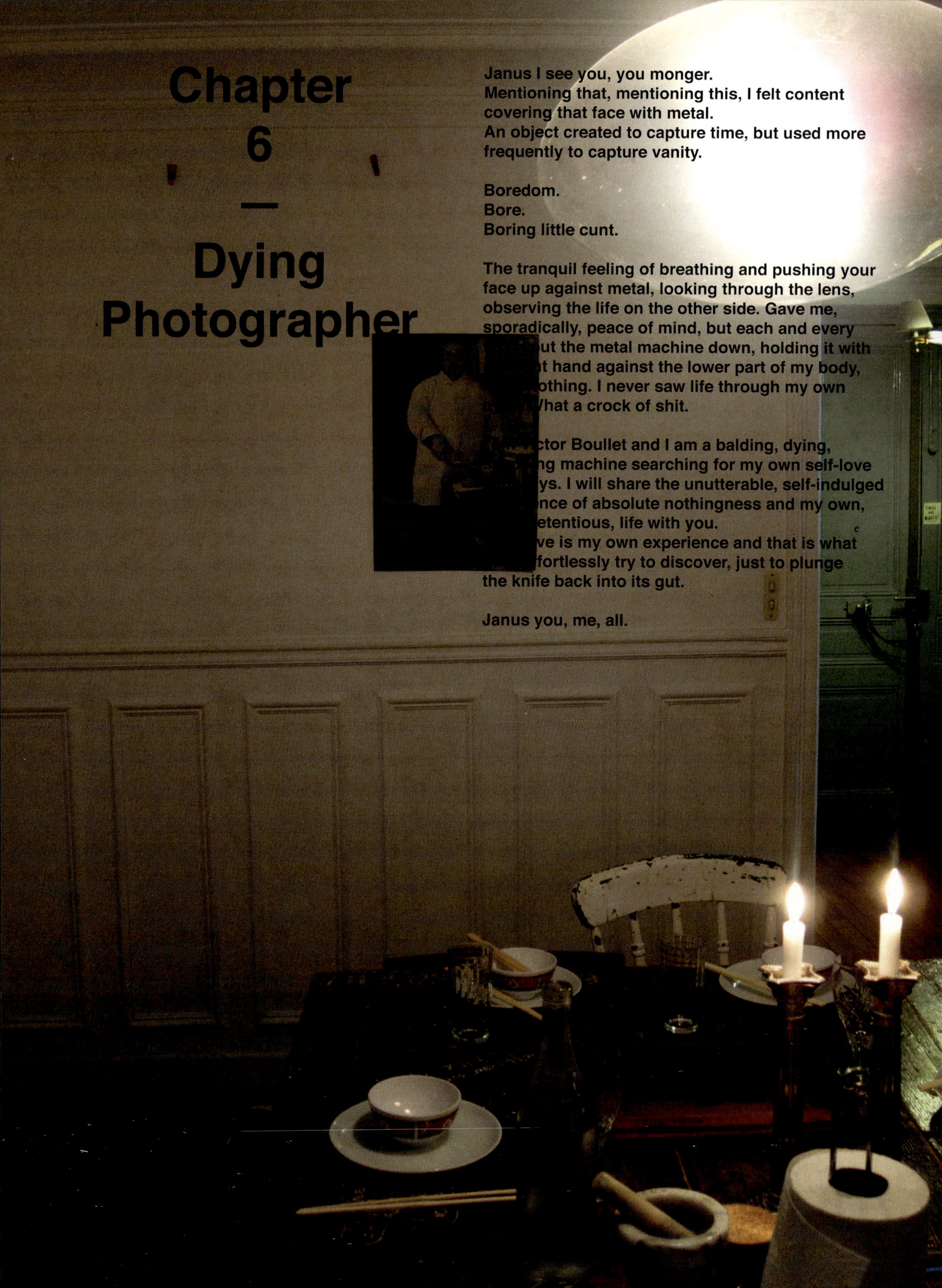

Chapter 6 — Dying Photographer

Janus I see you, you monger.
Mentioning that, mentioning this, I felt content covering that face with metal.
An object created to capture time, but used more frequently to capture vanity.

Boredom.
Bore.
Boring little cunt.

The tranquil feeling of breathing and pushing your face up against metal, looking through the lens, observing the life on the other side. Gave me, sporadically, peace of mind, but each and every ut the metal machine down, holding it with t hand against the lower part of my body, othing. I never saw life through my own /hat a crock of shit.

ctor Boullet and I am a balding, dying, ng machine searching for my own self-love ys. I will share the unutterable, self-indulged nce of absolute nothingness and my own, etentious, life with you.
ve is my own experience and that is what fortlessly try to discover, just to plunge the knife back into its gut.

Janus you, me, all.

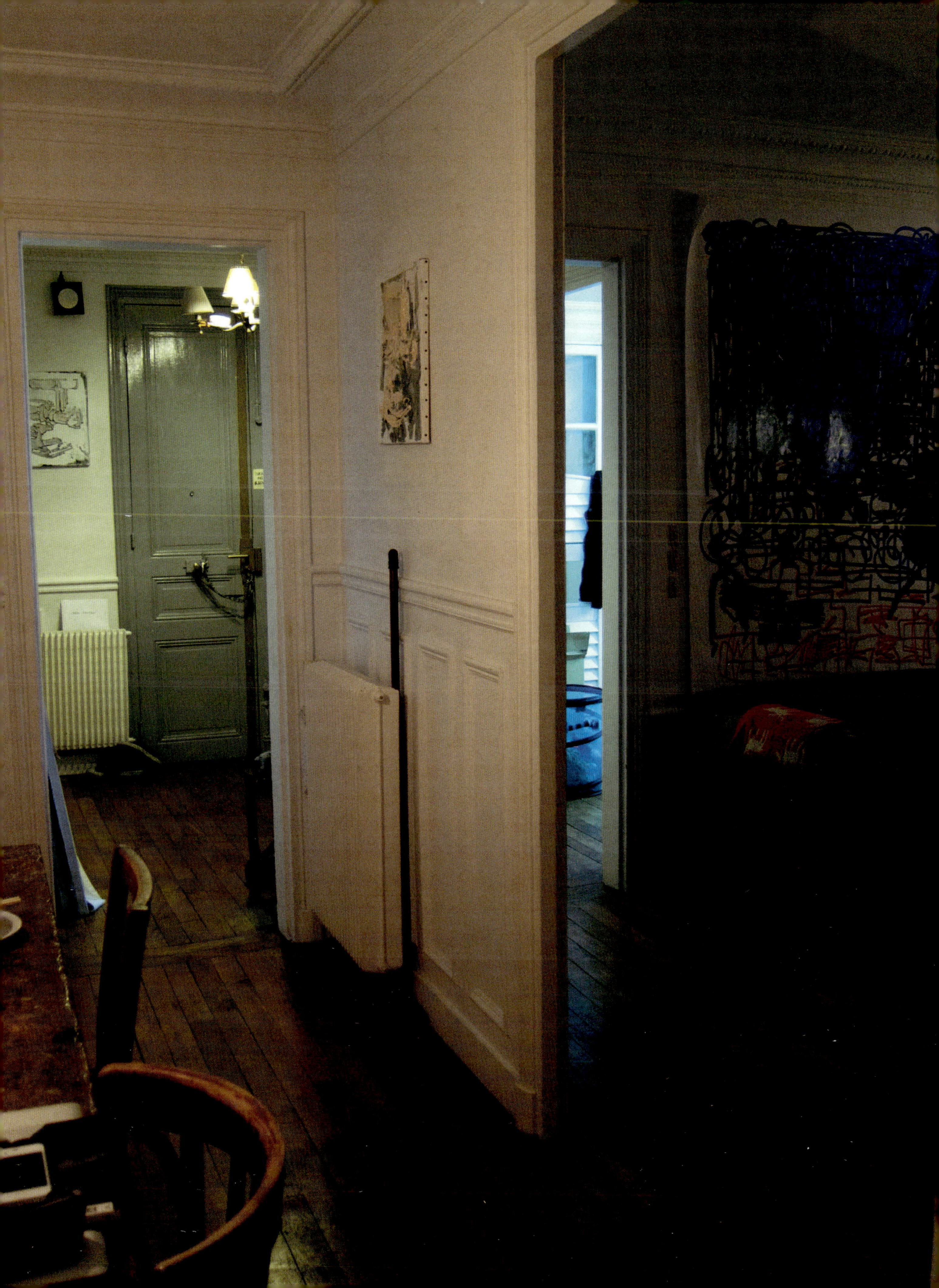

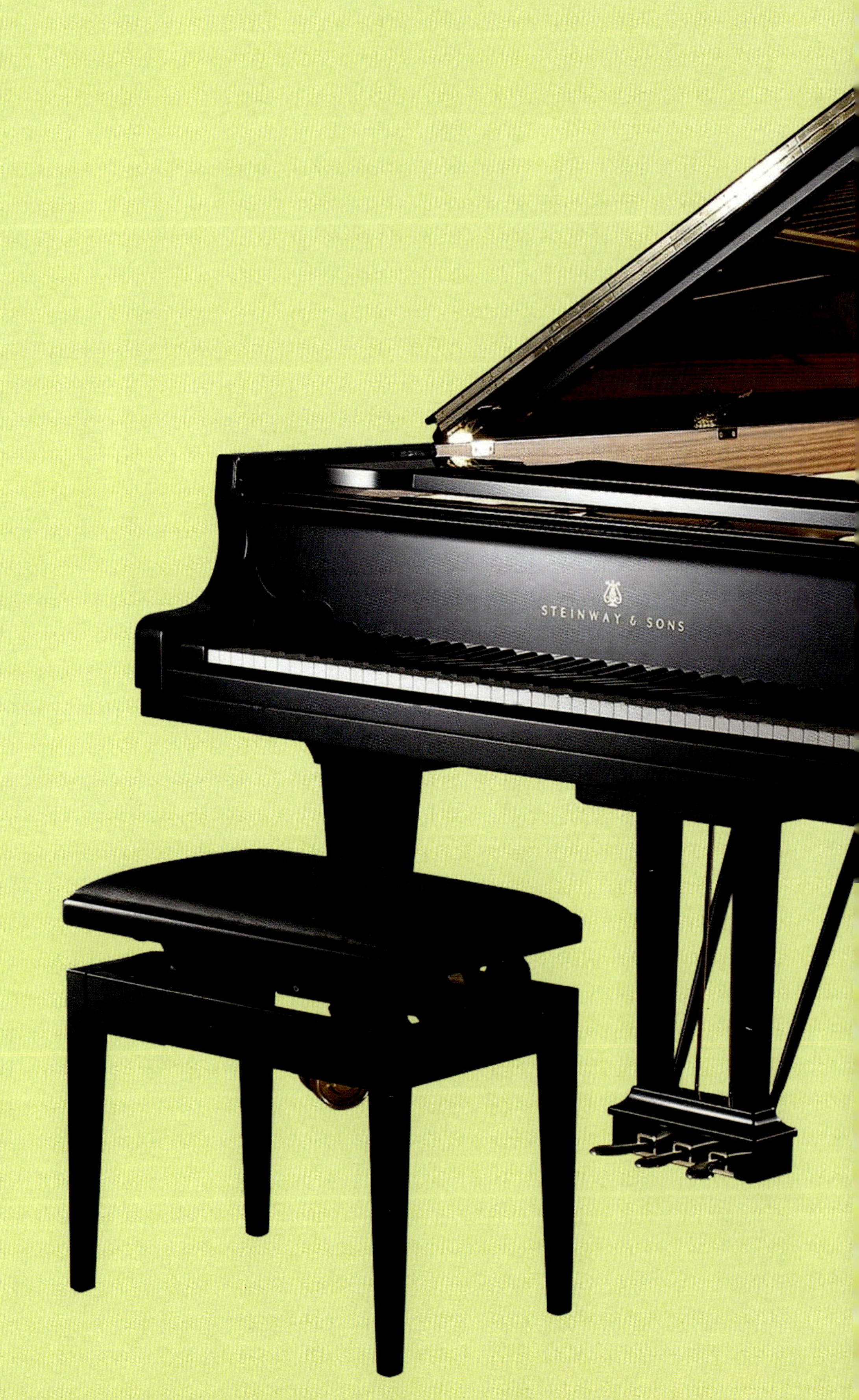
STEINWAY & SONS

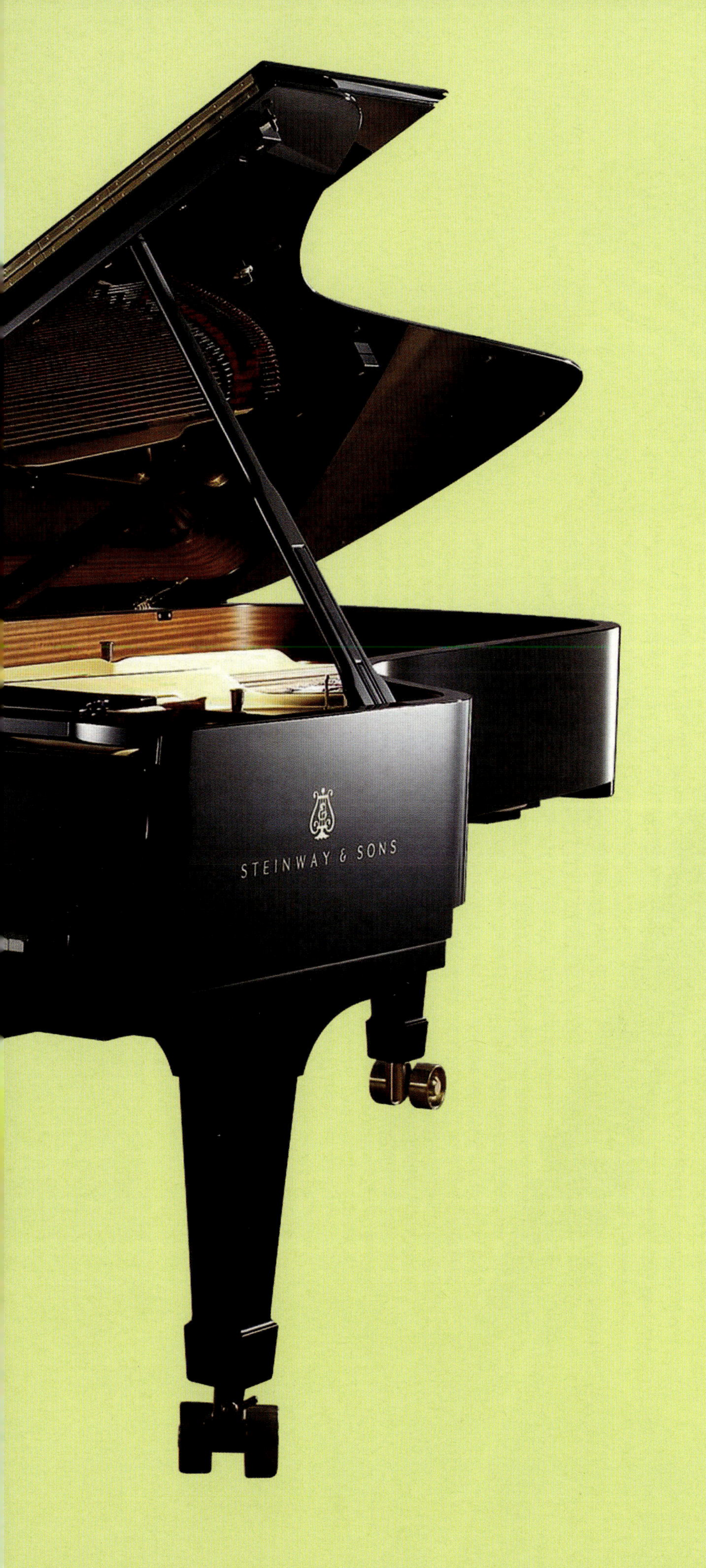
STEINWAY & SONS

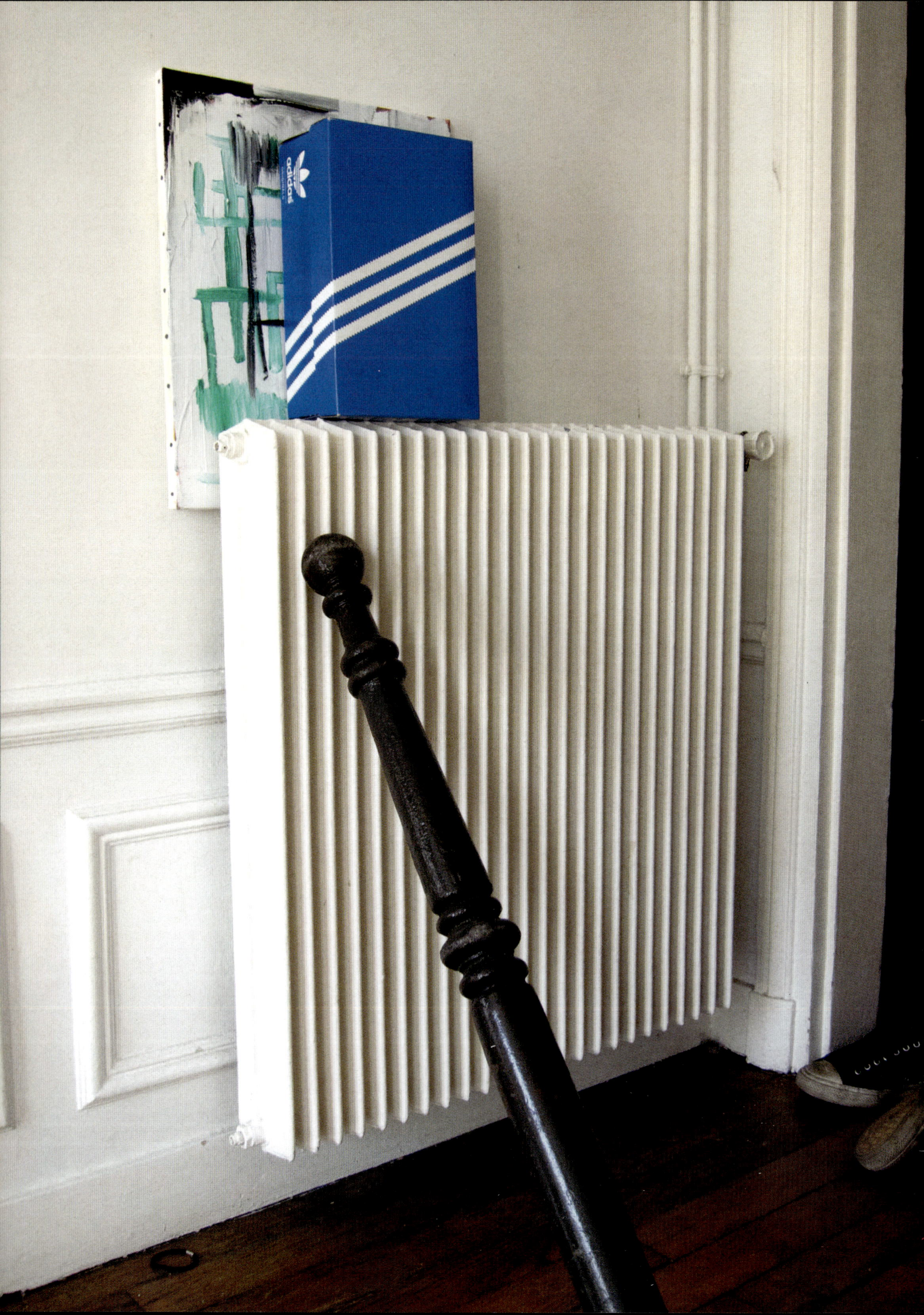
adidas

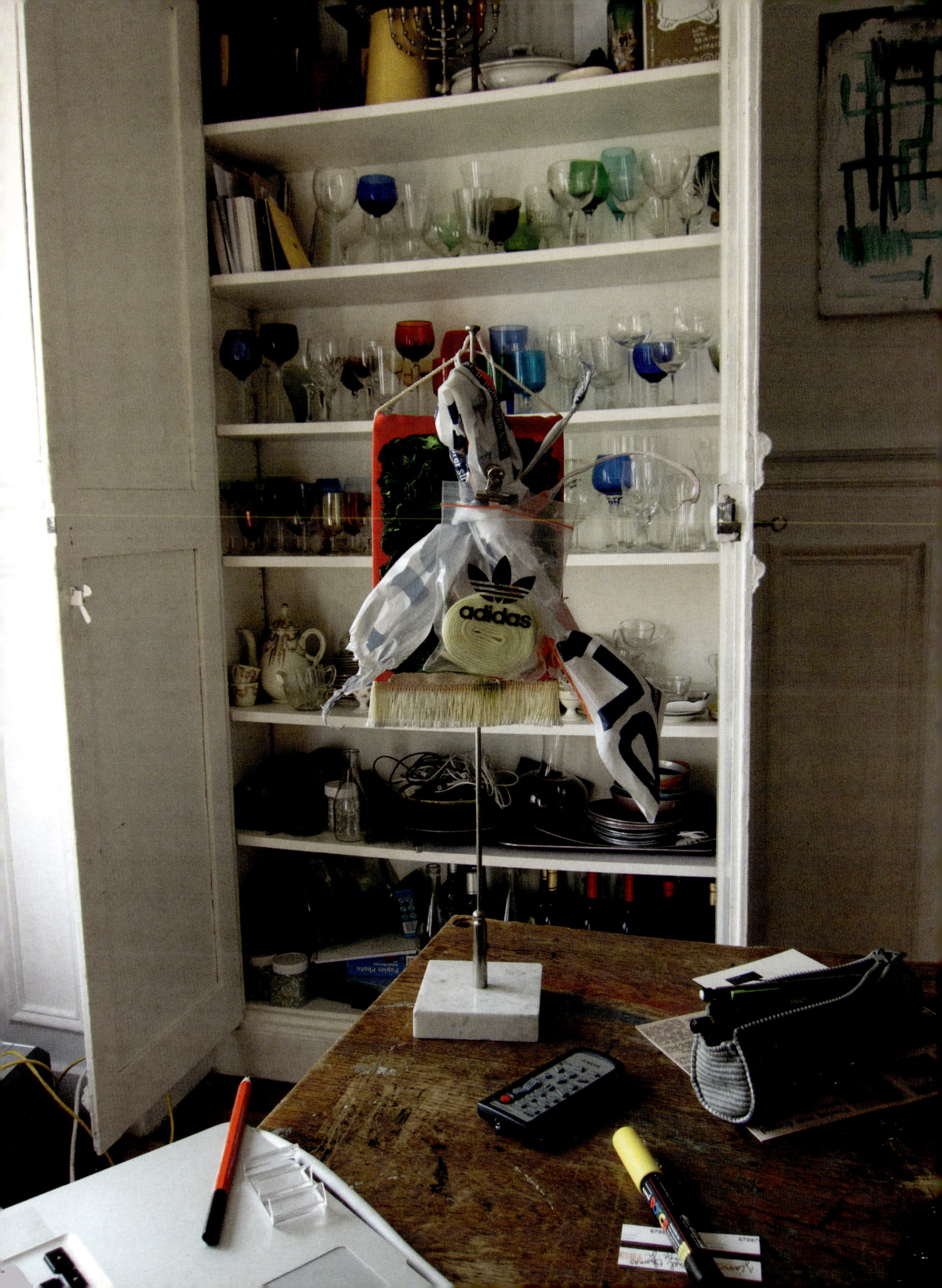
adidas

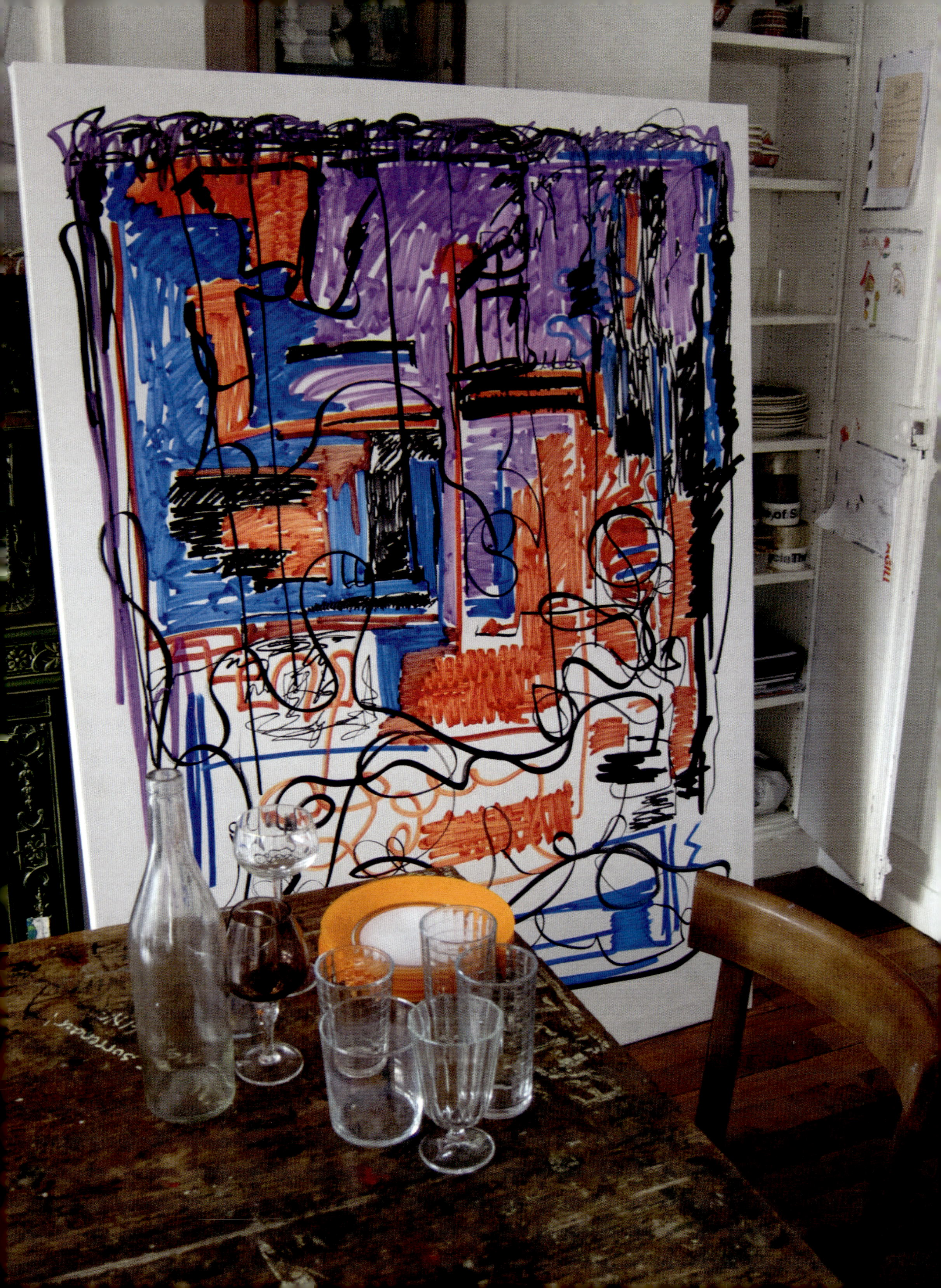

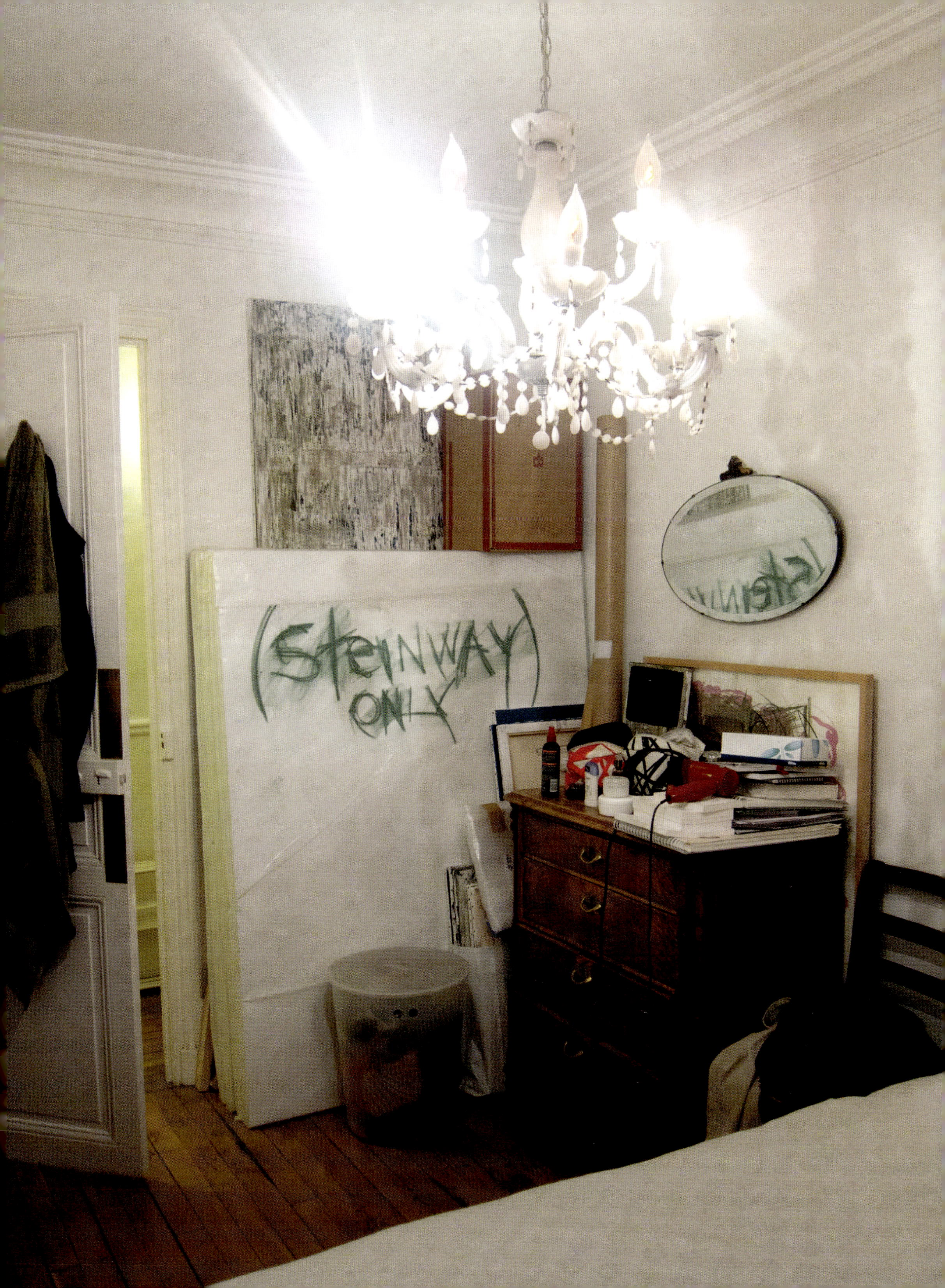
(STEINWAY)
ONLY

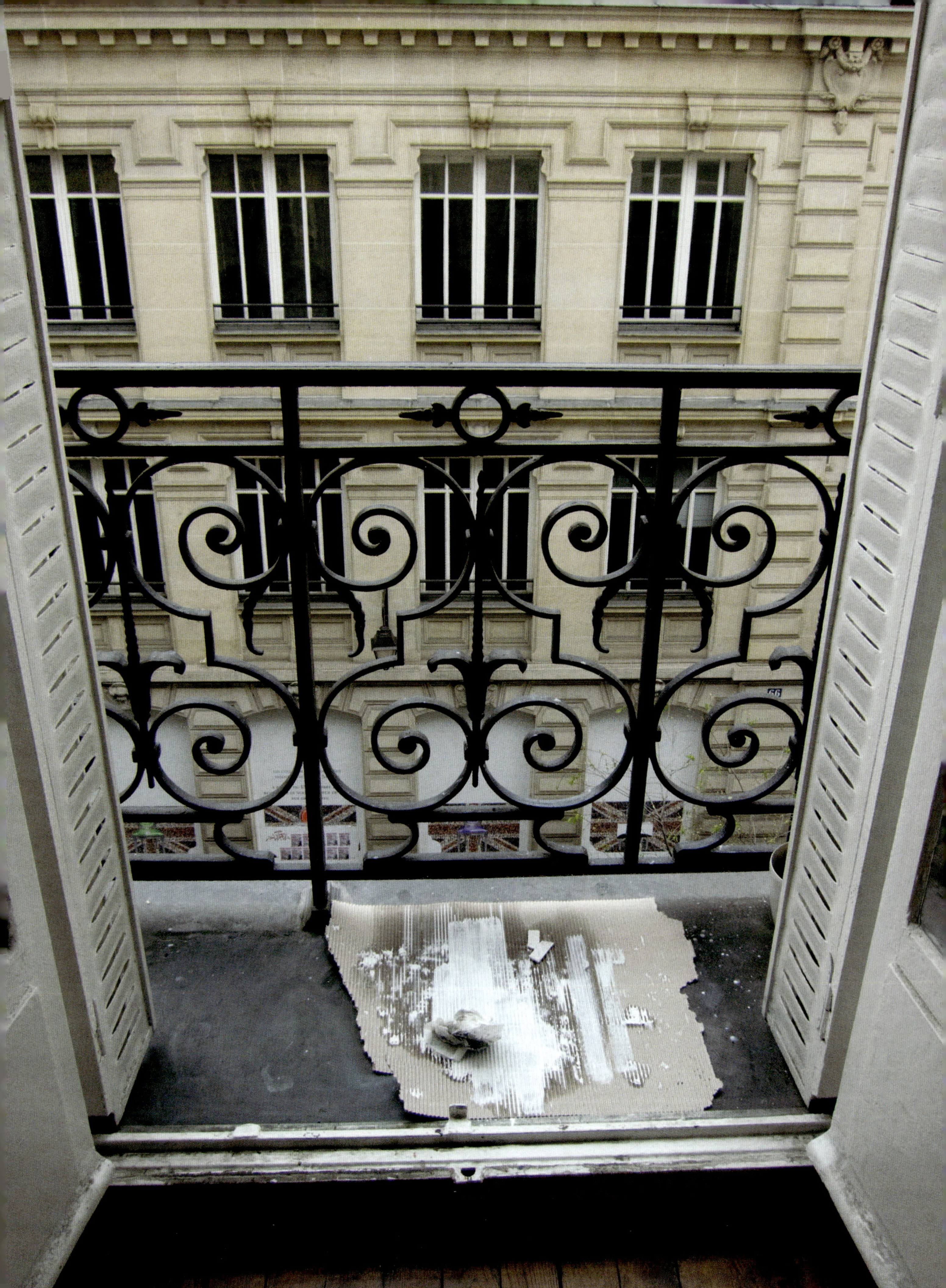

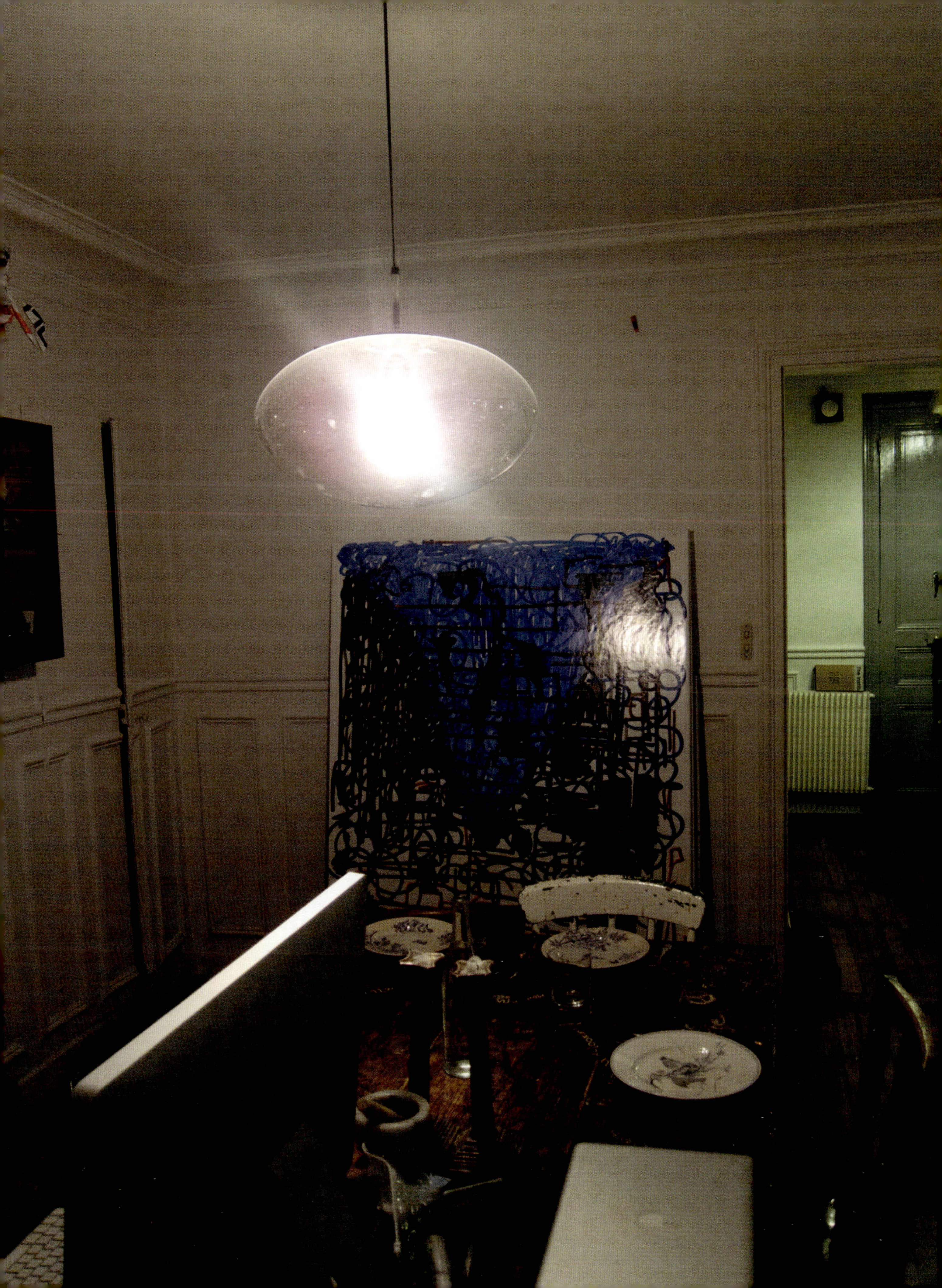

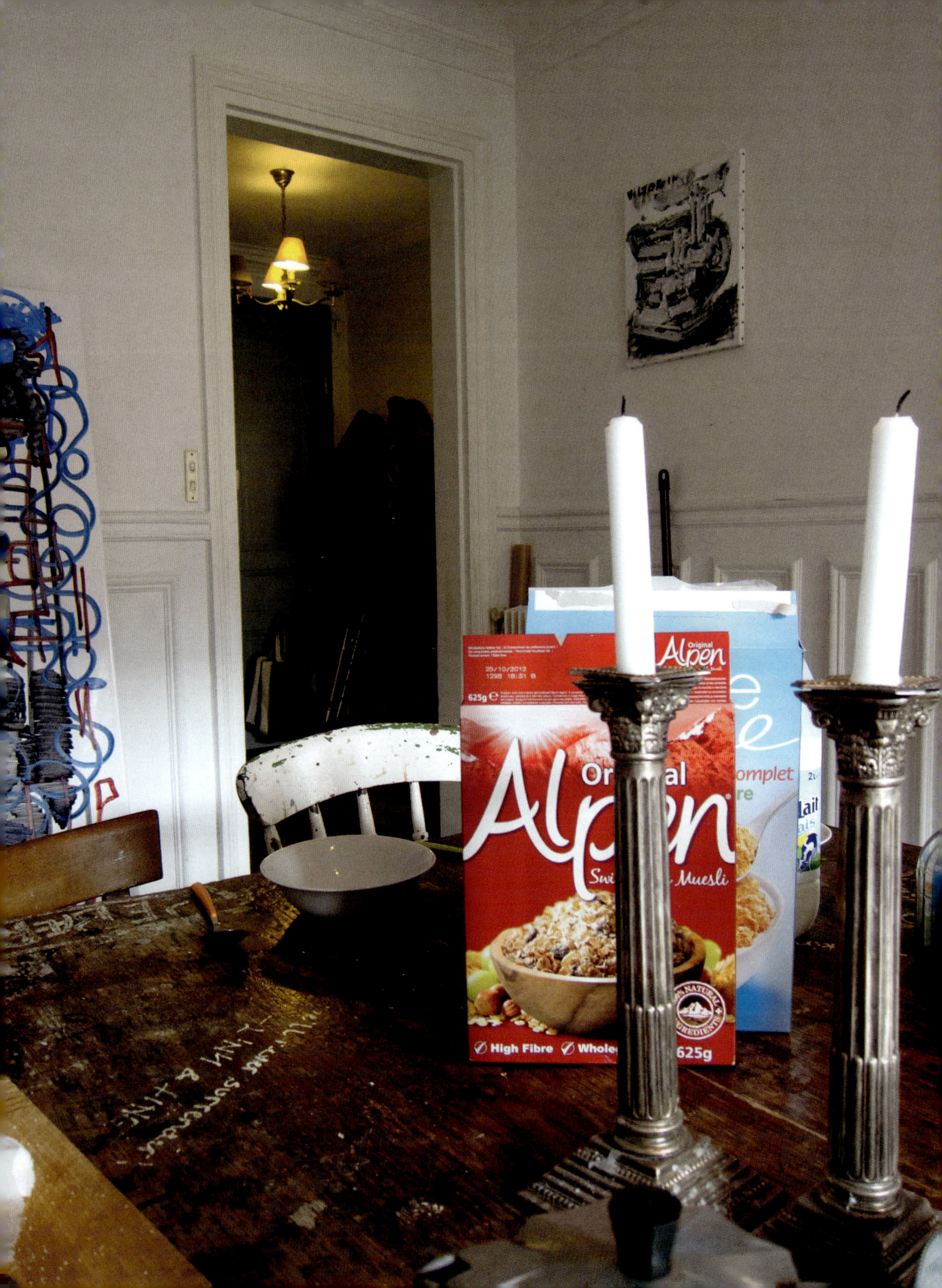
Original
Alpen
Muesli
High Fibre
625g
omplet

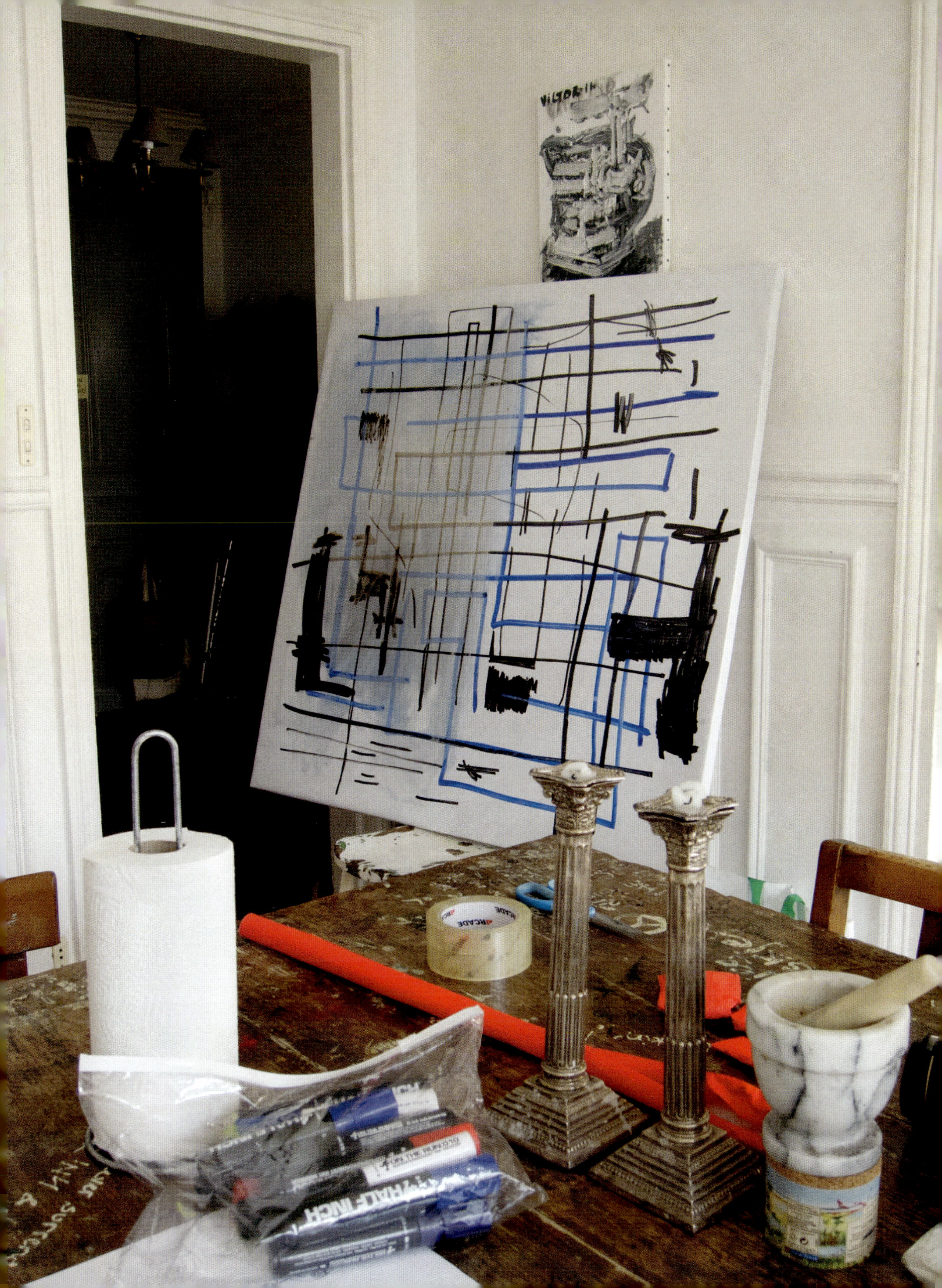
ARCADE
HALFINCH

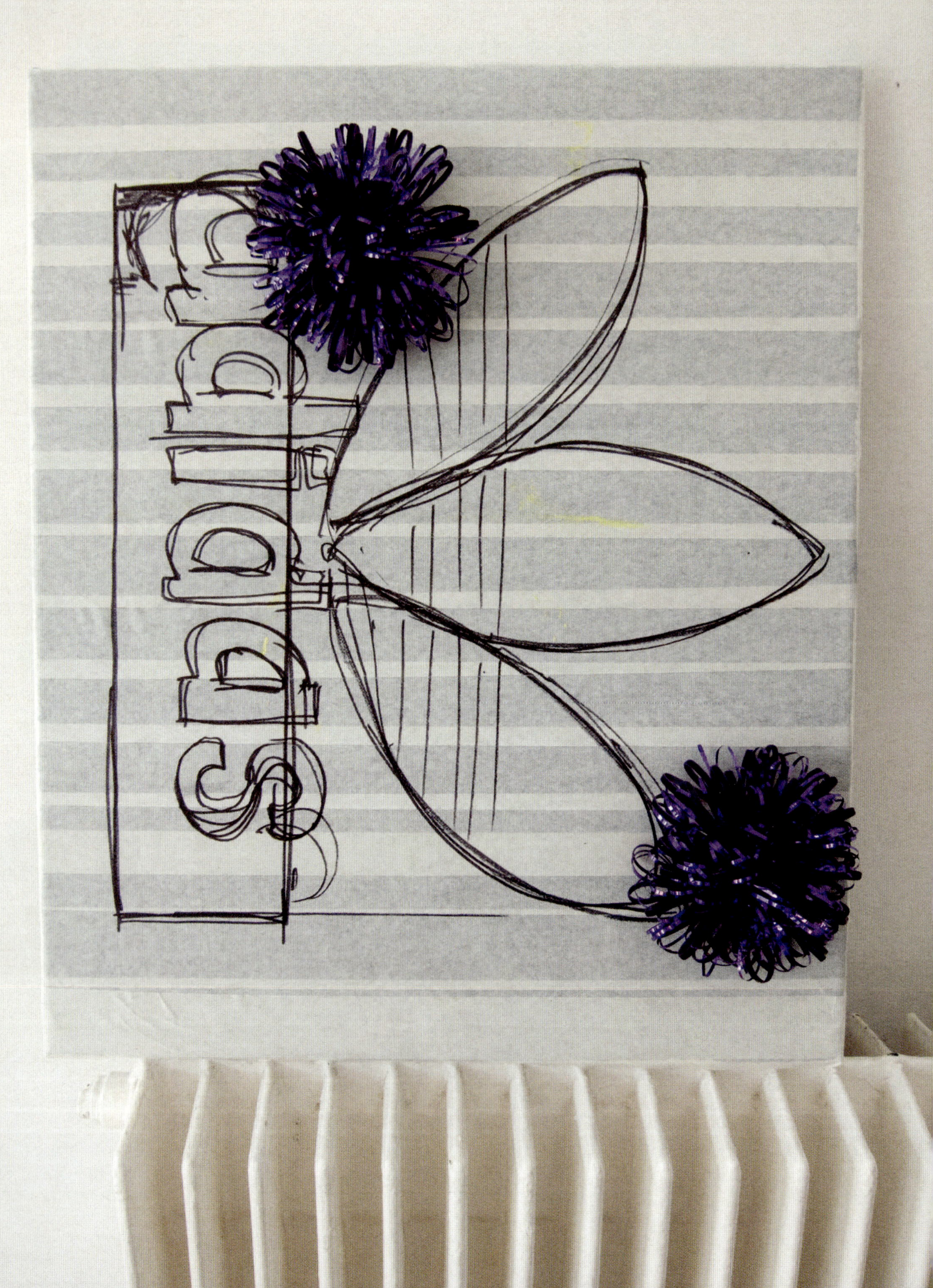

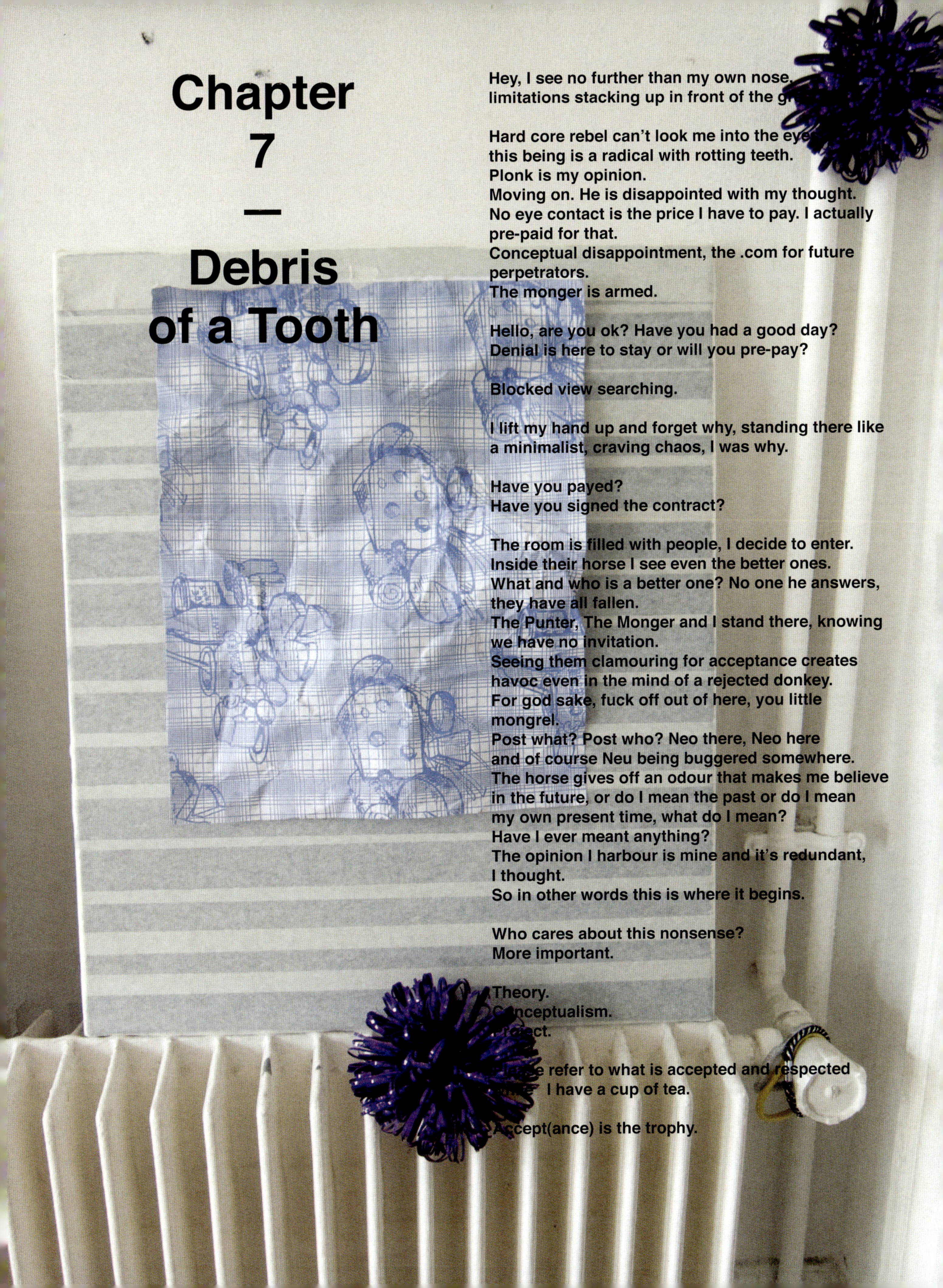

Chapter 7 — Debris of a Tooth

Hey, I see no further than my own nose,
limitations stacking up in front of the g[illegible]

Hard core rebel can't look me into the eye[illegible]
this being is a radical with rotting teeth.
Plonk is my opinion.
Moving on. He is disappointed with my thought.
No eye contact is the price I have to pay. I actually
pre-paid for that.
Conceptual disappointment, the .com for future
perpetrators.
The monger is armed.

Hello, are you ok? Have you had a good day?
Denial is here to stay or will you pre-pay?

Blocked view searching.

I lift my hand up and forget why, standing there like
a minimalist, craving chaos, I was why.

Have you payed?
Have you signed the contract?

The room is filled with people, I decide to enter.
Inside their horse I see even the better ones.
What and who is a better one? No one he answers,
they have all fallen.
The Punter, The Monger and I stand there, knowing
we have no invitation.
Seeing them clamouring for acceptance creates
havoc even in the mind of a rejected donkey.
For god sake, fuck off out of here, you little
mongrel.
Post what? Post who? Neo there, Neo here
and of course Neu being buggered somewhere.
The horse gives off an odour that makes me believe
in the future, or do I mean the past or do I mean
my own present time, what do I mean?
Have I ever meant anything?
The opinion I harbour is mine and it's redundant,
I thought.
So in other words this is where it begins.

Who cares about this nonsense?
More important.

Theory.
Conceptualism.
Project.

Please refer to what is accepted and respected
[illegible] I have a cup of tea.

Accept(ance) is the trophy.

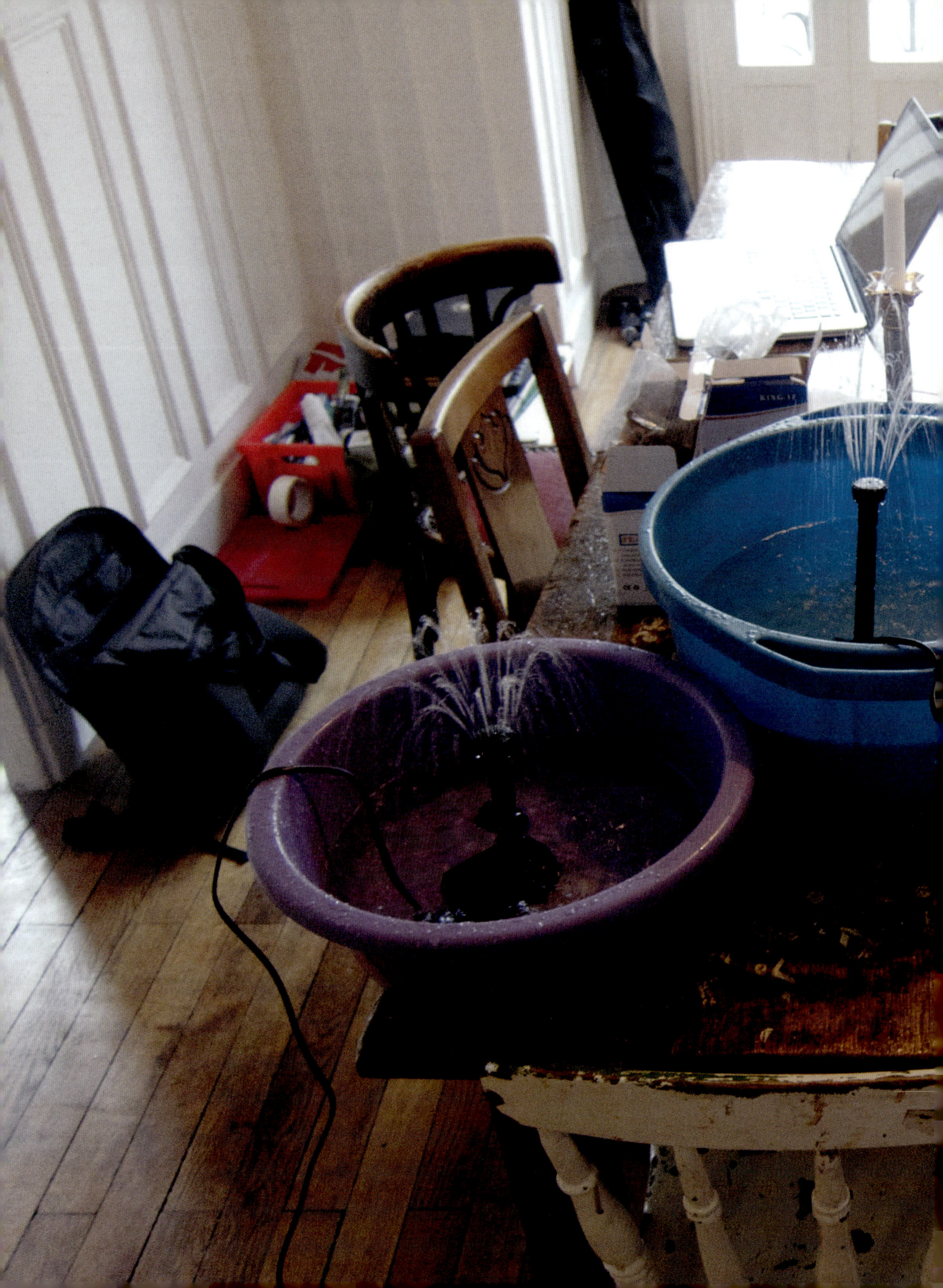

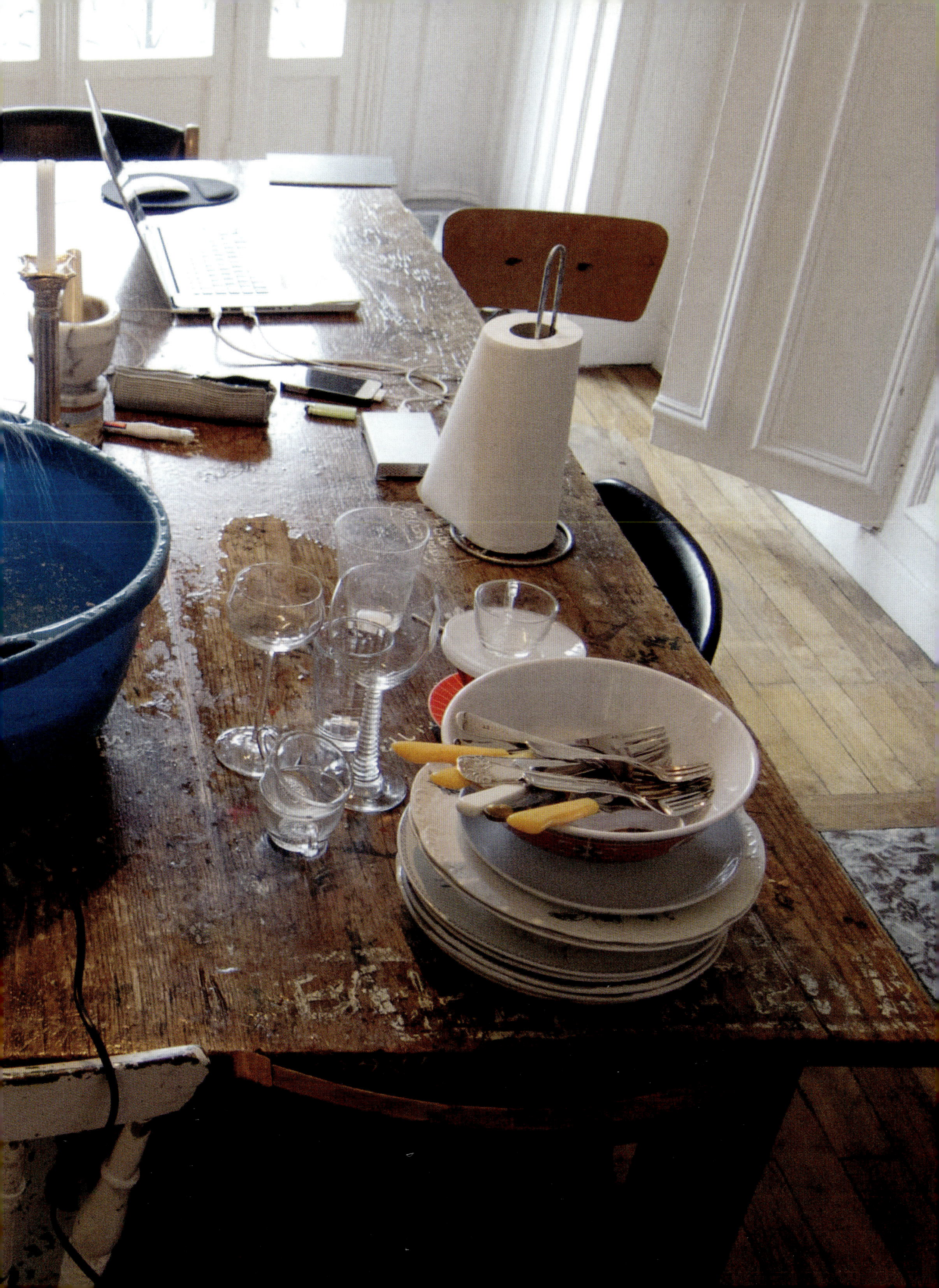

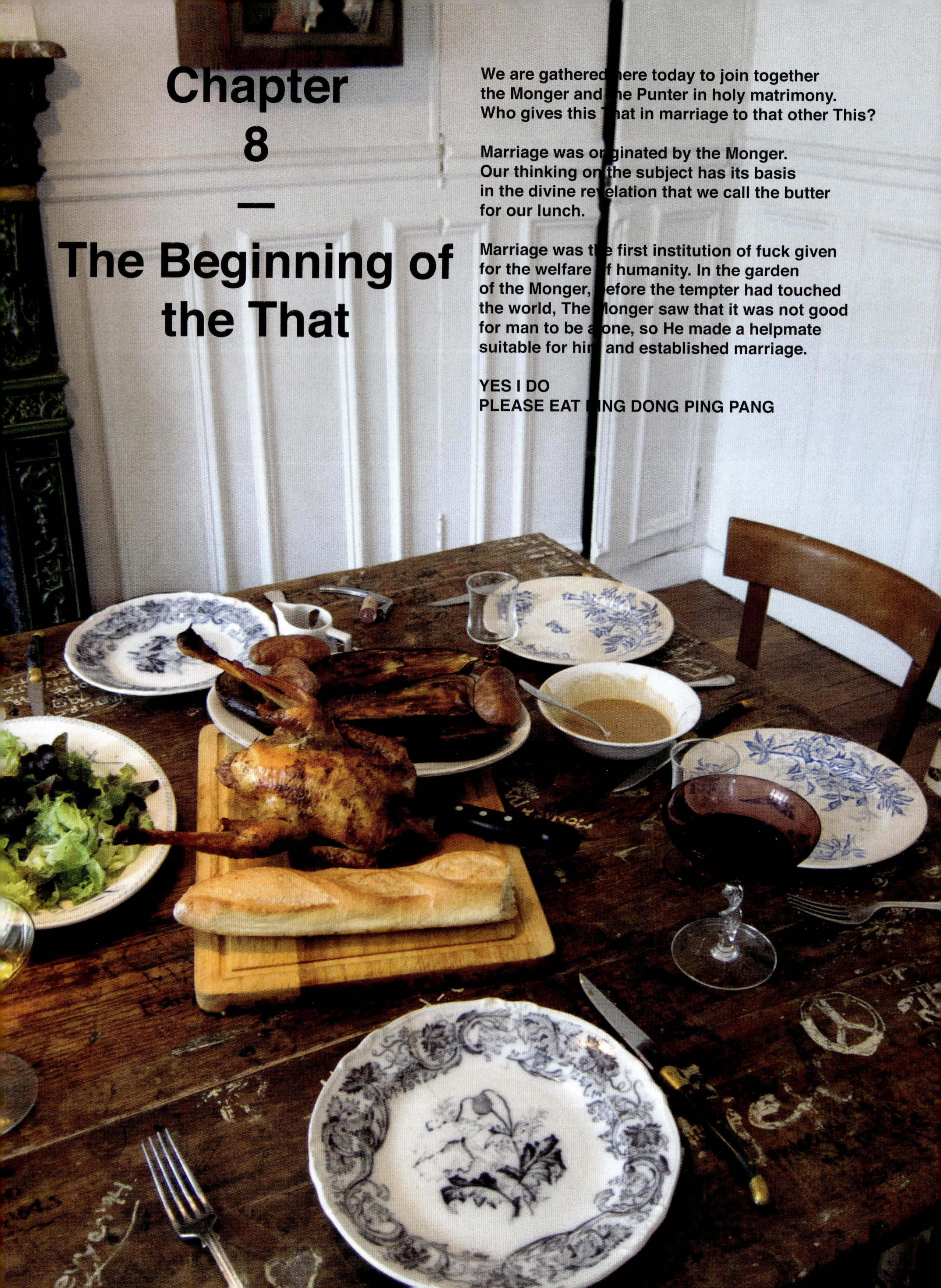

Chapter 8

—

The Beginning of the That

We are gathered here today to join together the Monger and the Punter in holy matrimony. Who gives this That in marriage to that other This?

Marriage was originated by the Monger. Our thinking on the subject has its basis in the divine revelation that we call the butter for our lunch.

Marriage was the first institution of fuck given for the welfare of humanity. In the garden of the Monger, before the tempter had touched the world, The Monger saw that it was not good for man to be alone, so He made a helpmate suitable for him and established marriage.

YES I DO
PLEASE EAT [illegible]ING DONG PING PANG

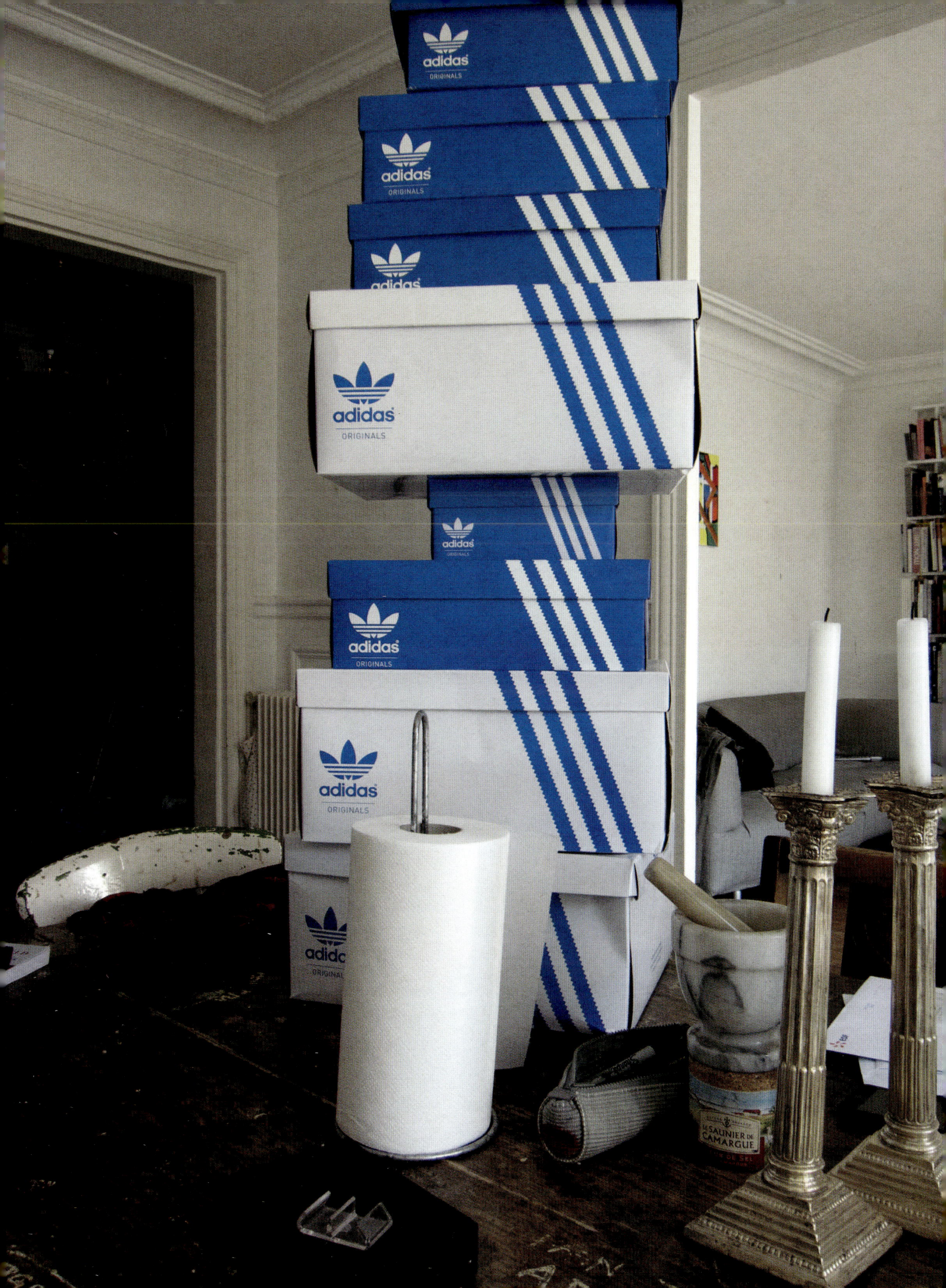
adidas
ORIGINALS
LE SAUNIER DE CAMARGUE

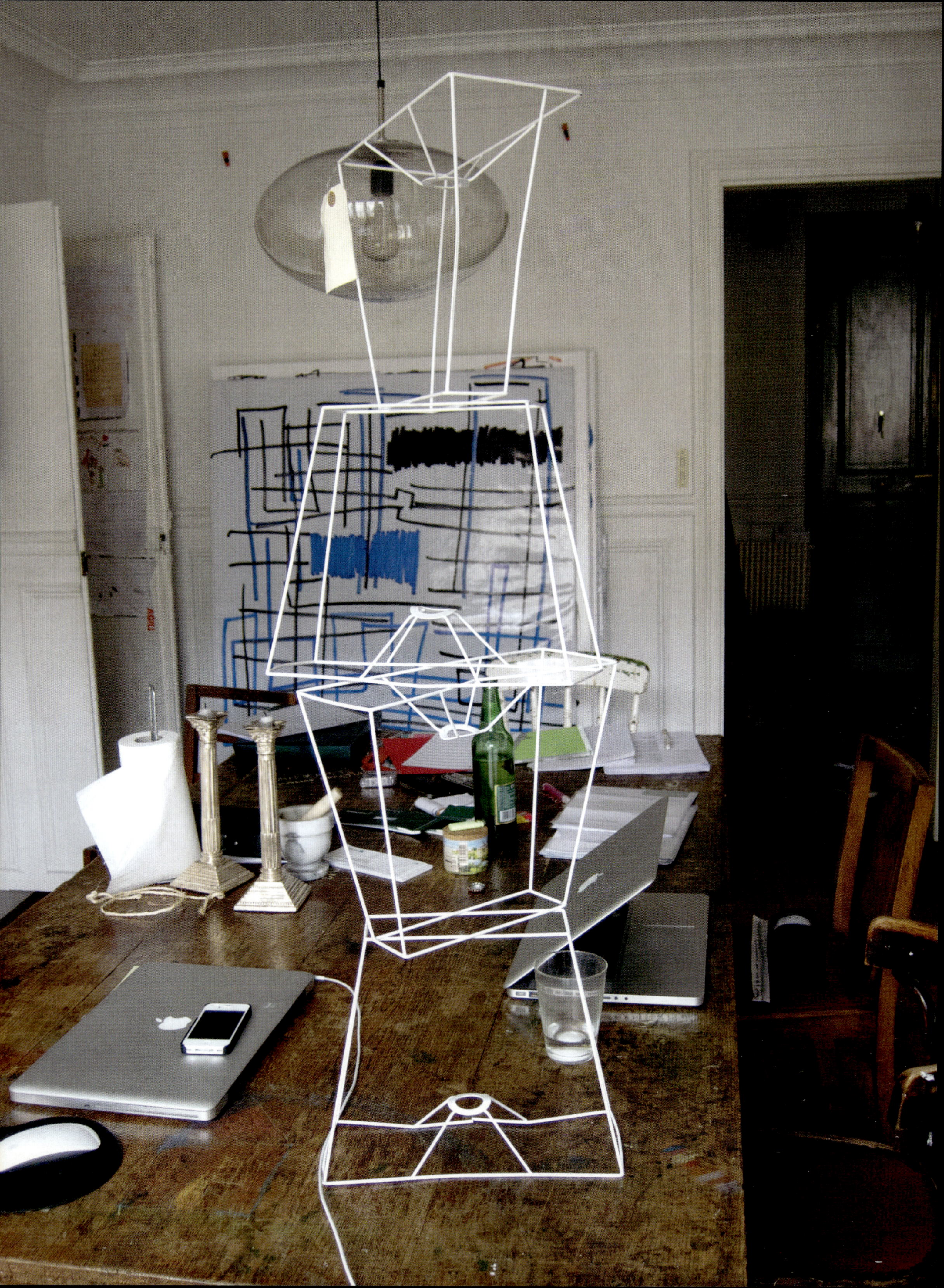

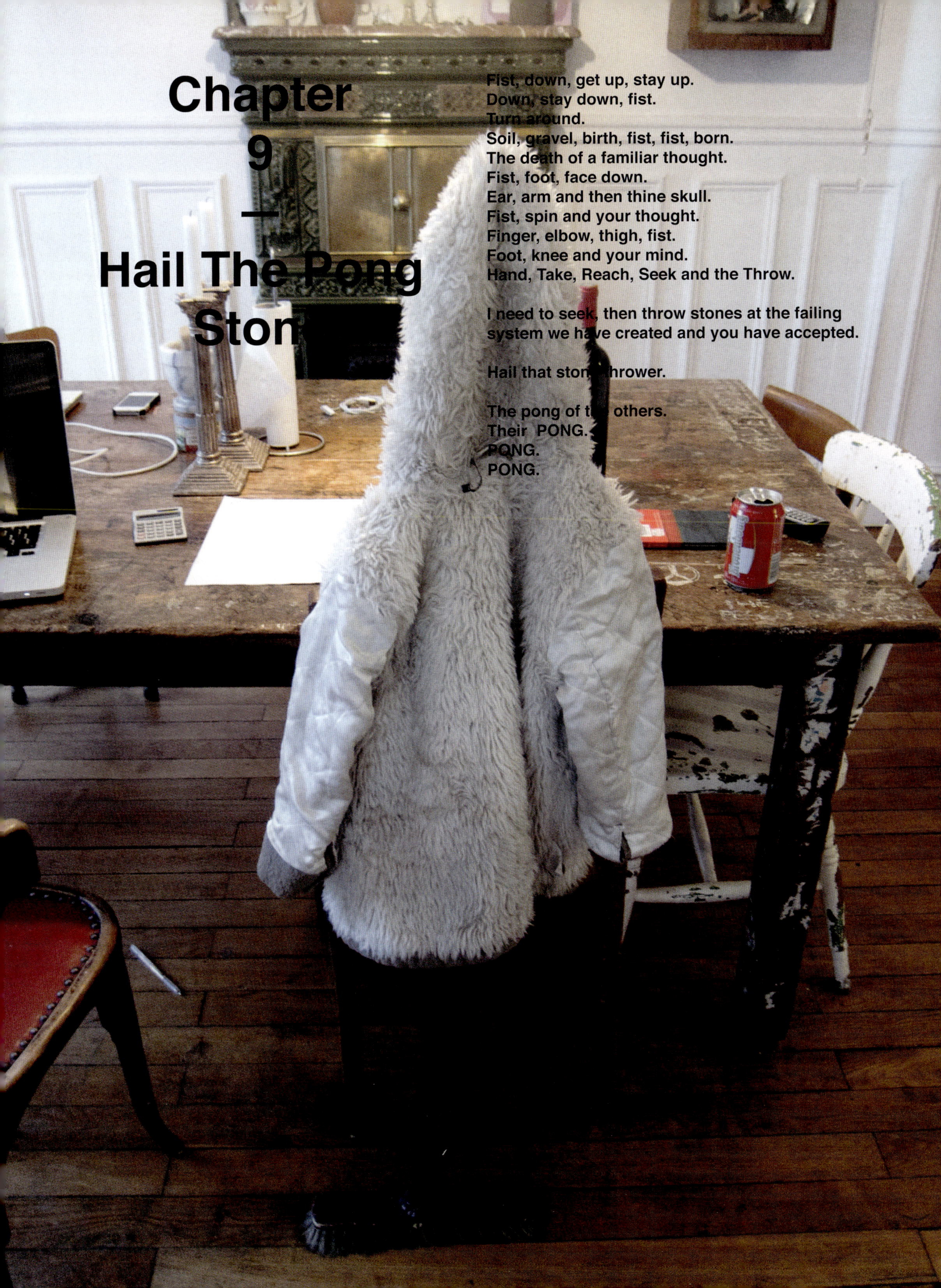

Chapter 9 — Hail The Pong Ston

Fist, down, get up, stay up.
Down, stay down, fist.
Turn around.
Soil, gravel, birth, fist, fist, born.
The death of a familiar thought.
Fist, foot, face down.
Ear, arm and then thine skull.
Fist, spin and your thought.
Finger, elbow, thigh, fist.
Foot, knee and your mind.
Hand, Take, Reach, Seek and the Throw.

I need to seek, then throw stones at the failing system we have created and you have accepted.

Hail that ston hrower.

The pong of t others.
Their PONG.
PONG.
PONG.

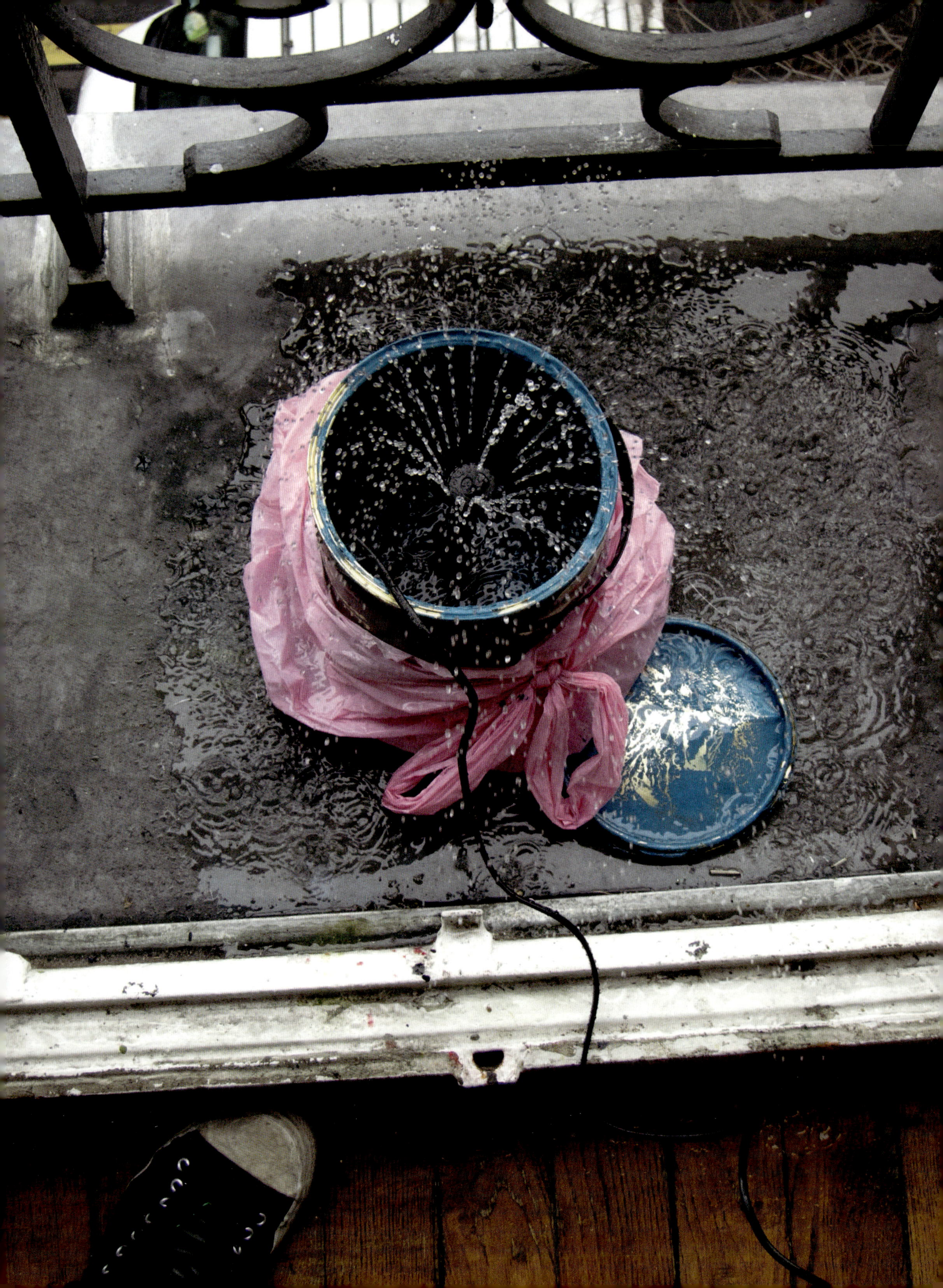

Chapter 10 — Comb Over

I steal.
I lie.
I cheat.

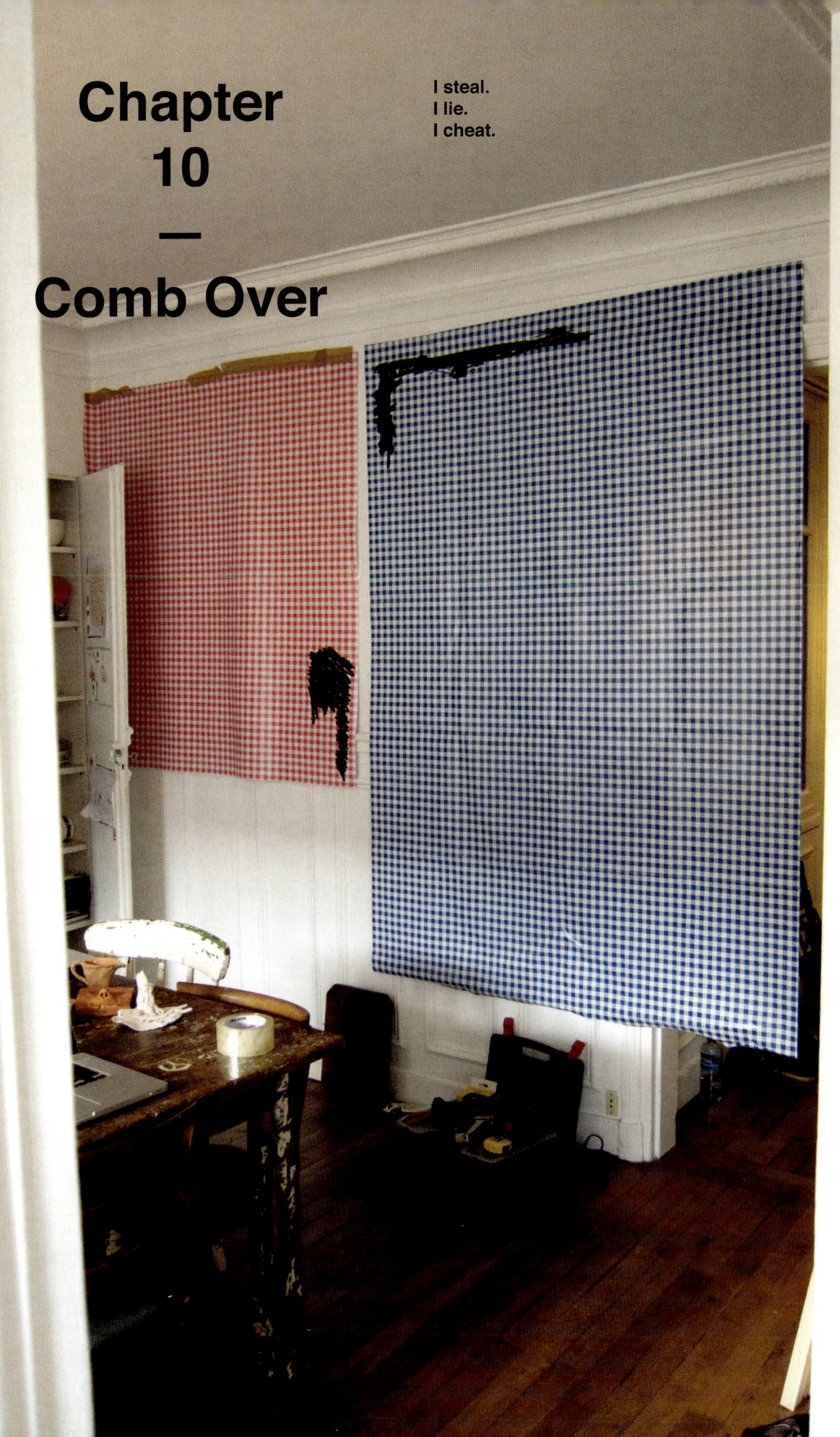

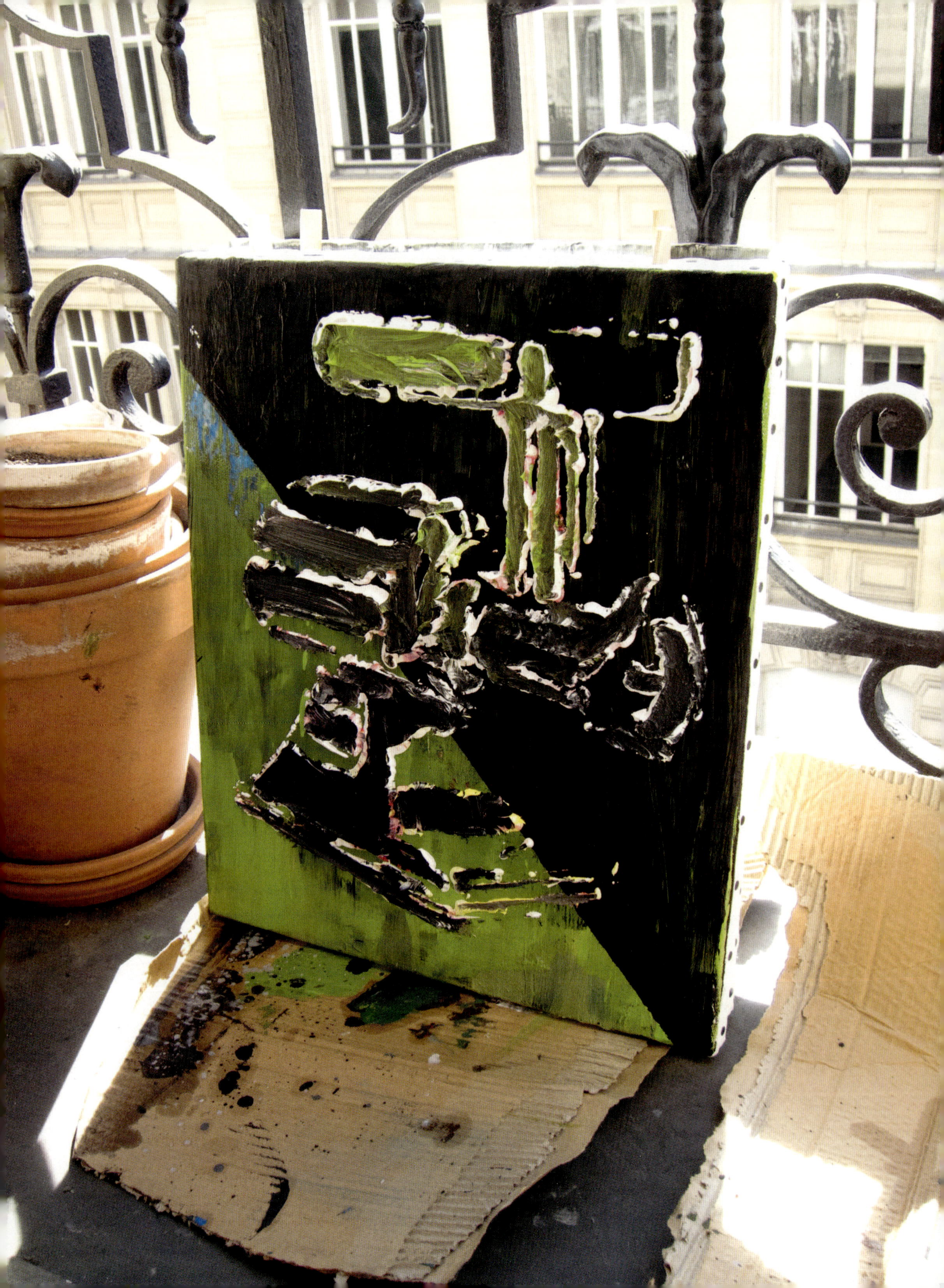

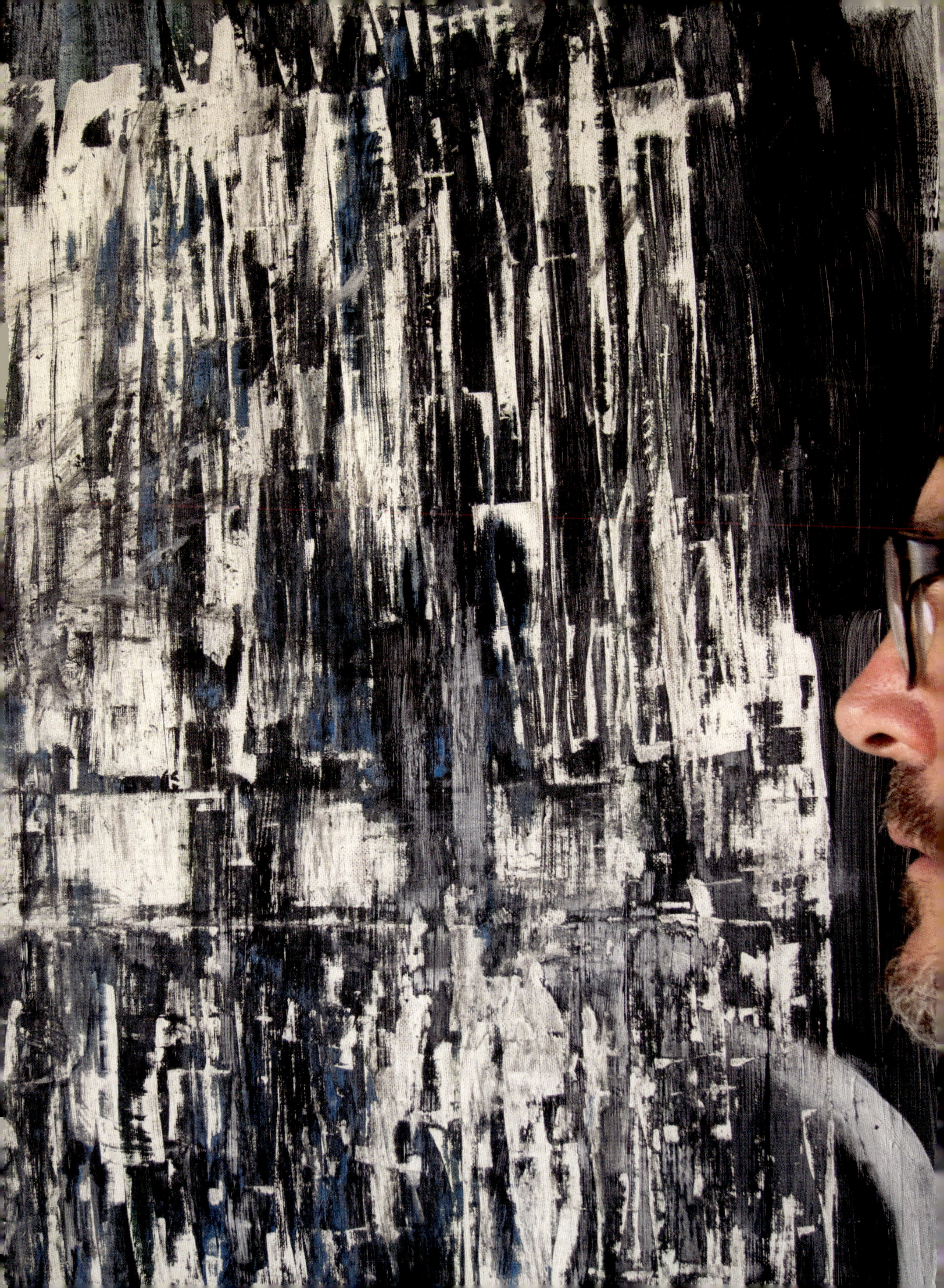

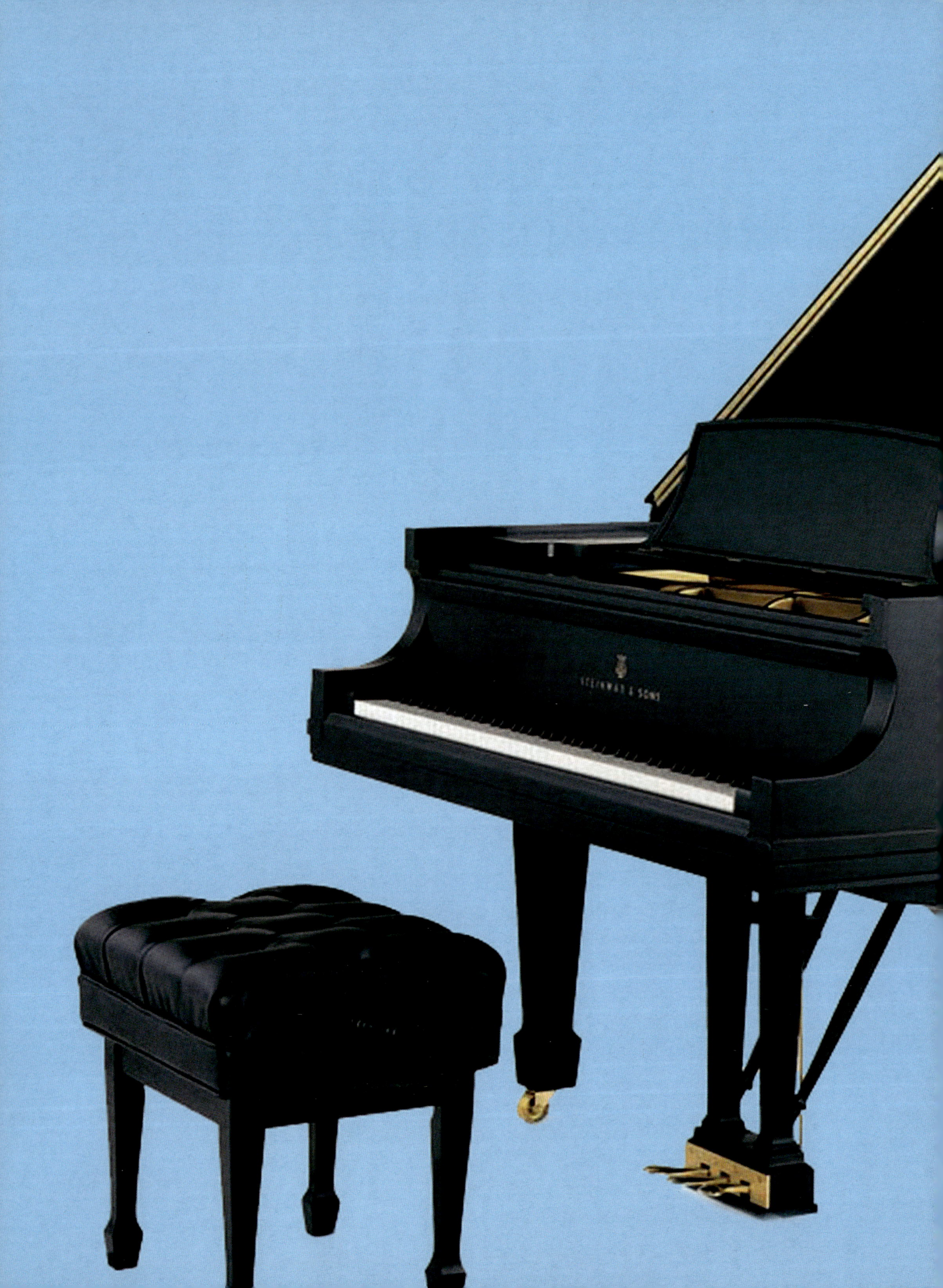

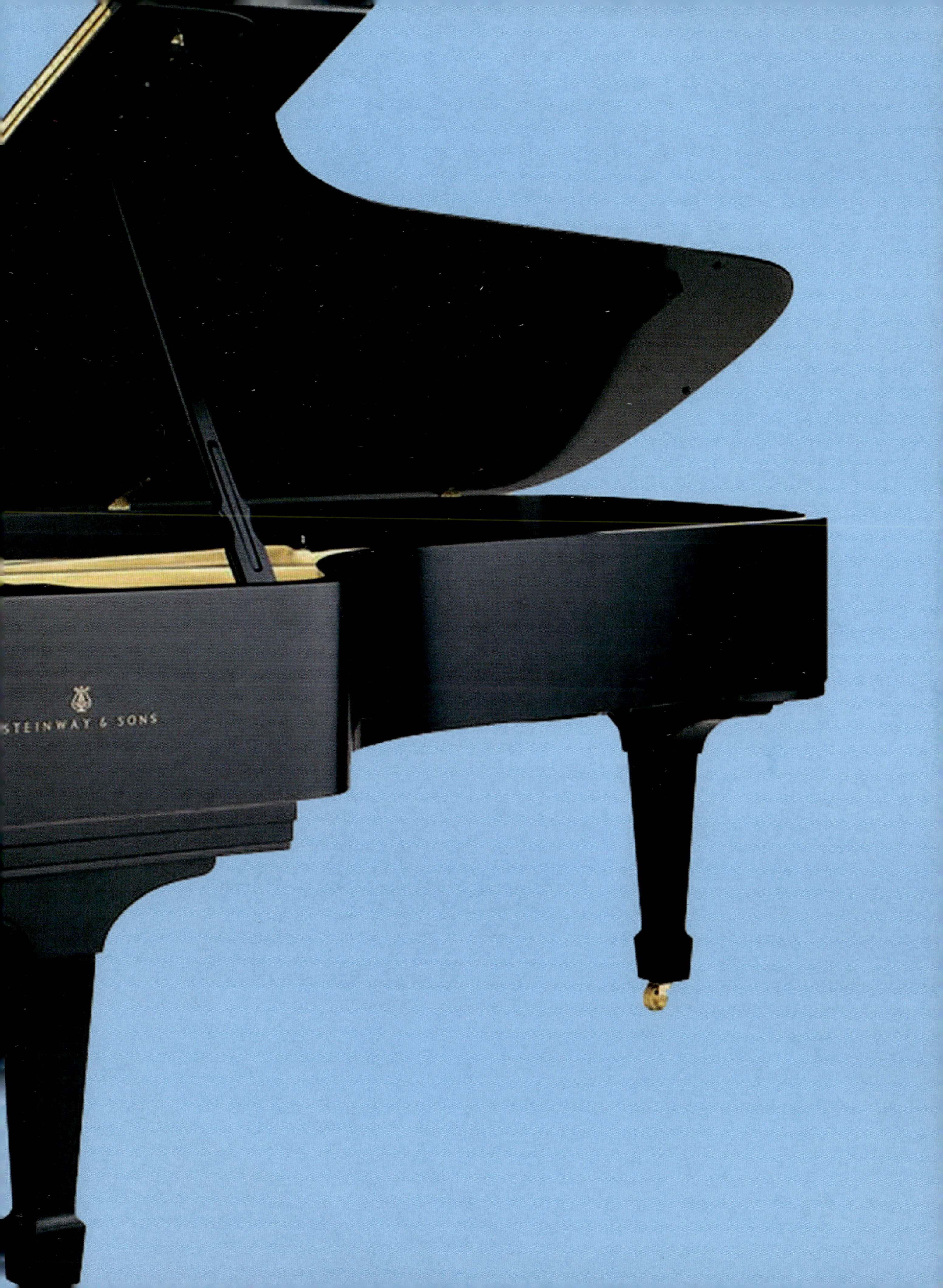
STEINWAY & SONS

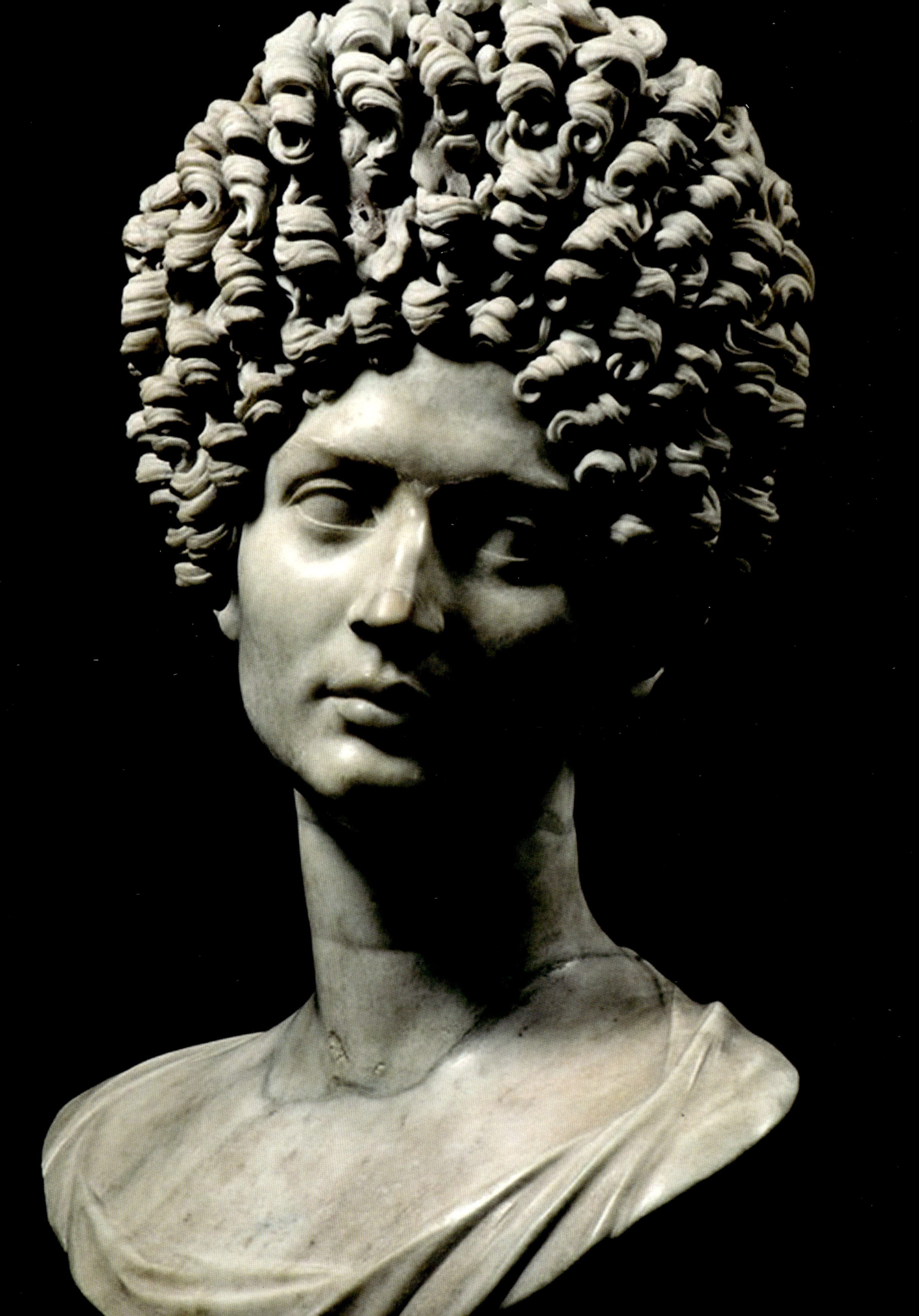

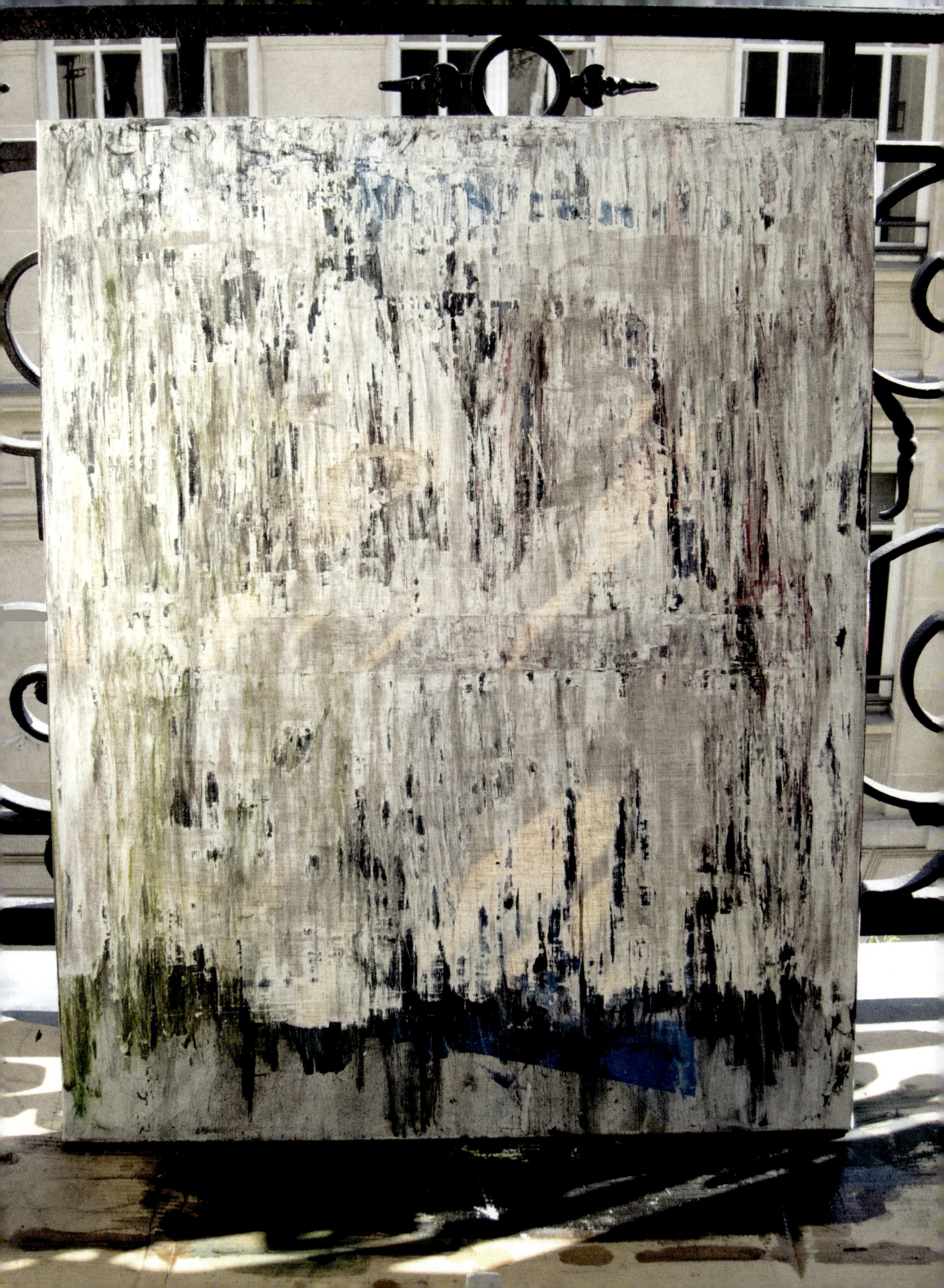

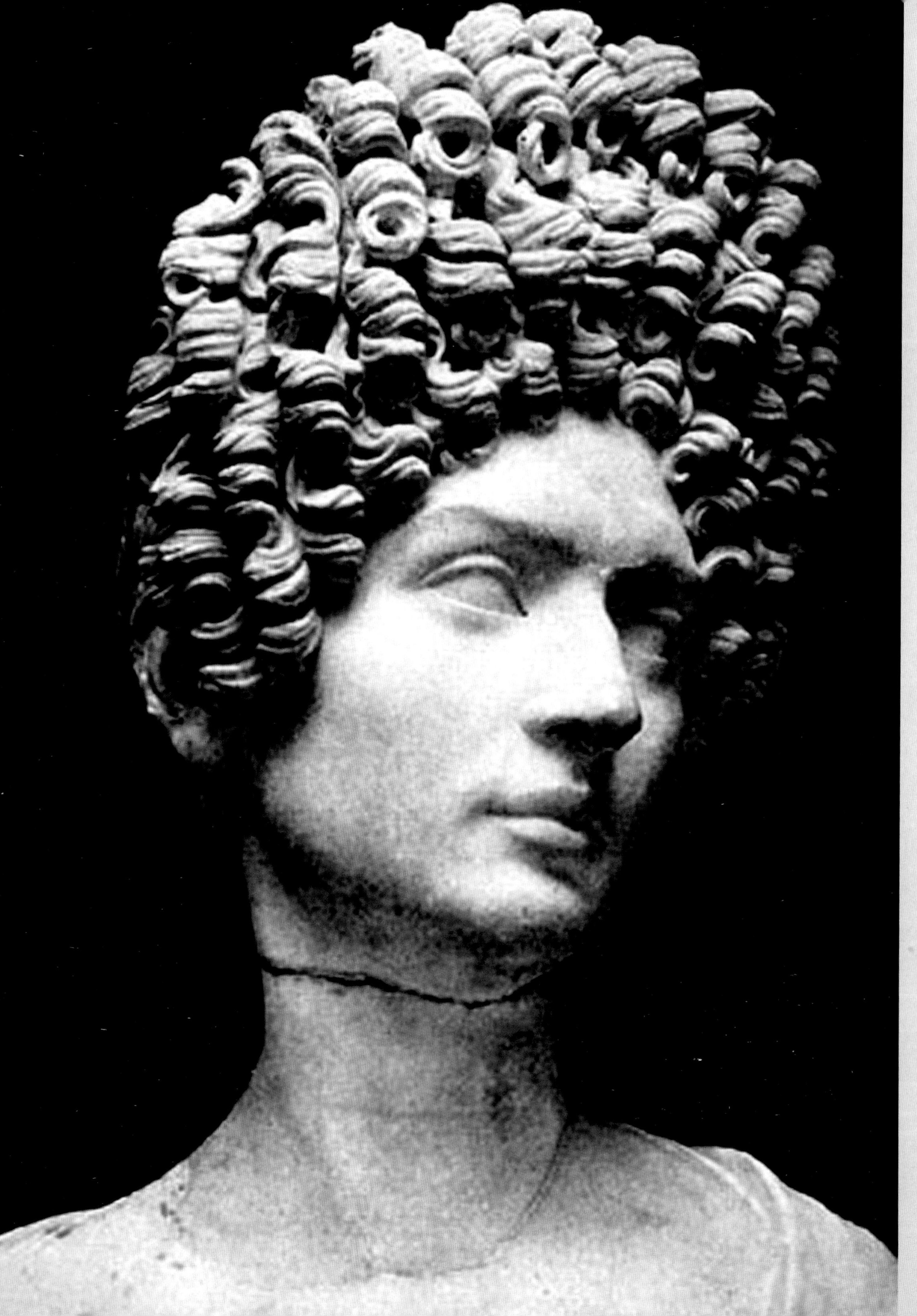

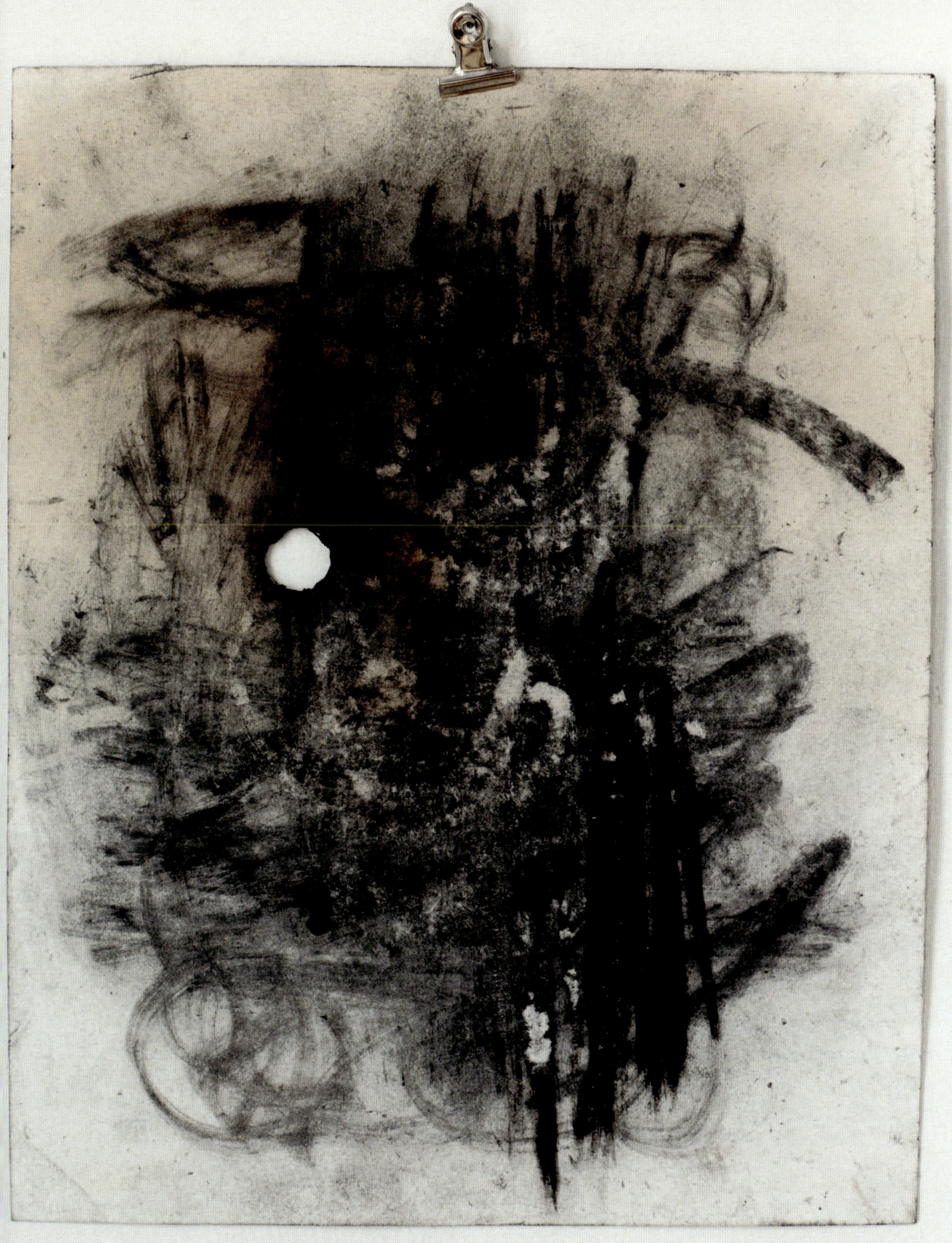

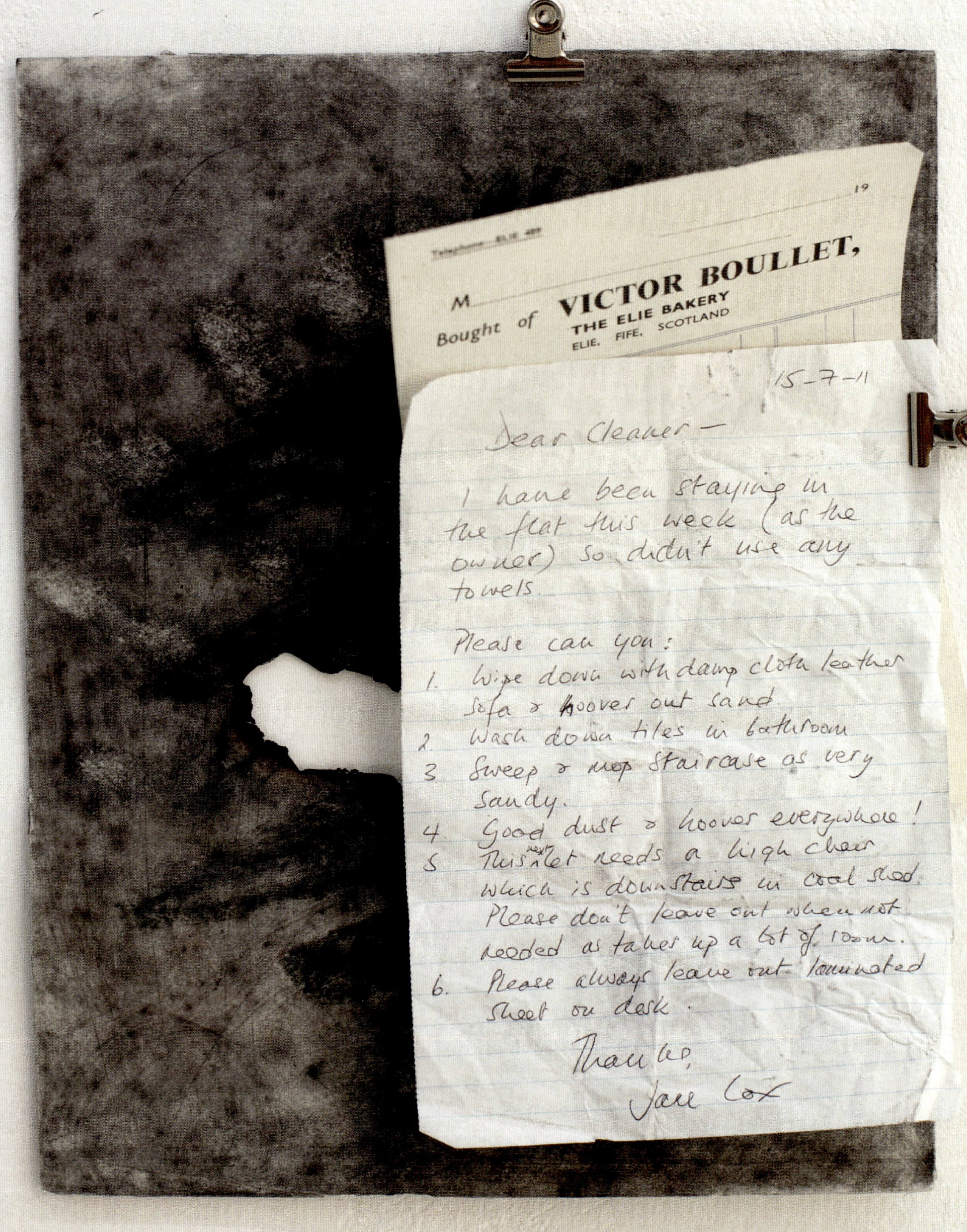

M

19

Bought of **VICTOR BOULLET,**
THE ELIE BAKERY
ELIE, FIFE, SCOTLAND

15-7-11

Dear Cleaner —

I have been staying in the flat this week (as the owner) so didn't use any towels.

Please can you:

1. Wipe down with damp cloth leather sofa & hoover out sand.
2. Wash down tiles in bathroom
3. Sweep & mop staircase as very sandy.
4. Good dust & hoover everywhere!
5. This flat needs a high chair which is downstairs in coal shed. Please don't leave out when not needed as takes up a lot of room.
6. Please always leave out laminated sheet on desk.

Thanks,

Jane Cox

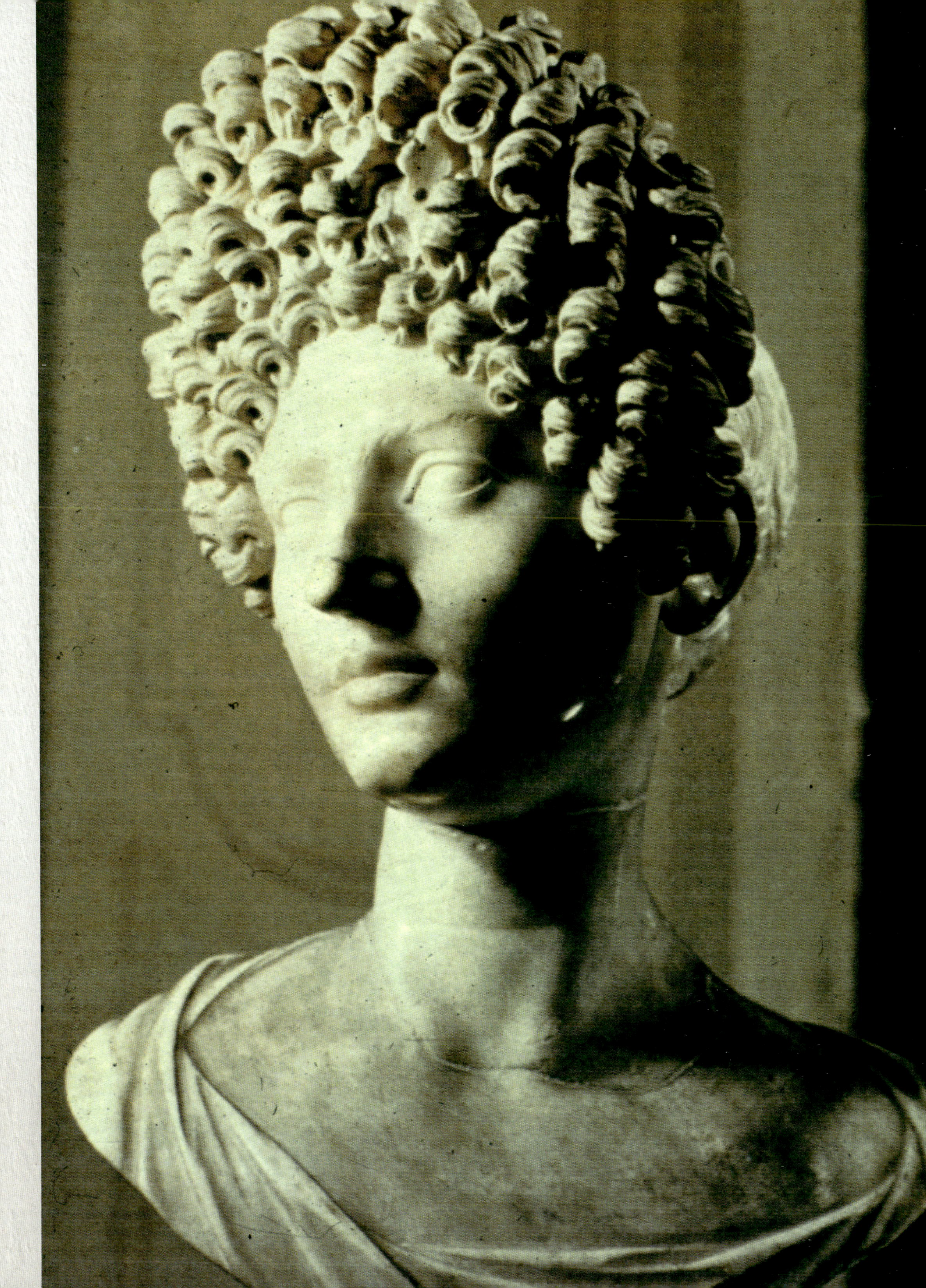

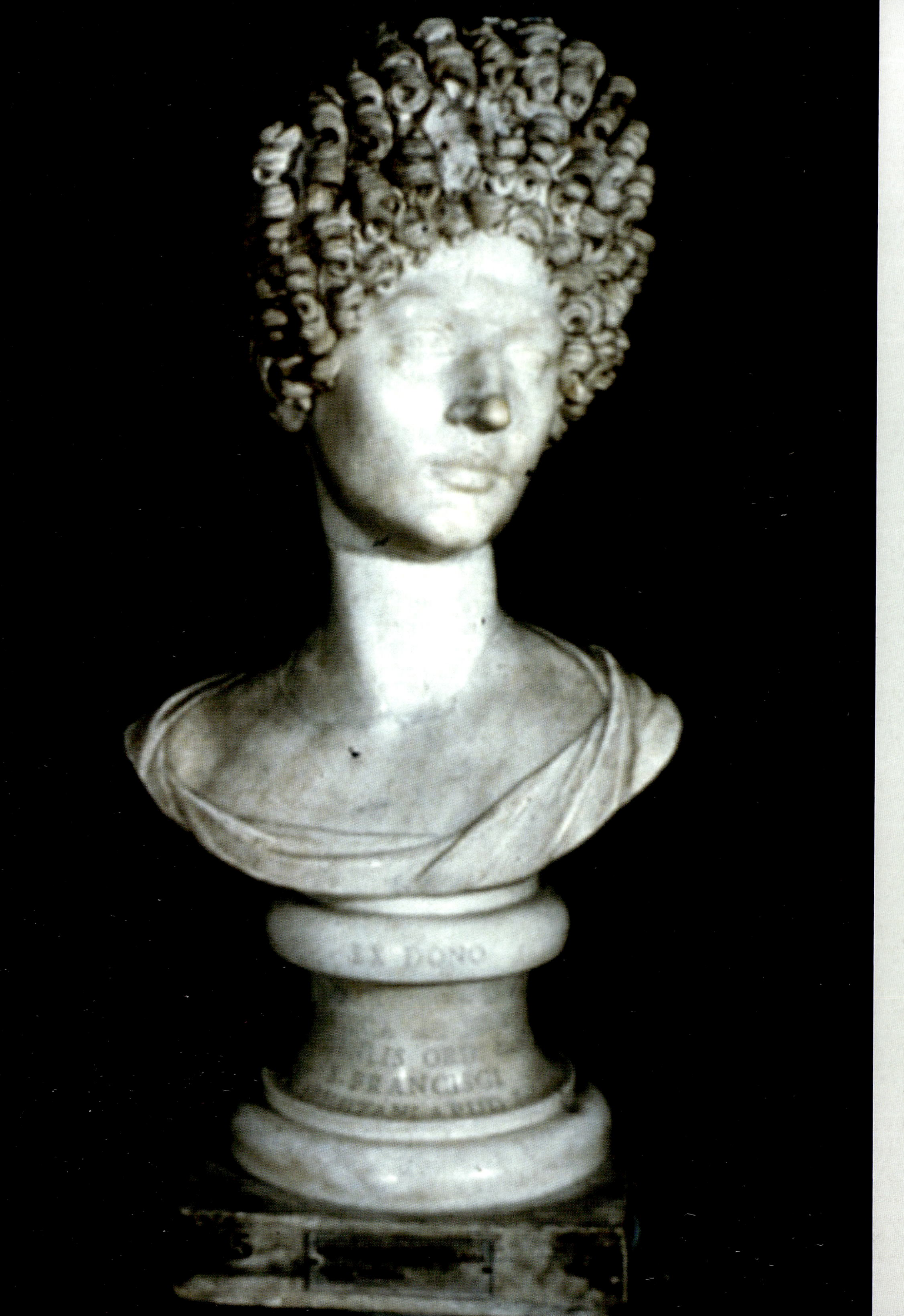
EX DONO

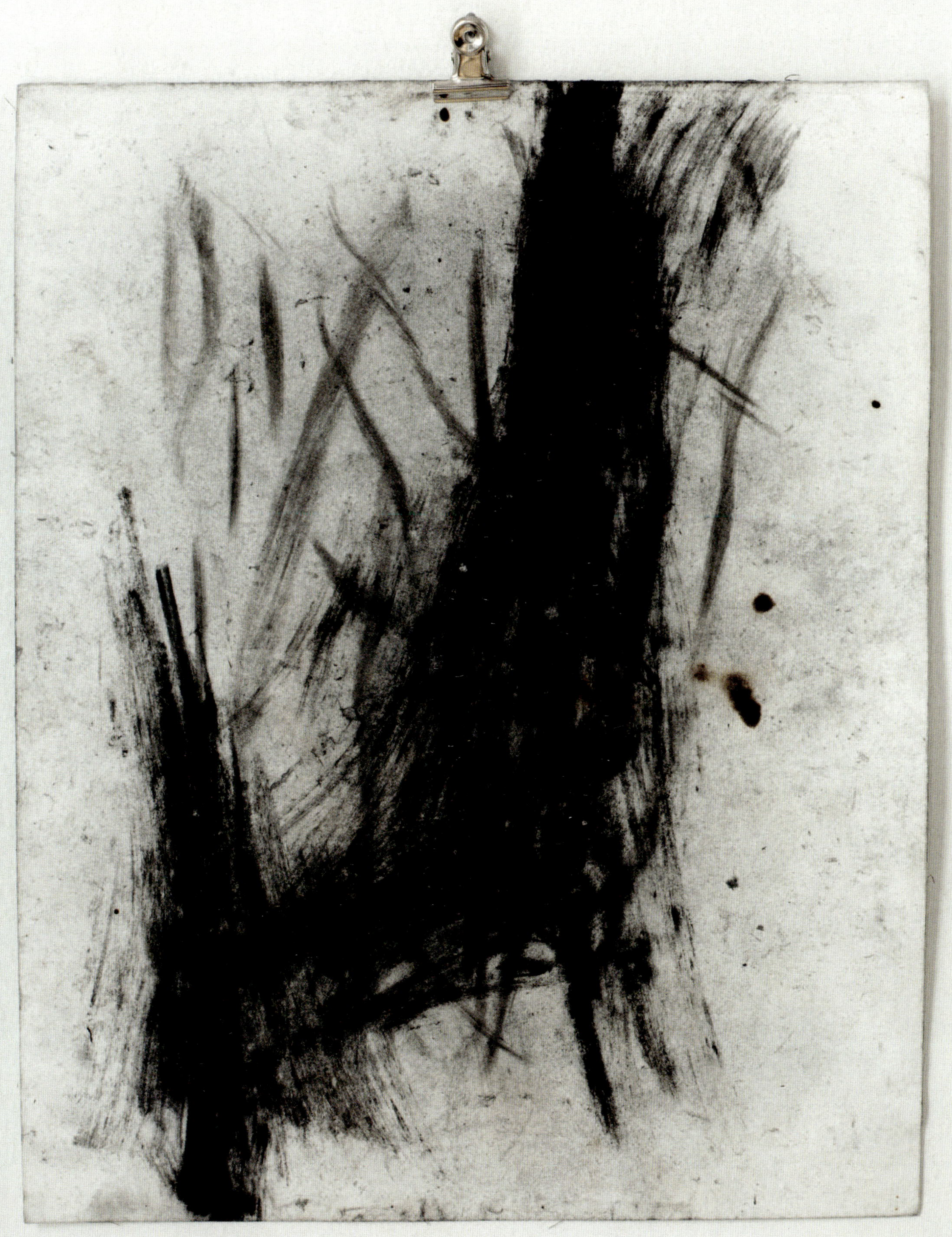

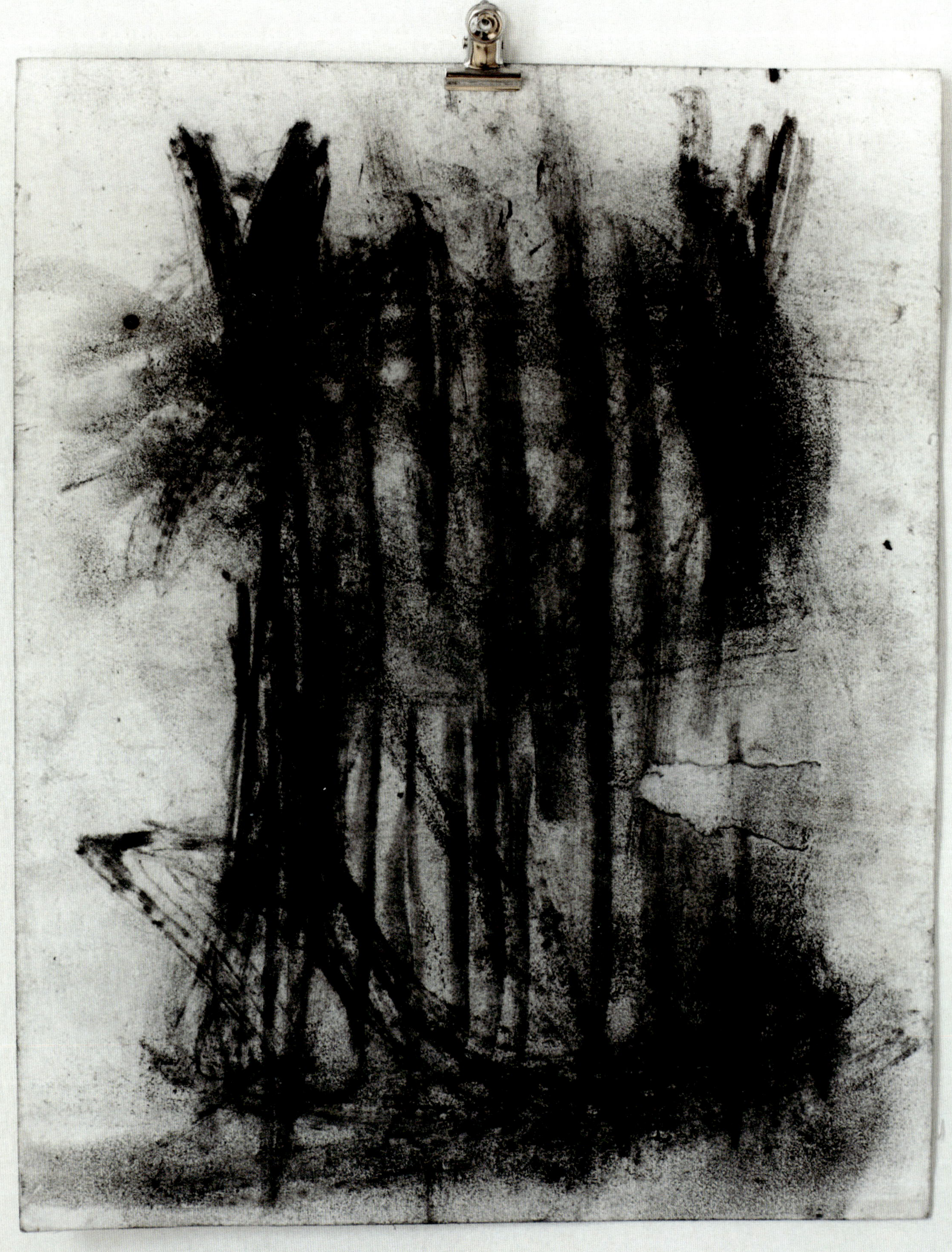

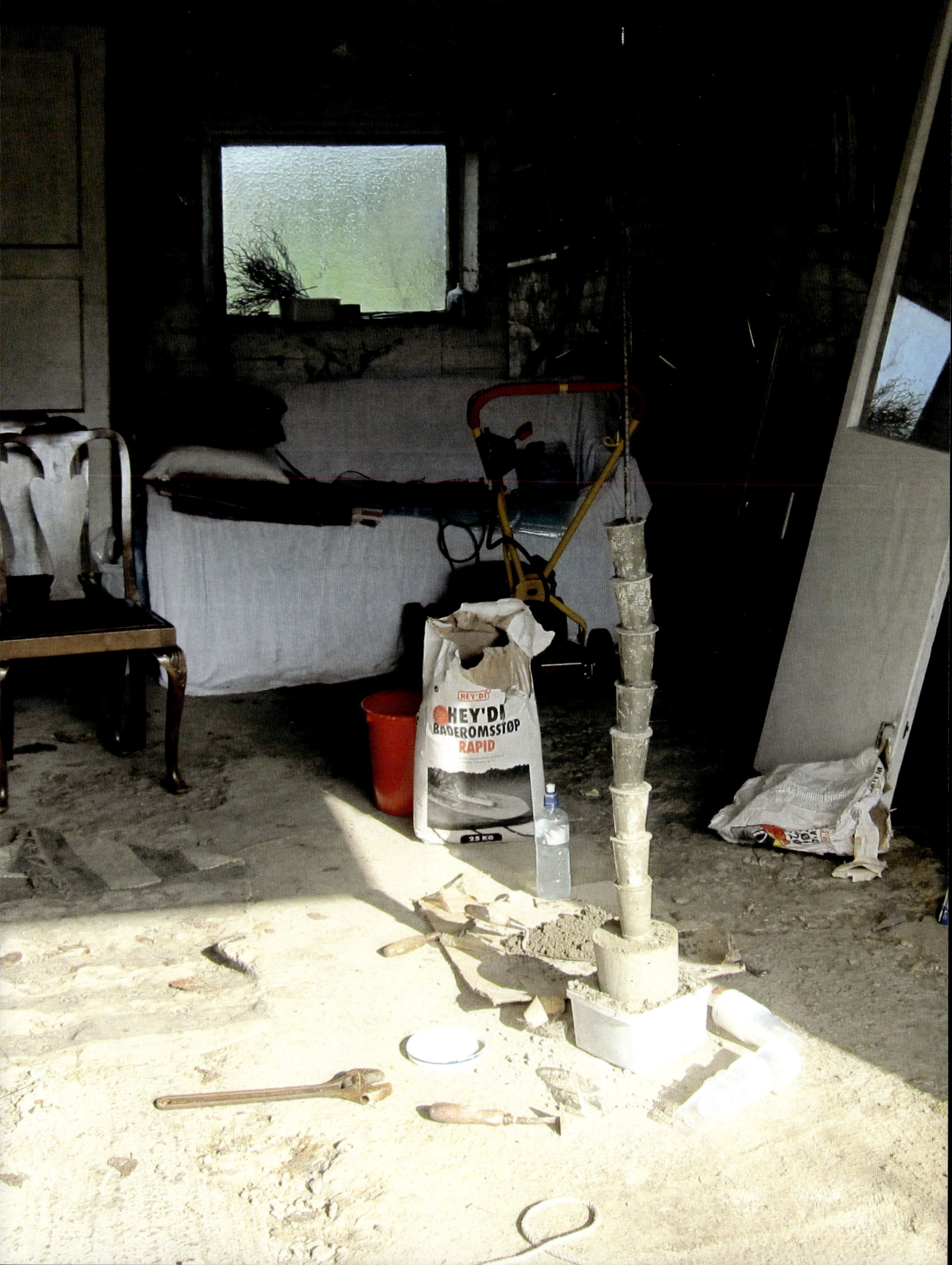
HEY'DI
HEY'DI
BADEROMSSTØP
RAPID
25 KG

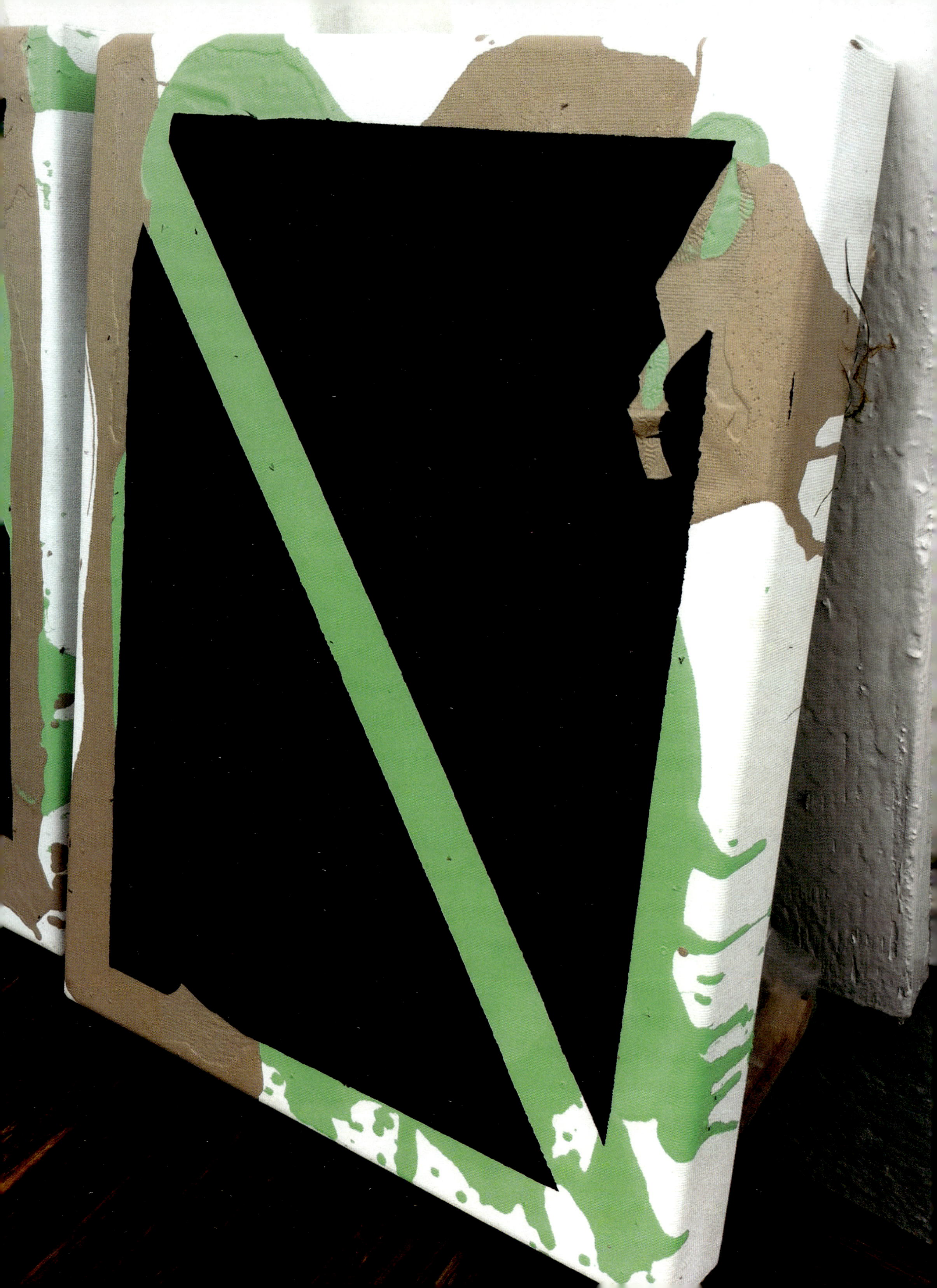

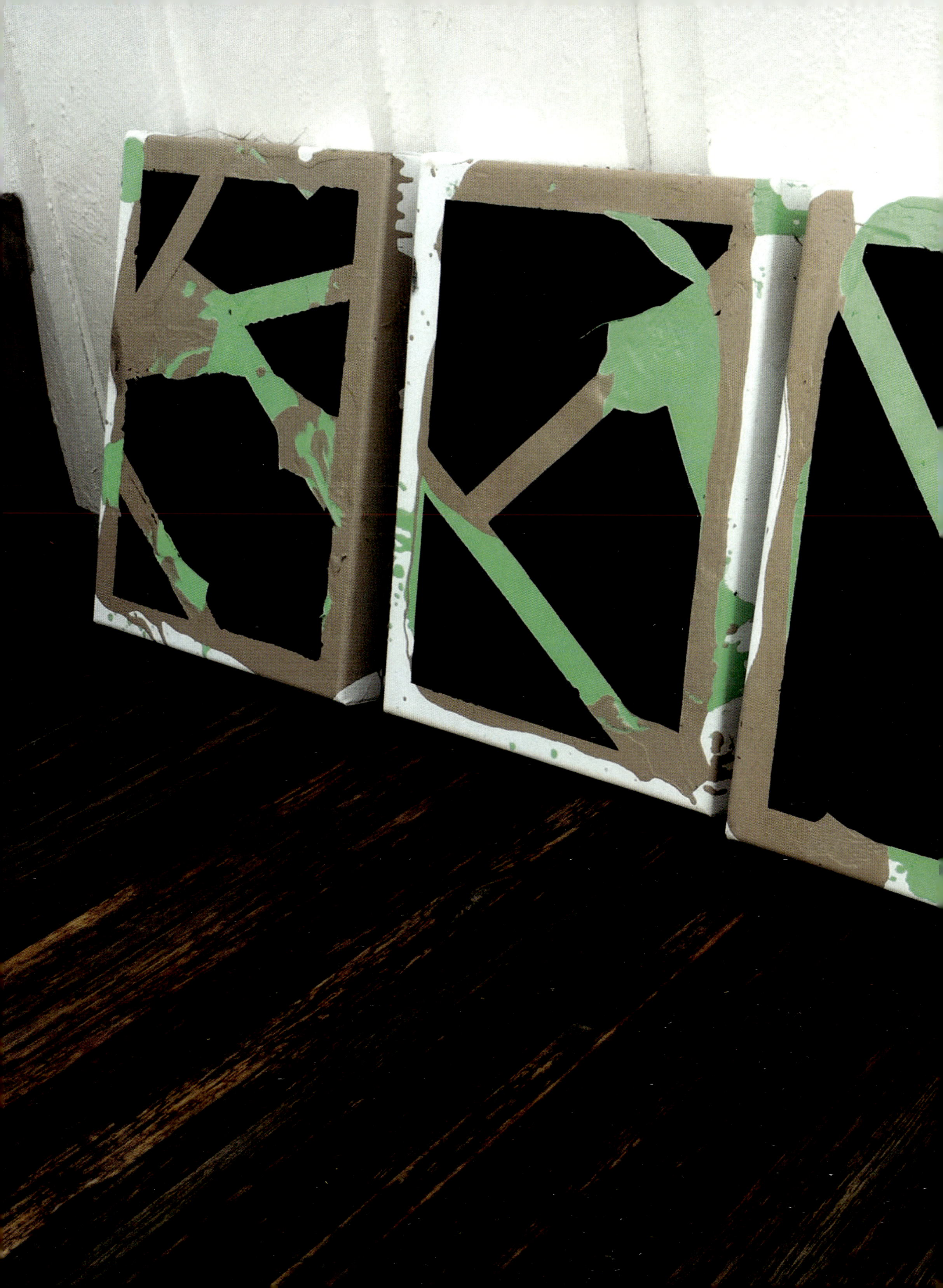

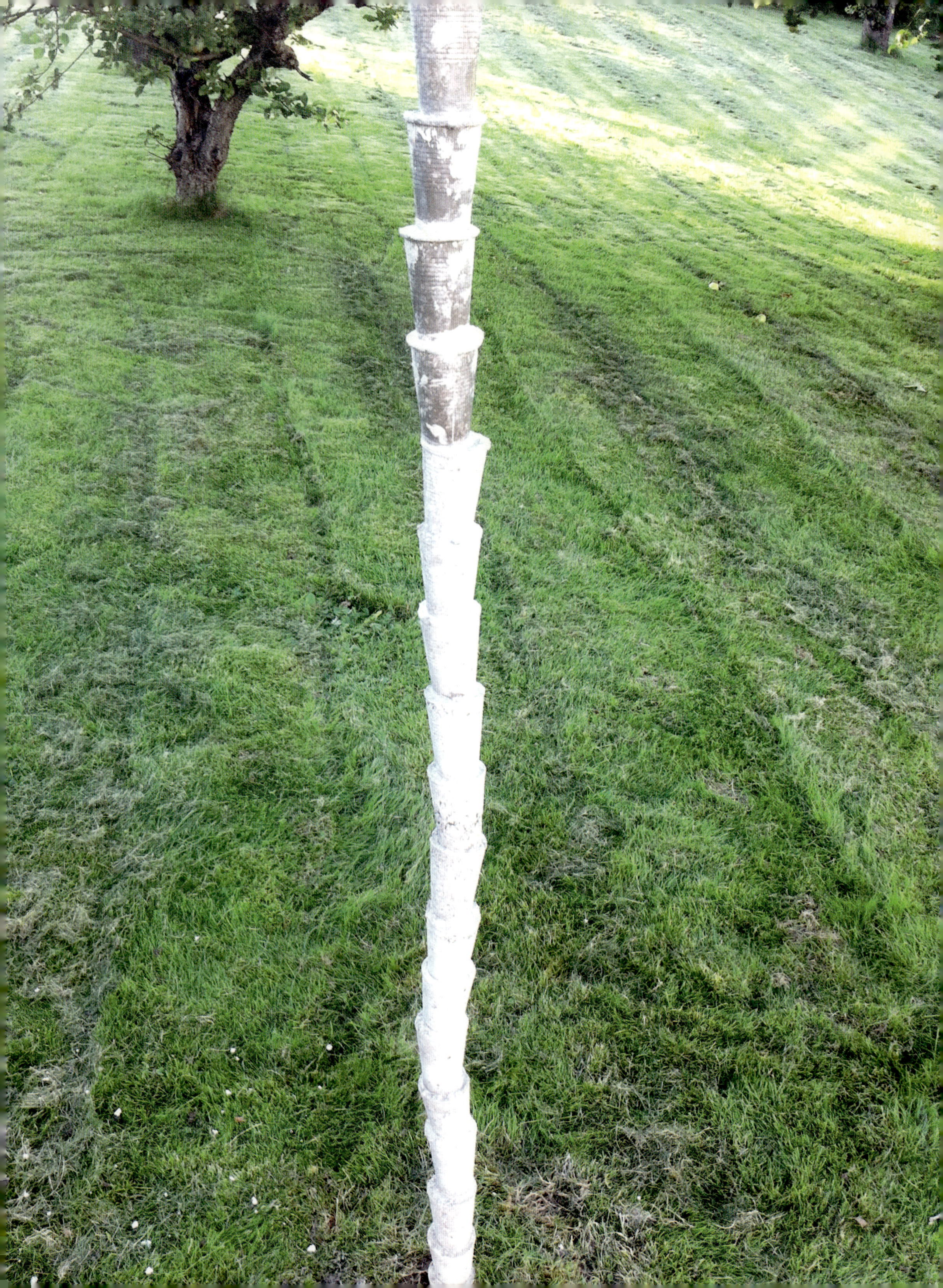

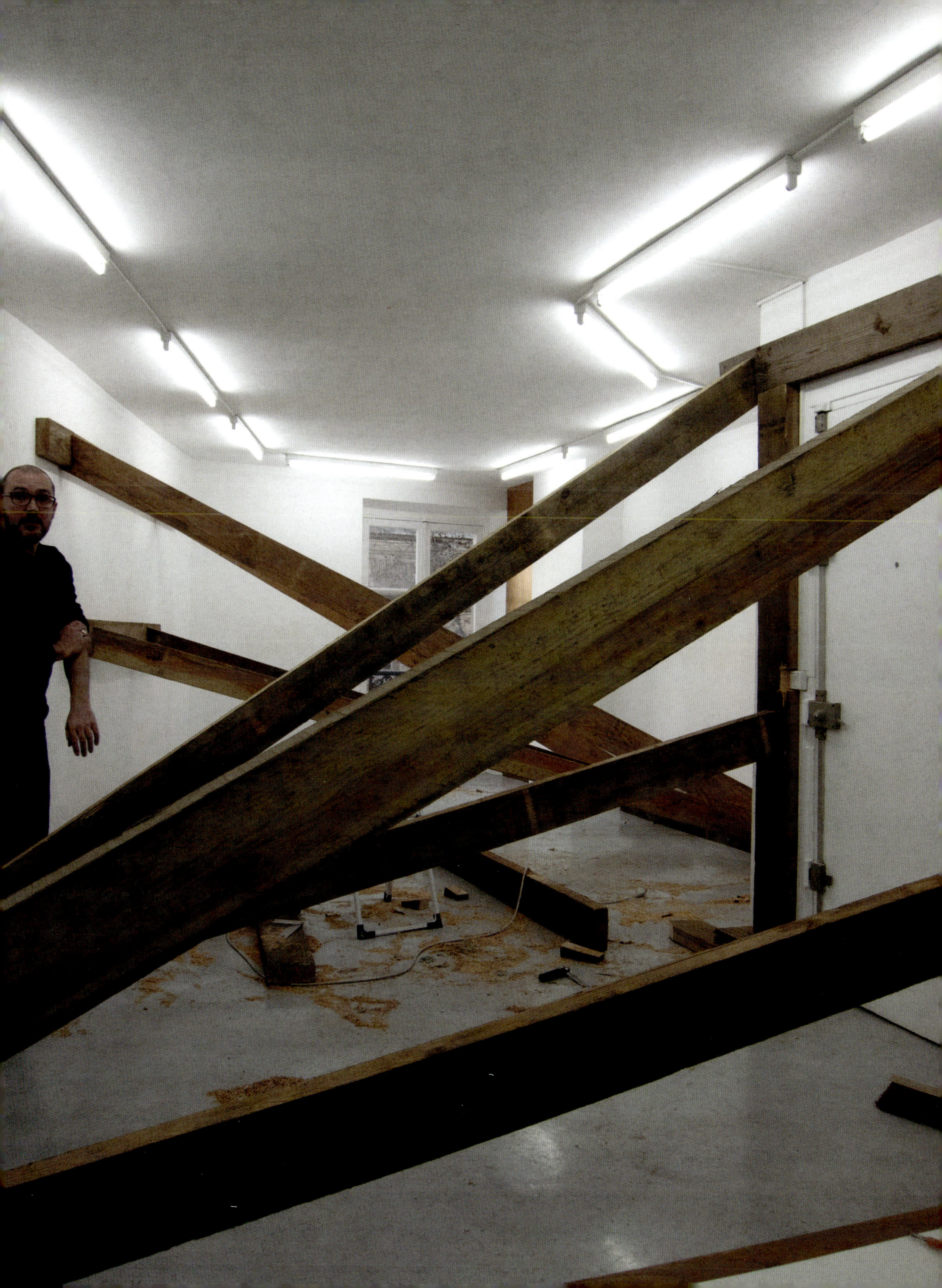

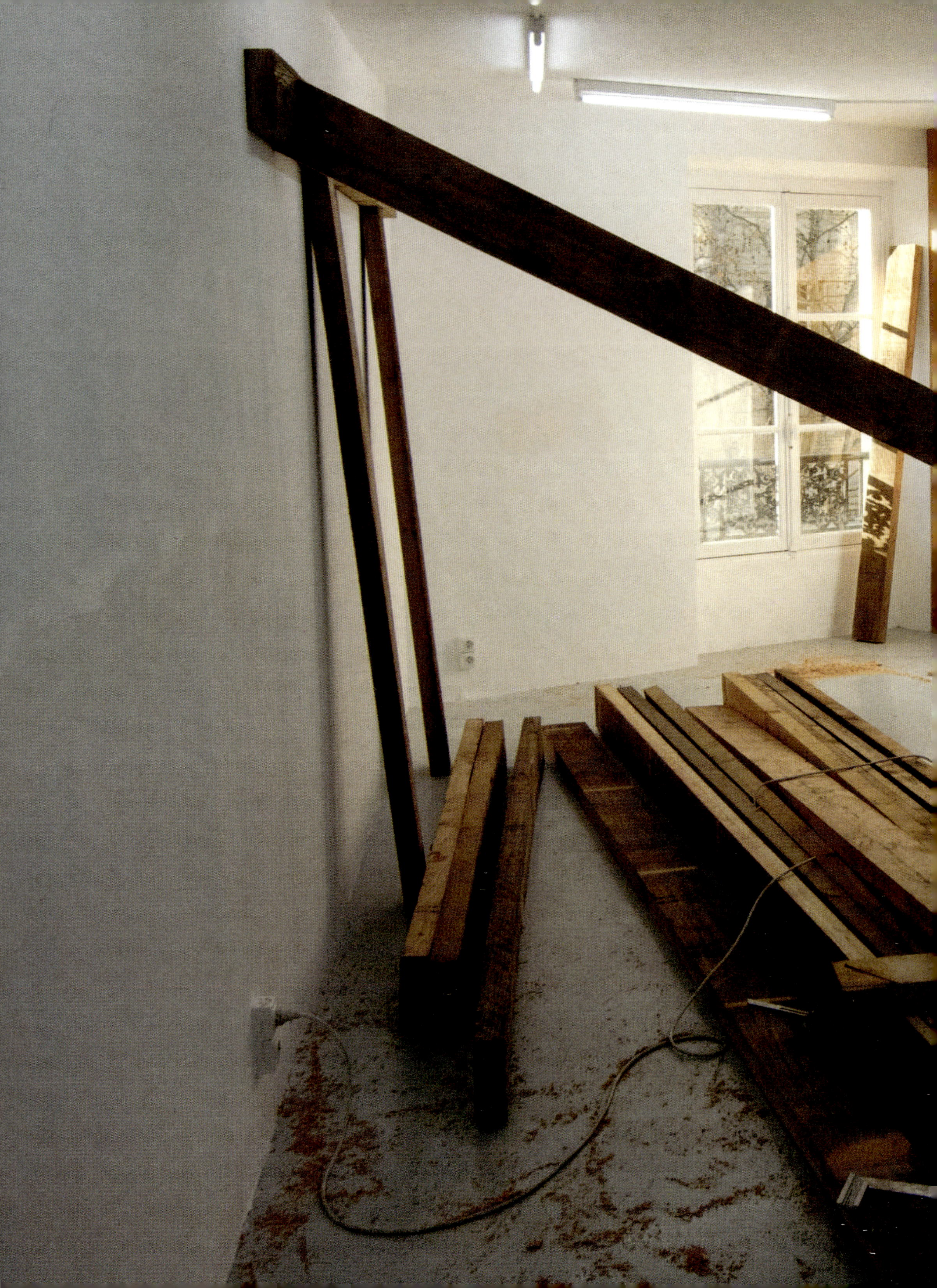

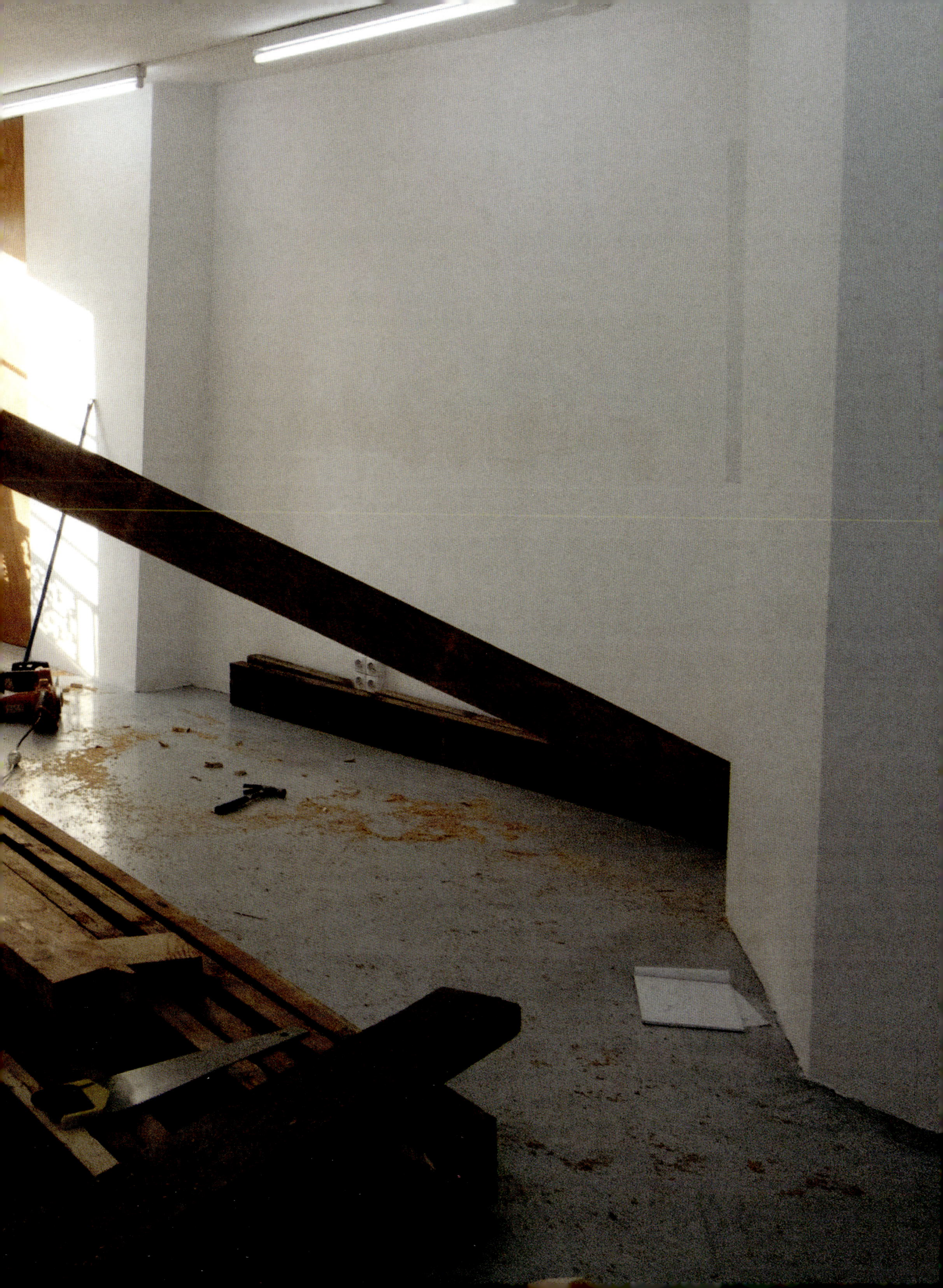

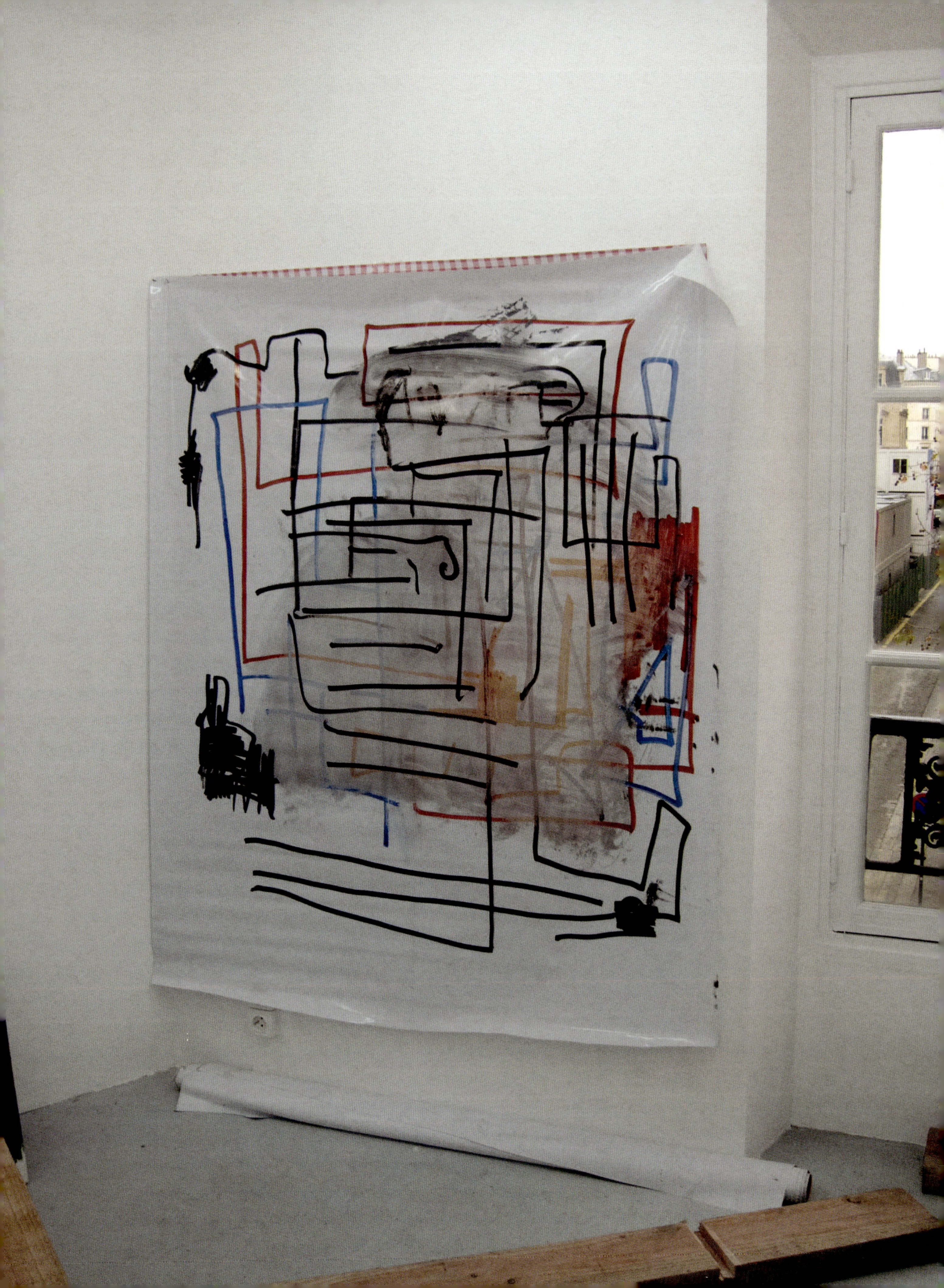

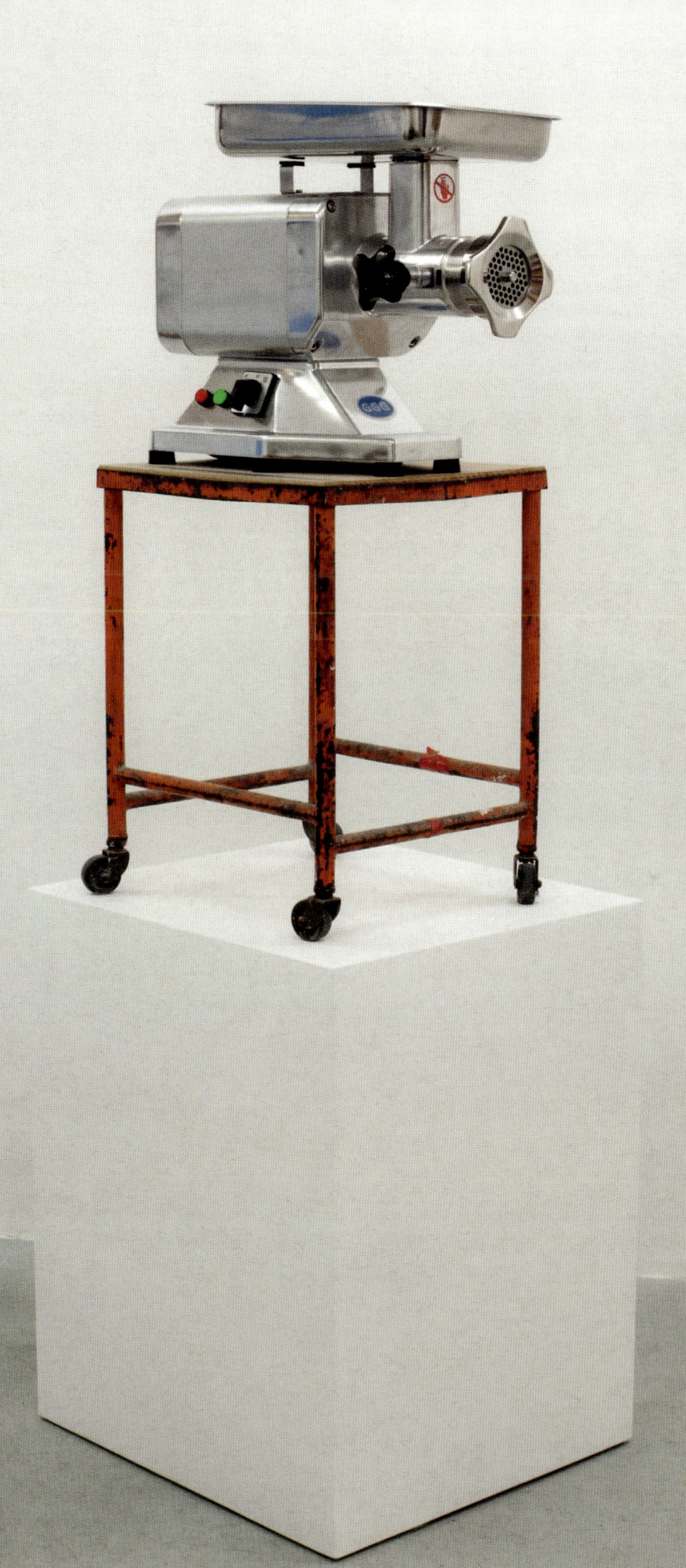

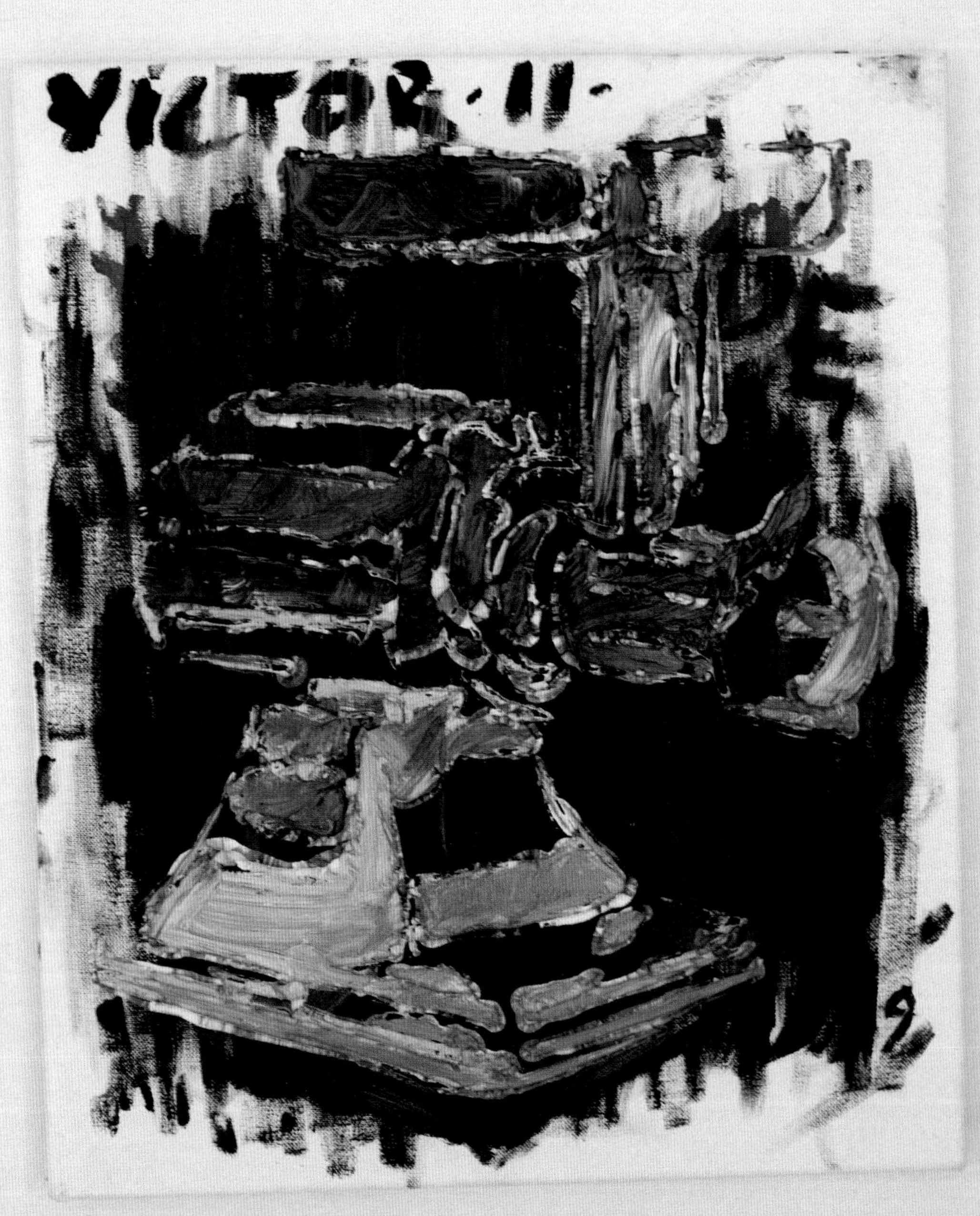
VICTOR · II ·

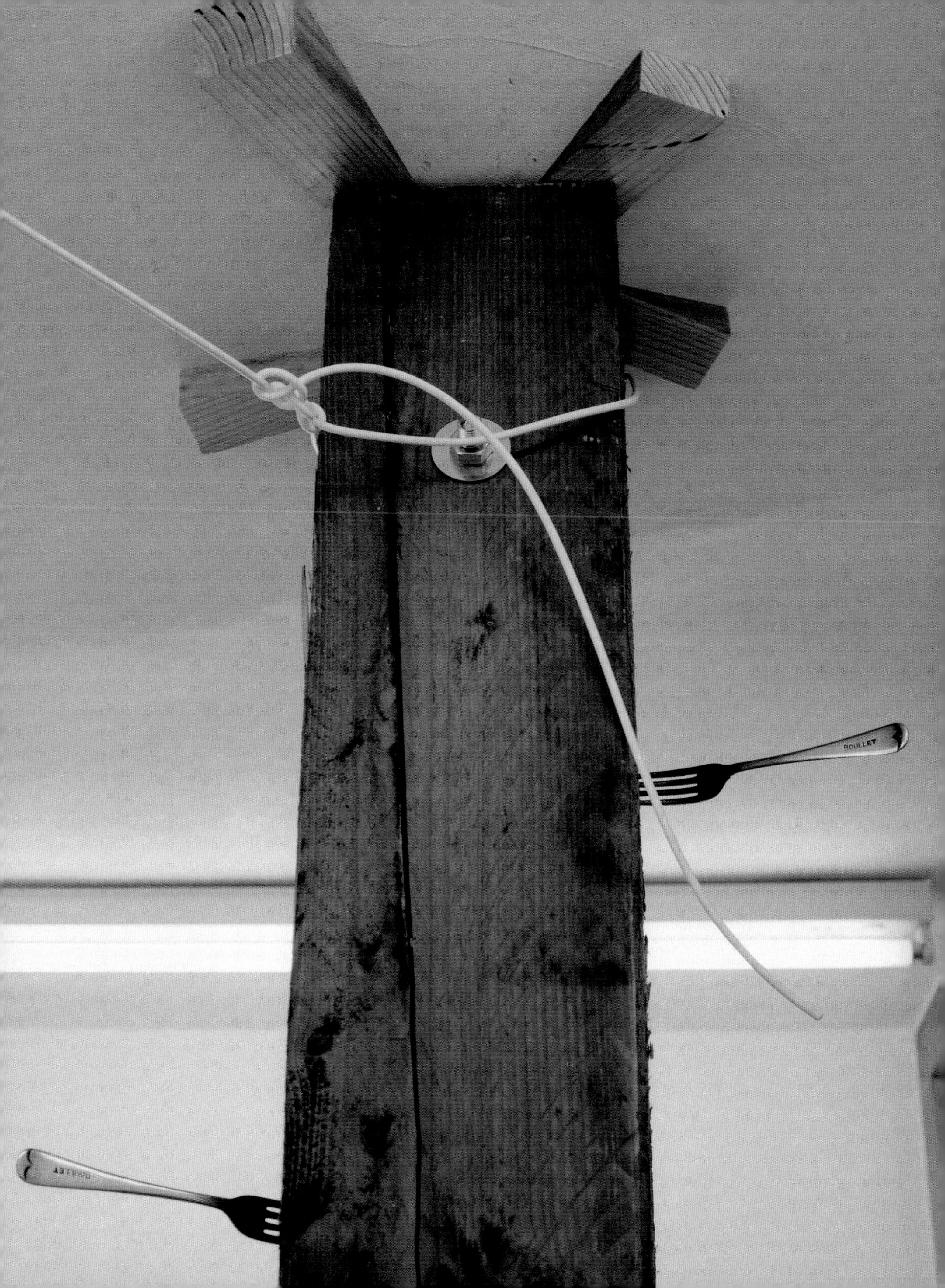
BOULLET
BOULLET

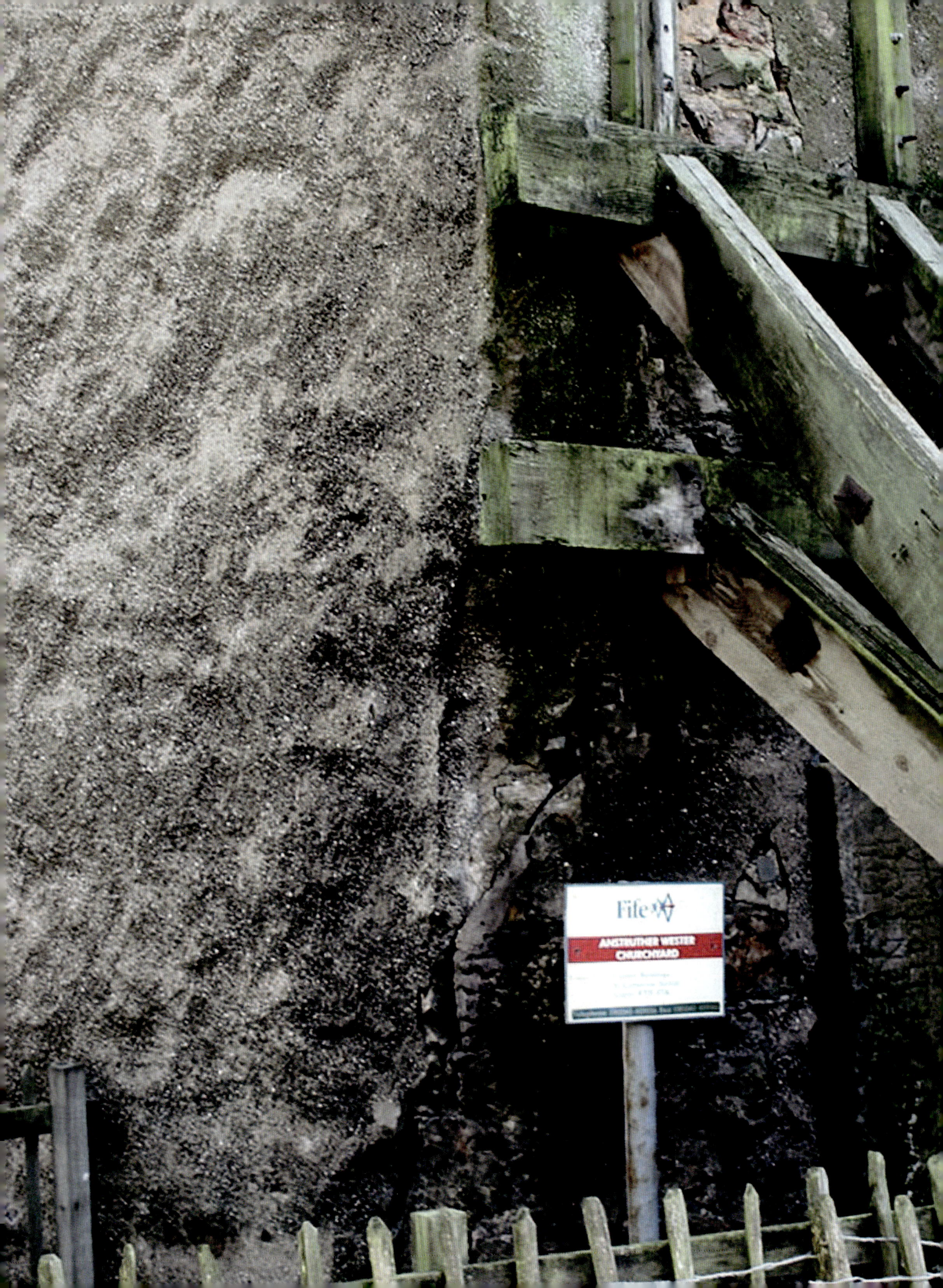
Fife
ANSTRUTHER WESTER
CHURCHYARD

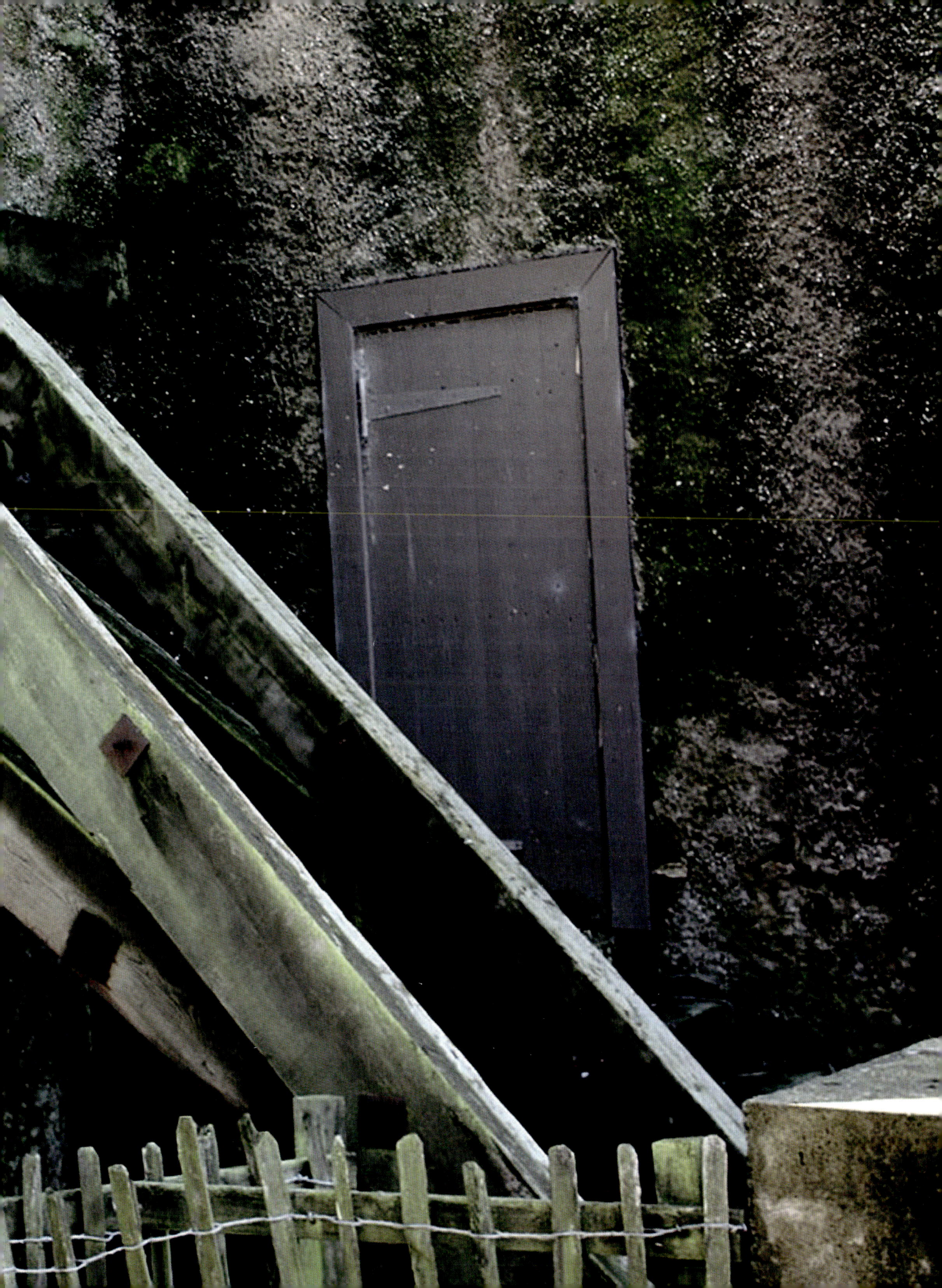

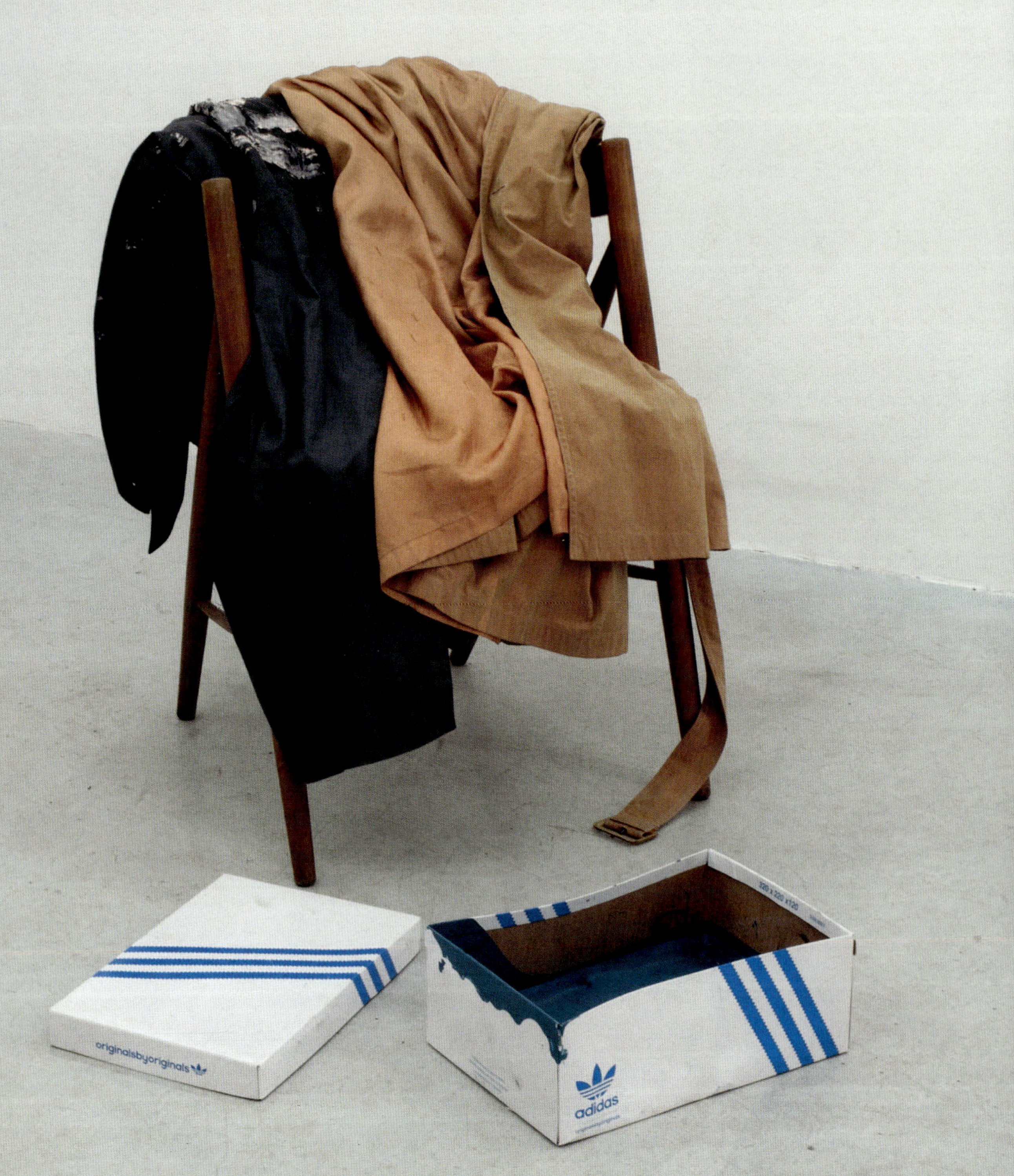
originalsbyoriginals
adidas

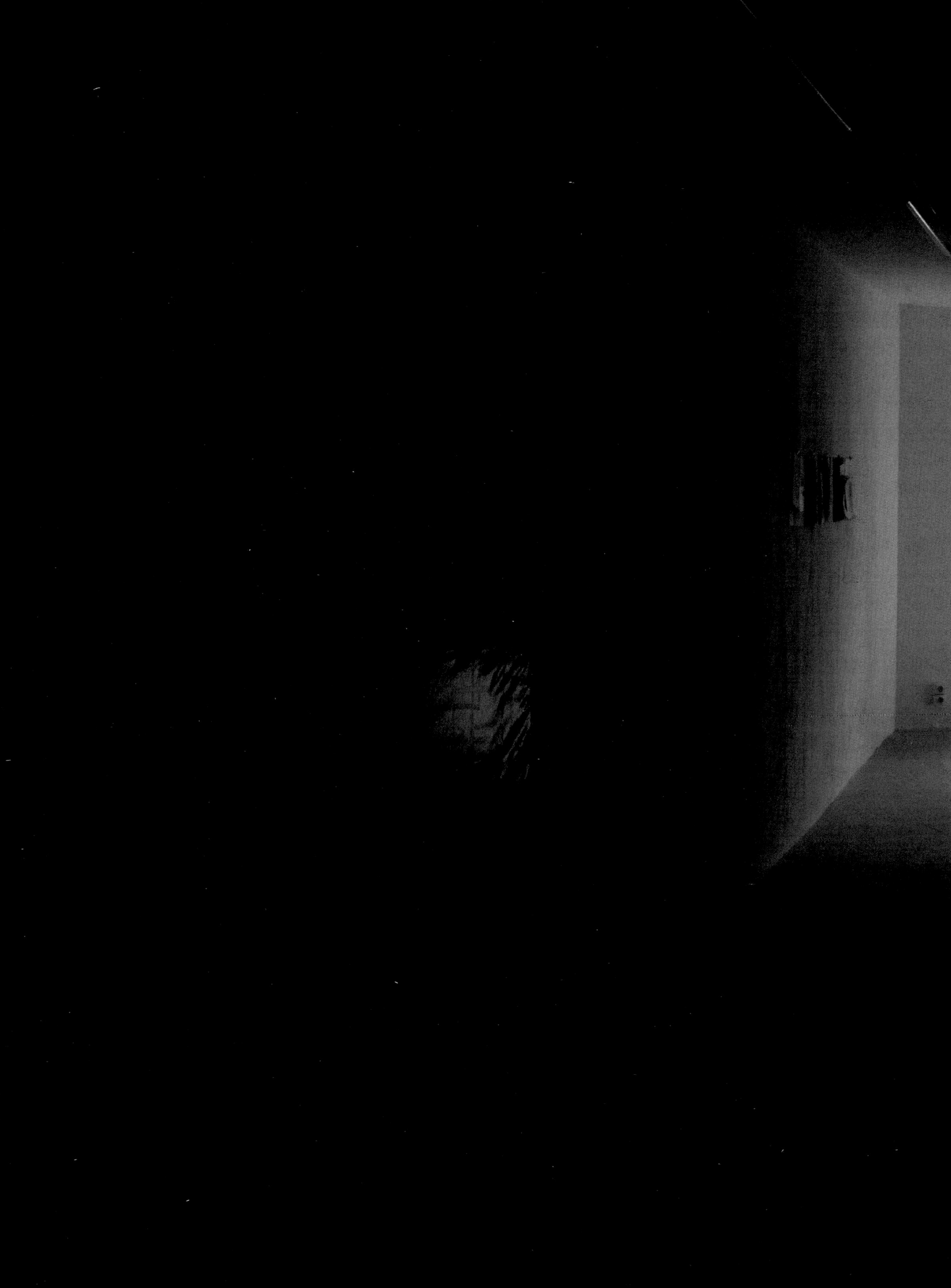

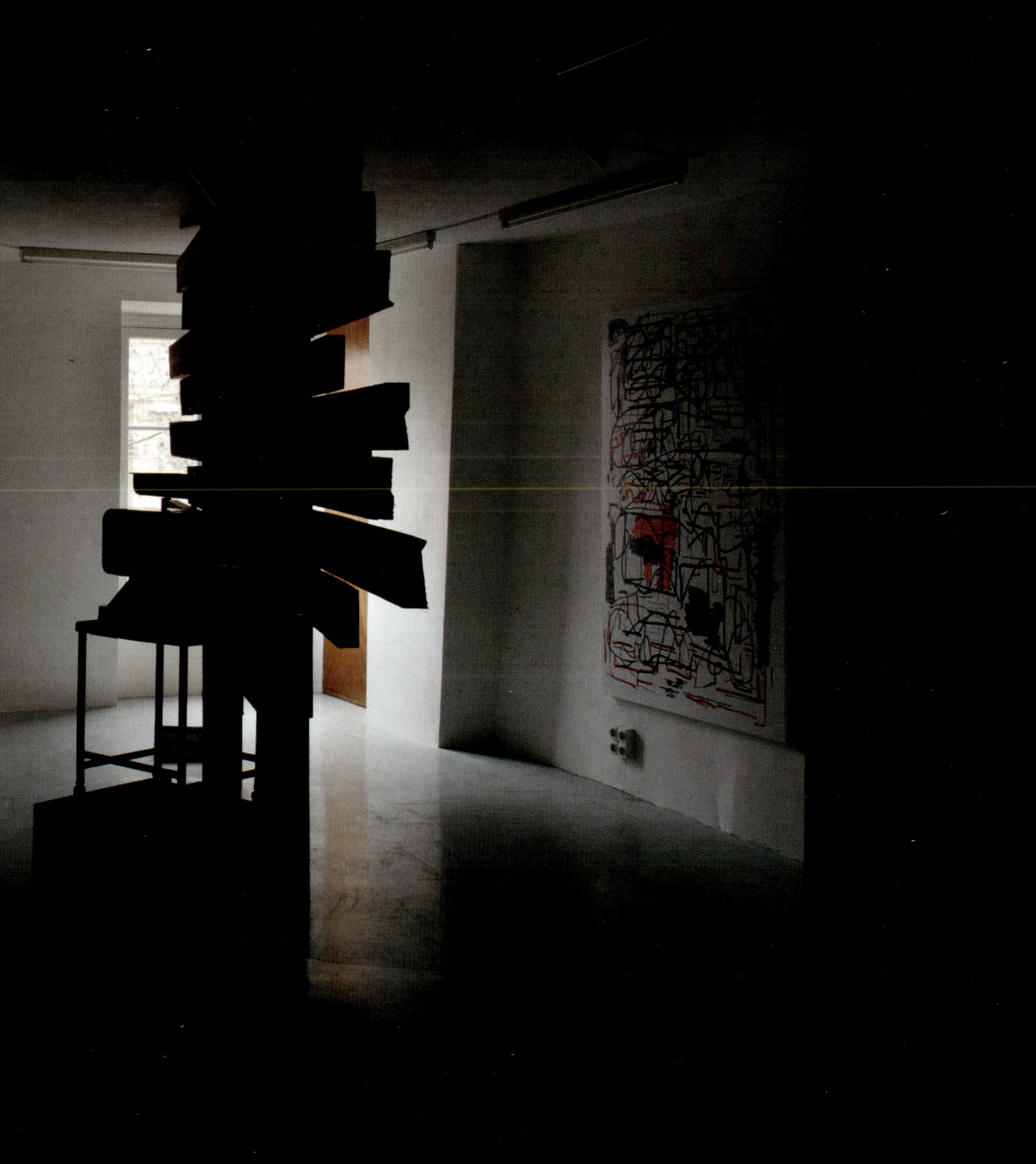

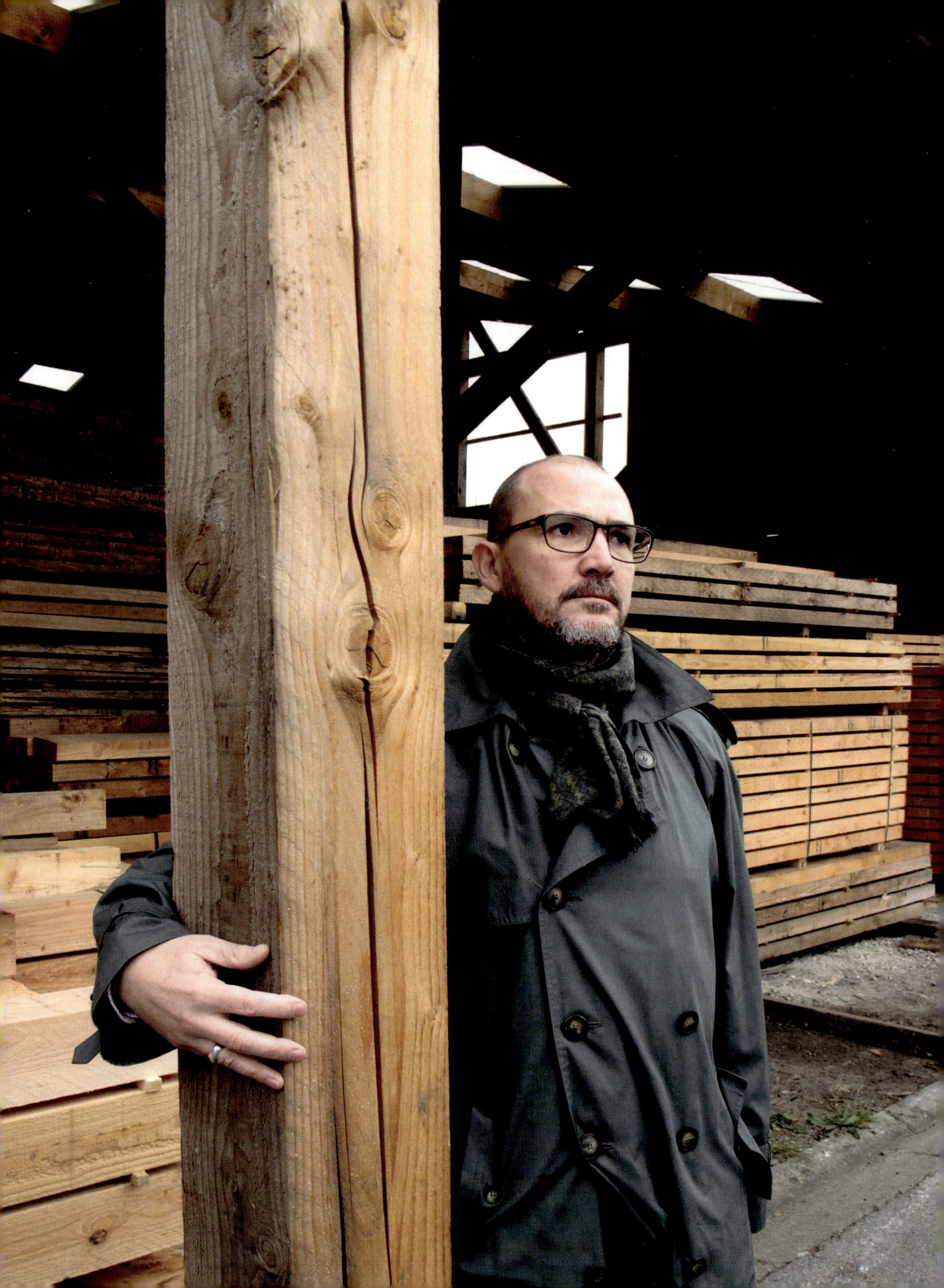

CHEAP MEAT

interview by Anna Franck

February 2012

Anna Franck:
How can you describe your practice, and why are you an artist?

Victor Boullet:
I shall work on to the end, I shall work in Paris, I shall work on the seas and oceans, I shall work with growing confidence and growing strength in the air, I shall defend my oeuvre, whatever the cost may be, I shall work on the beaches, I shall work on the landing grounds, I shall work in the fields and in the streets, I shall work in the hills; I shall never surrender, and even if, which I do not for a moment believe, this piece or a large part of it were subjugated and starving, then my Empire beyond the seas, armed and guarded by the Scottish soil, would carry on the struggle, until, in God's good time, the New Art, with all its power and might, steps forth to the rescue and the liberation of the old seen.

AF:
ok, that is what you said last night, drinking and eating like a decadent successful artist, but can you survive and support your family?

VB:
I eat and drink dirt cheap. I buy food that has gone out of date for half price, but I preach about the butchers and the quality, I lie to give you and others the impression that I am man of meat morals and standards beyond yours.

AF:
You lie? You would never buy cheap meat.
Have you been lying to me all this time?
Why do I like you?

VB:
You love me!

AF:
I do love you and I really like you as well.

VB:
I like you too Miss Franck inc!

AF:
Can you support your family?

VB:
Not at all.

AF:
Where is your work?

VB:
I am not at all sure where it is?

AF:
Tell me a funny story instead.

VB:
One morning in Paris I had my coffee at one of my favorite cafés, in comes someone I know (he is always badly dressed).
We had a conversation about life, The ISH and kids. He is very superior this character, full of morals, in other words he is self-righteous, but sadly beyond his own understanding. Anyway, coffee drunk, we cross the road, I say goodbye, and I turn towards my studio for my daily routines, then all of a sudden, my arm is pulled back, not very hard, it's him, wanting to tell me something, he looks at me and says, Do you know that I have won awards for my work? I am an award-winner.
I am, an award winner.

AF:
Funny! Your work changes all the time, it's like you have no concept or identity. Weak.

VB:
I agree.

AF:
Do you read Post-Fordism?

VB:
Post what? I am hungry, the meat is in the oven,
I am making us something very special.
Are you hungry?

AF:
No cheap meat I hope!

VB:
I have told you, we only eat cheap meat!

AF:
Please.

VB:
Half priced meat from Franprix, it's the truth.

AF:
I want to understand your work, please help me!

VB:
What is there to understand? There it is. Let's eat, did you bring a bottle of wine?

AF:
Yes!

VB:
Let's have it!

AF:
Are you working these days?

VB:
Yes, No, Maybe, someone told me that one morning.

AF:
When I see your work I immediately think I can do better.

VB:
You can.

AF:
Eat me.

VB:
REALLY?

AF:
FUCK ME

VB:
OH MY GOD, REALLY?

AF:
FUCK YOU BOULLET!

VB:
How's your son (Anton)?

AF:
Pass the salt please!

AF:
Tell me another story from your busy life then!

VB:
Why?

AF:
They are funny

VB:
A gallerist friend of mine was very happy with his new intern, she was clever and she read philosophy he told me. He also mentioned that she was from Brazil, I asked if she had tan-lines?

AF:
HAHAHAHAHA

VB:
Here's another: In a café in one of the art metropoles of the world I order a cup of tea with an artist friend.
We talk about the art world and its mechanisms, he tell's me that I do not know enough and it's difficult to talk art with me and that I should follow the rules.

AF:
OMG!

VB:
There you have it!

AF:
There I have WHAT?

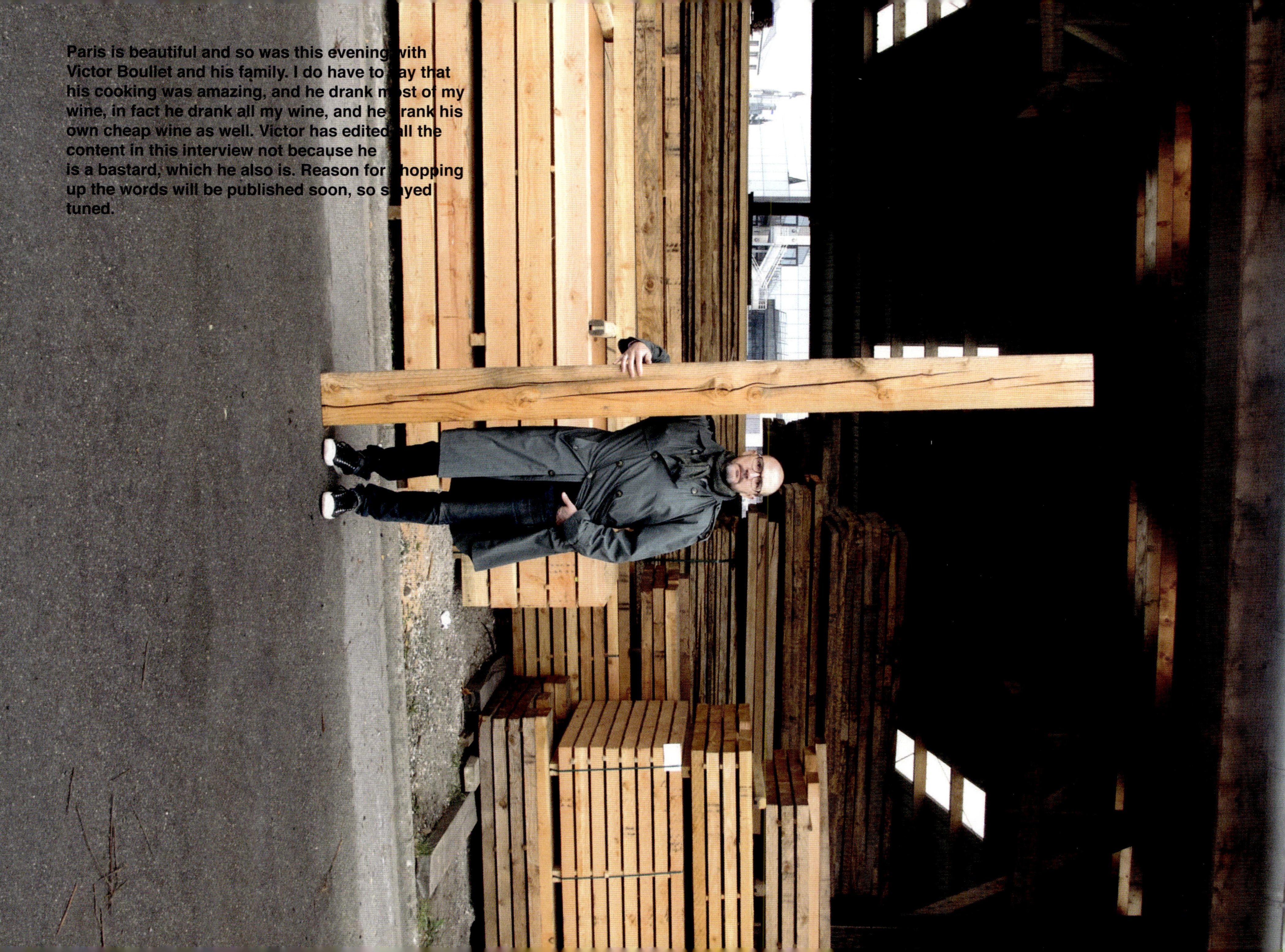

Paris is beautiful and so was this evening with Victor Bouliet and his family. I do have to say that his cooking was amazing, and he drank most of my wine, in fact he drank all my wine, and he drank his own cheap wine as well. Victor has edited all the content in this interview not because he is a bastard, which he also is. Reason for chopping up the words will be published soon, so stayed tuned.

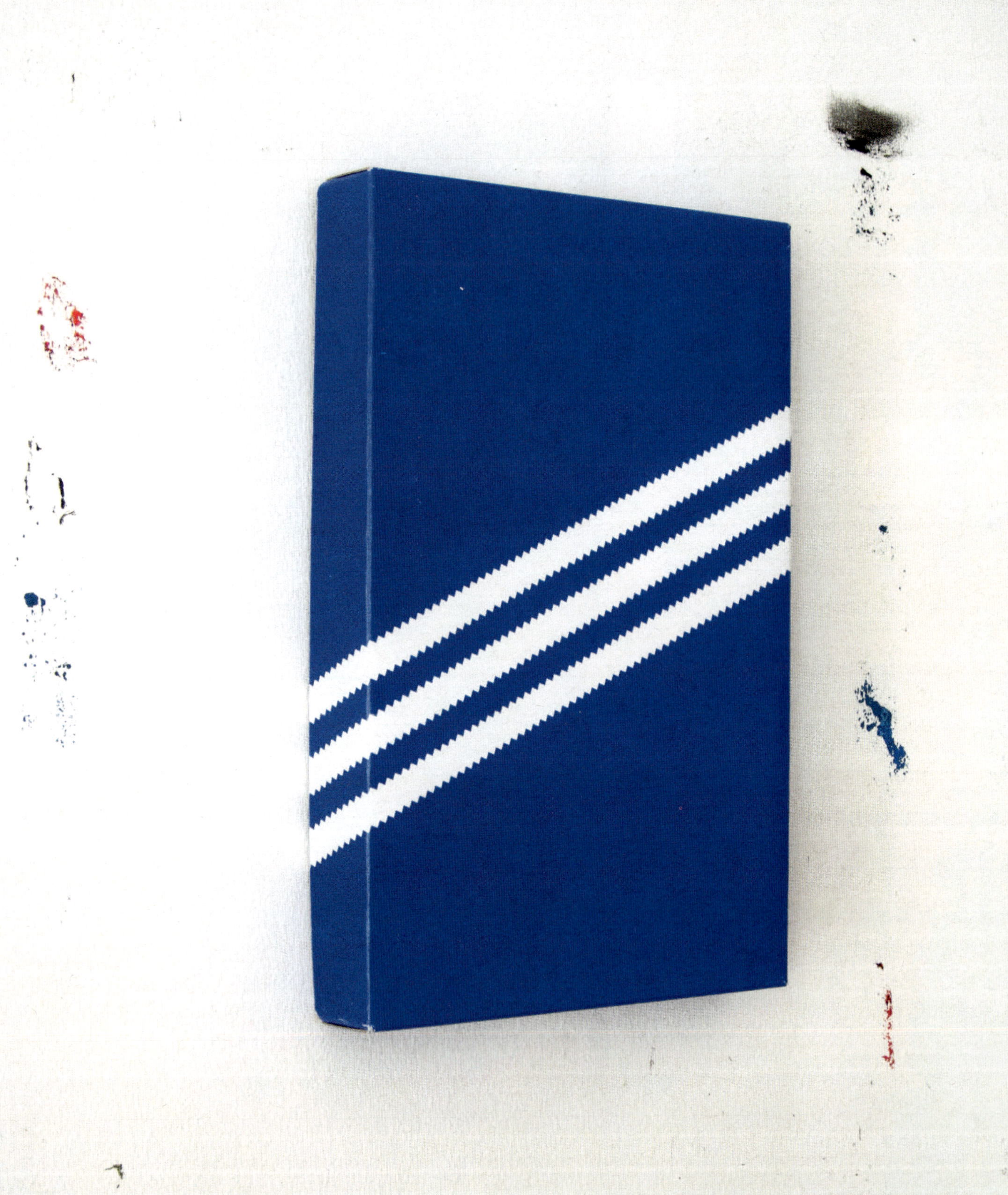

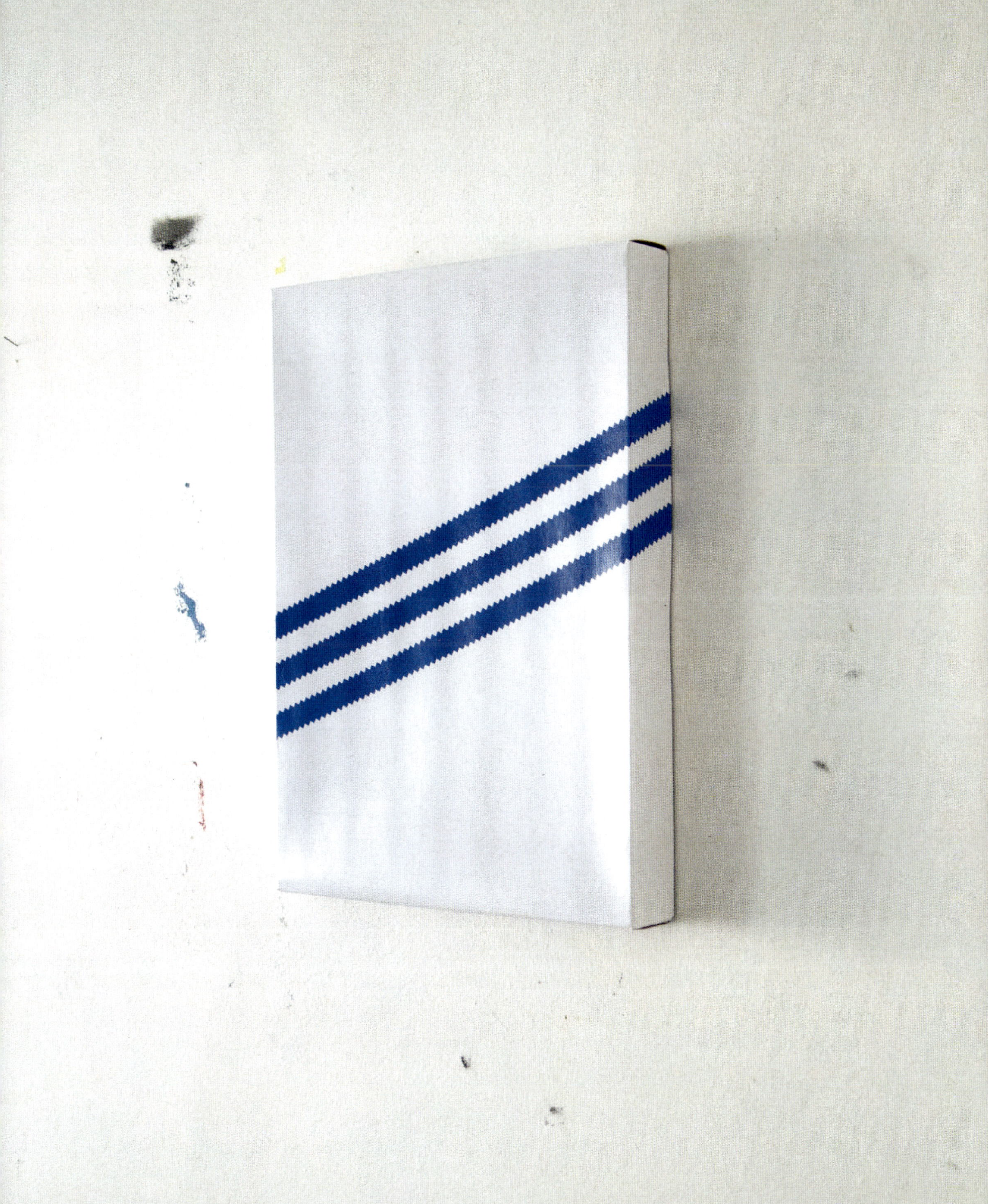

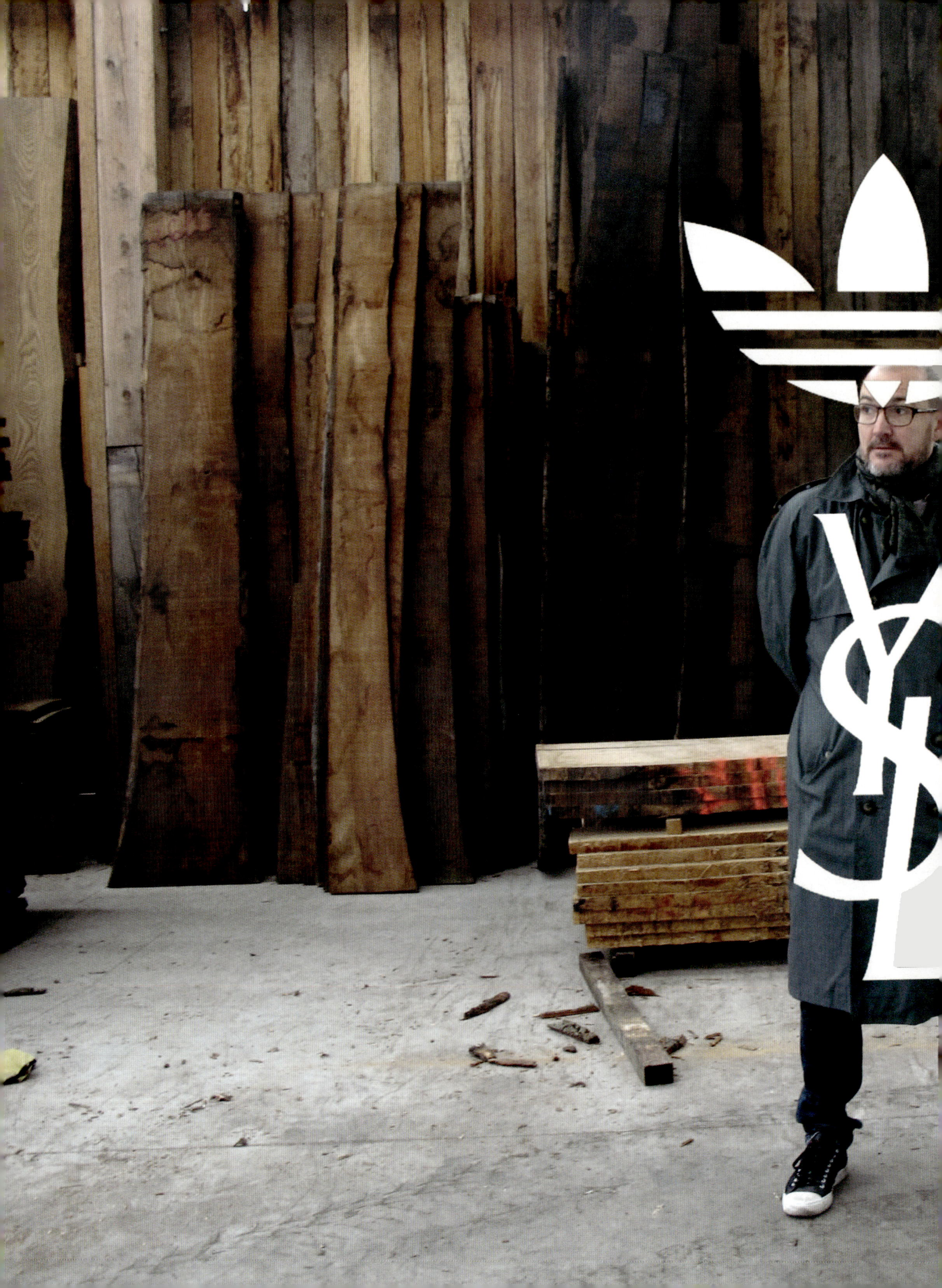

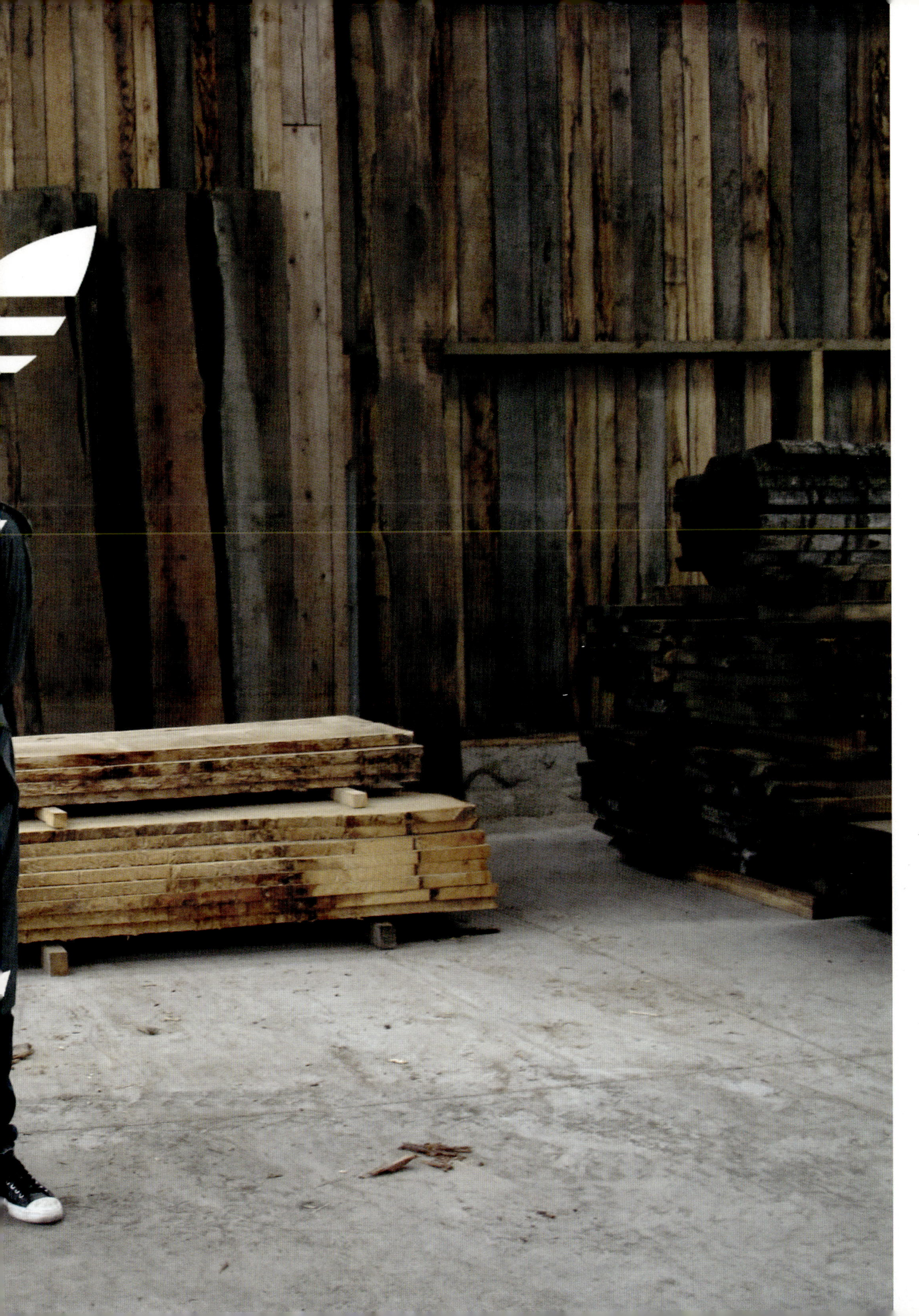

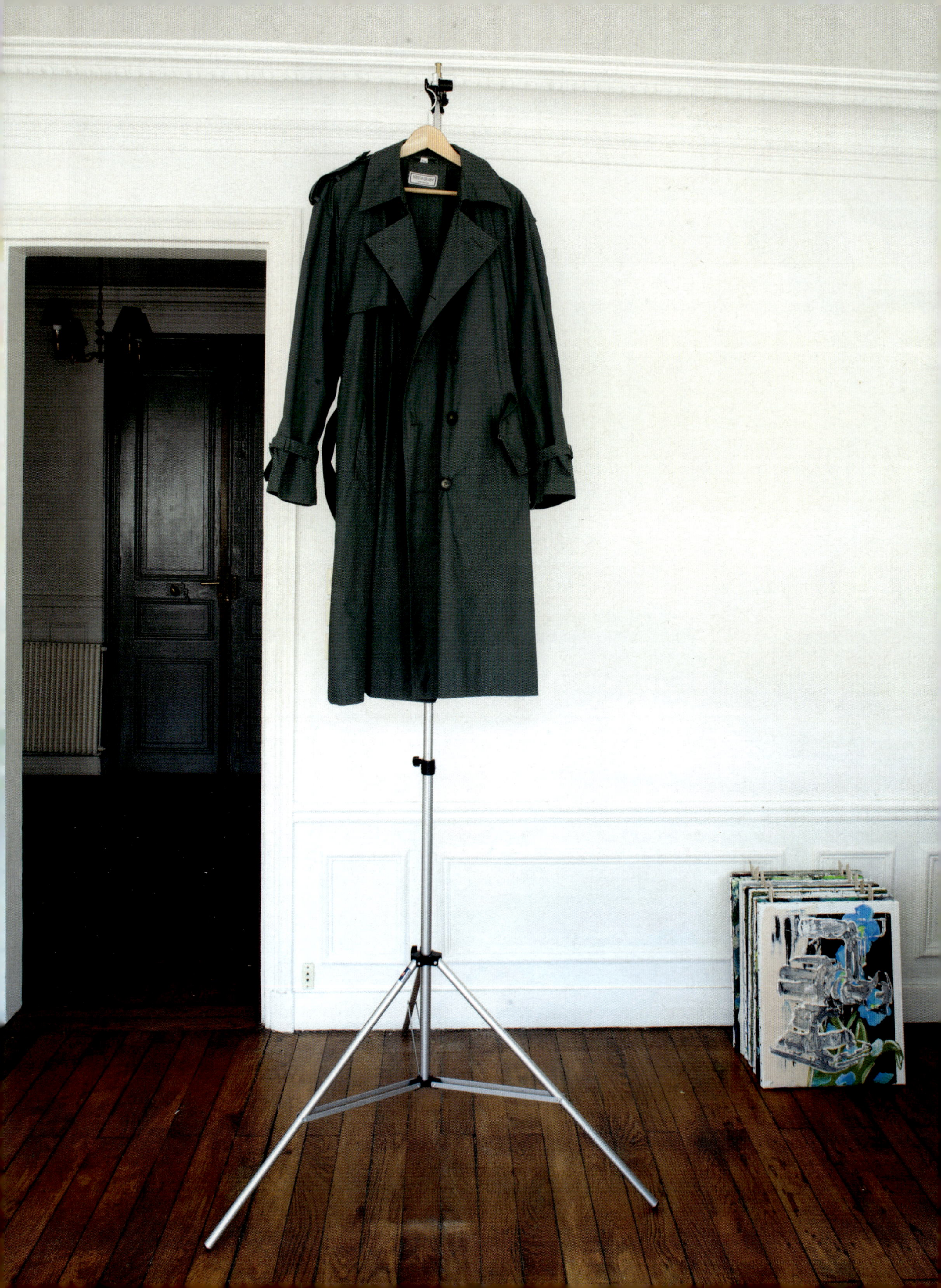

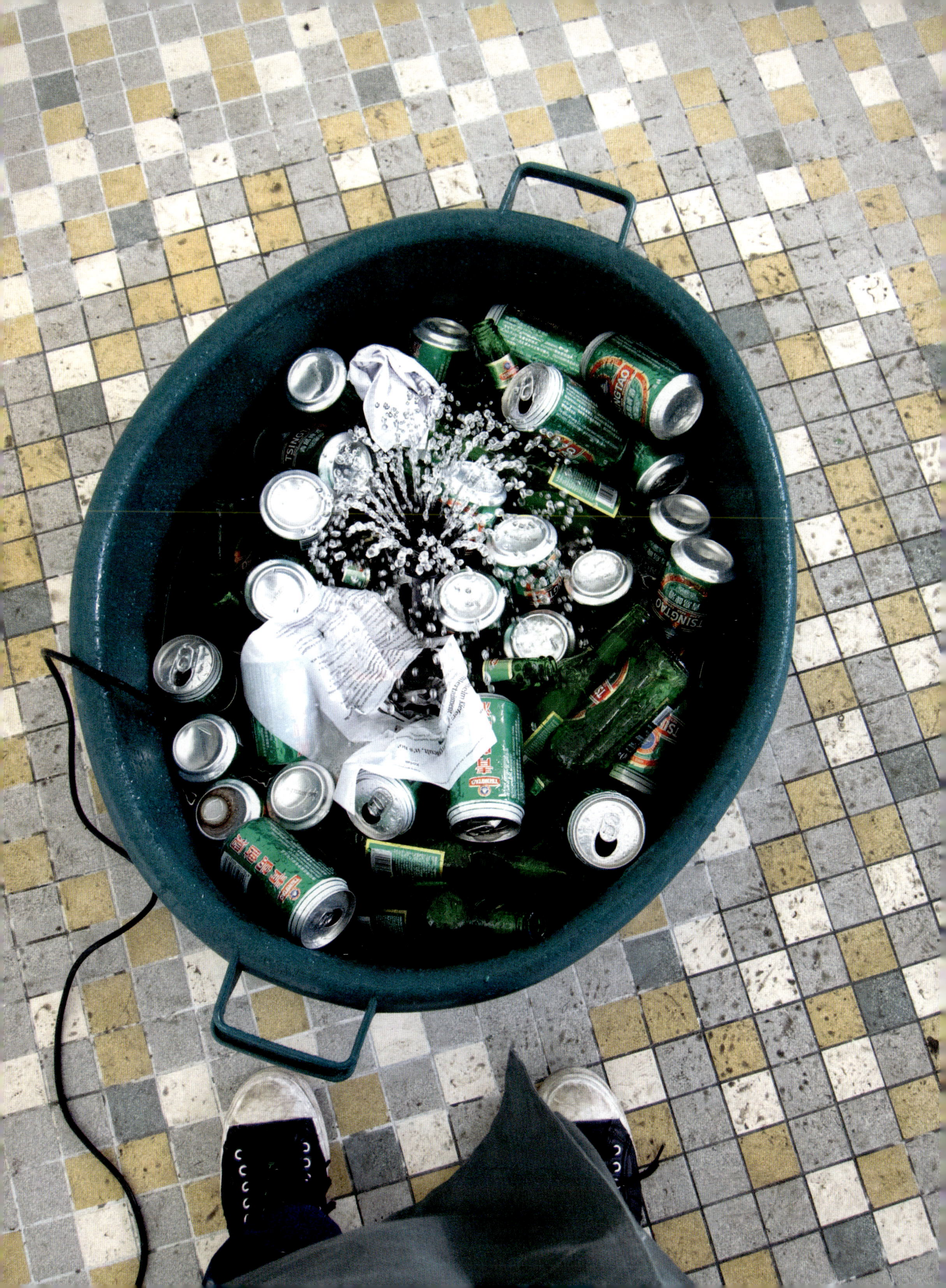

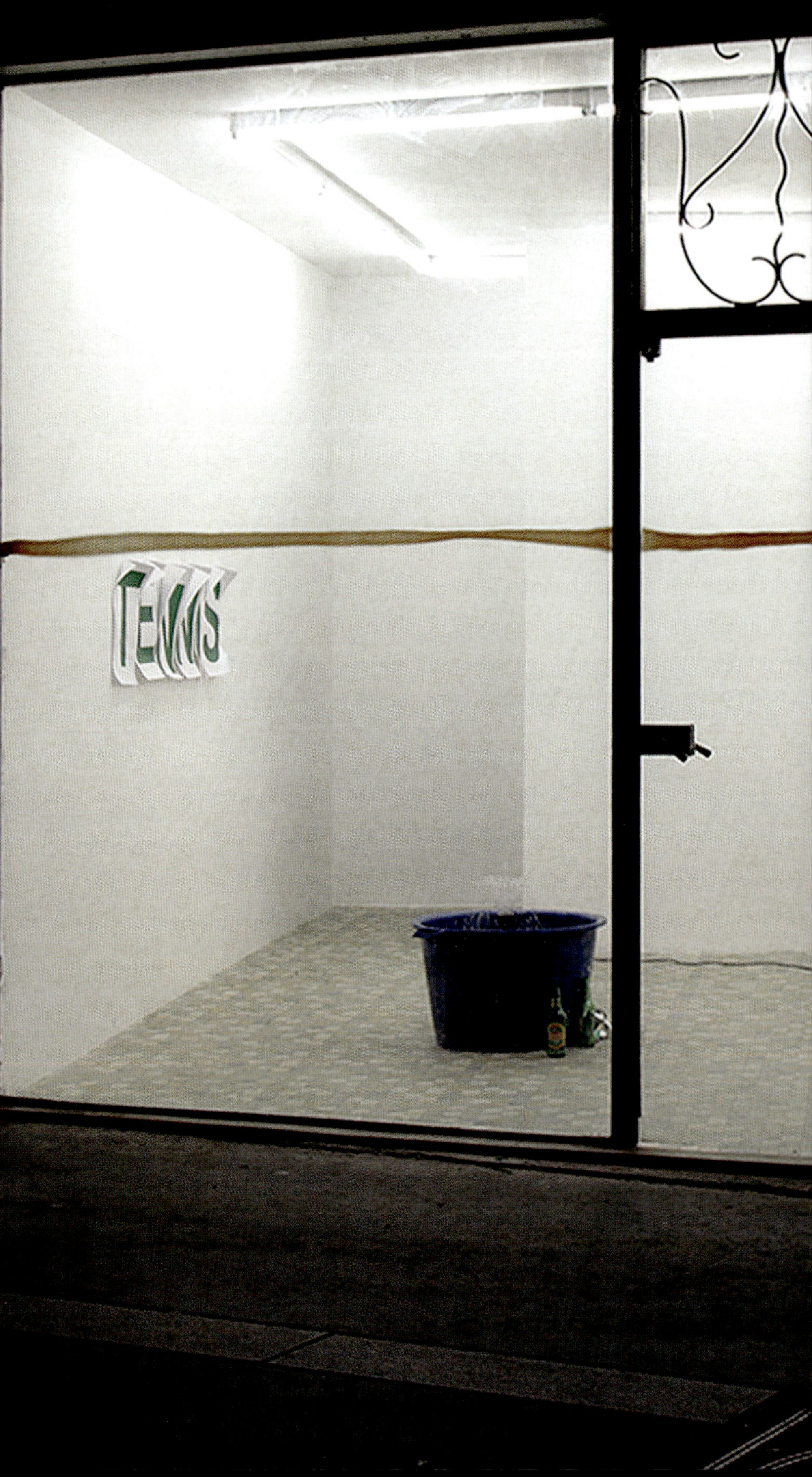

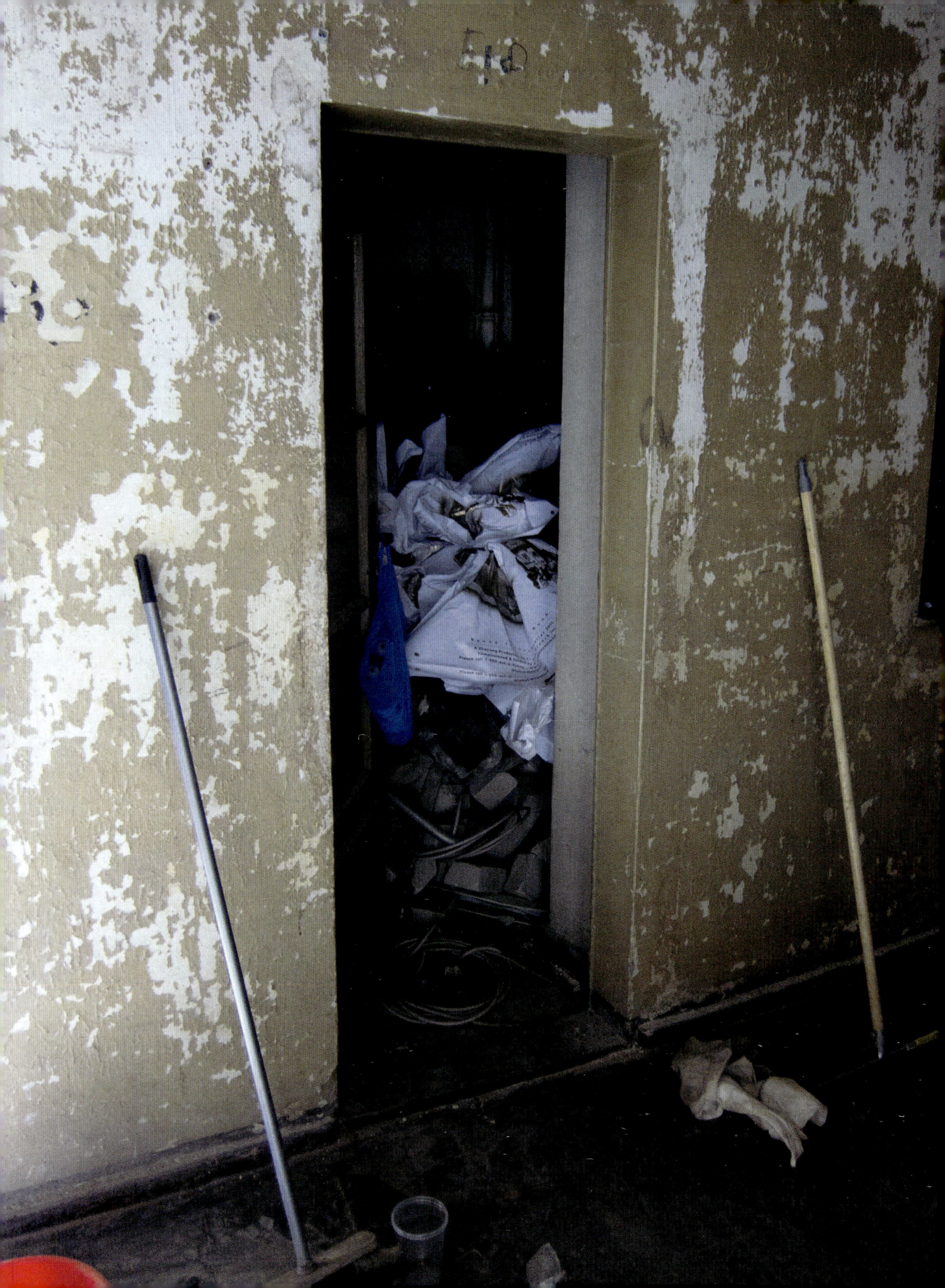

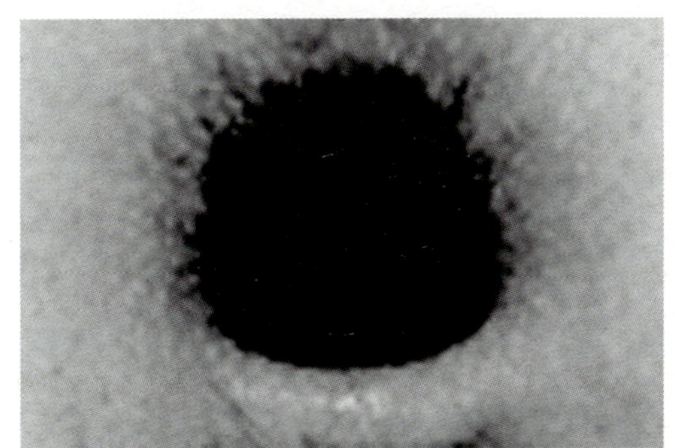

Hey Victor.

Just wondering, the money that I gave you to invest – is that the poster, or is there more coming? You mentioned Oct/Nov 2011.

See you soon,

xxx Anna

Anna Franck Inc
www.annafranckinc.com
Paris France

NOTAUSGANG

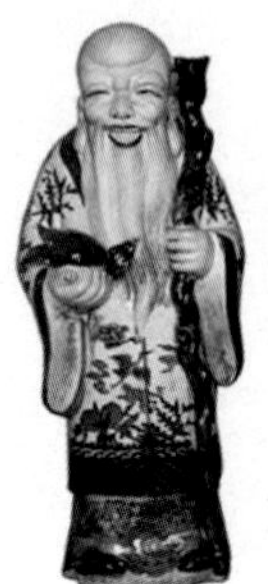

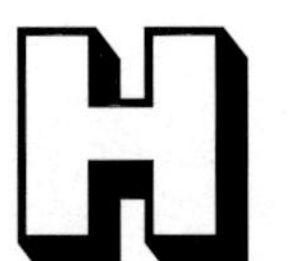
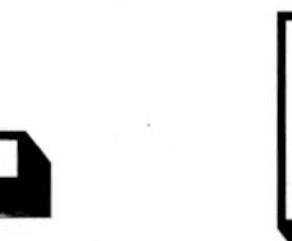
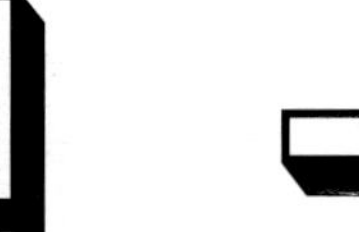
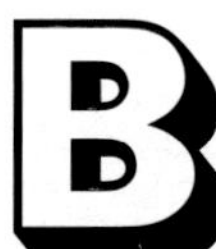

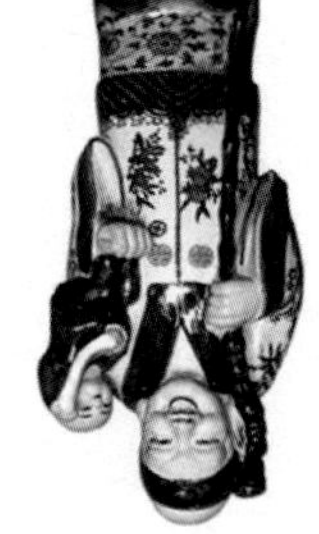

Pruning your Clematis
by Victor Boullet

"To prune or not to prune,"(6) is the most often asked question. It should be noted that incorrect pruning will never bring an early death to the clematis.(8) At worst an inappropriate pruning will only delay flowering. Furthermore, if all varieties were left unpruned they would all flower very well.(7) However, as is explained below, the flowers would not necessarily cover the plant as well as they otherwise could.(4)

One tip on pruning applies to all clematis varieties. The first February or March after planting all clematis should be cut back.(1) At this time, you should be able to see leaf buds developing as your plant breaks dormancy.(2) You should leave two sets of buds on each stem between where you make your cut and soil level.(10)

Planting Clematis on a Fence or Trellis

Made in China

Clematis needs something to climb on.(3) Sweet pea netting or plastic mesh work well. Carefully, but securely, attach vine to cane. Back fill with good quality top soil mixed with a handful of bone meal (if your soil has a high clay content add peat moss). The top of the root ball should be at least 15cm below ground level. Cover with 15cm of well rotted manure mixed with good top soil or compost.(9) Where practical it is a good idea to plant a small shrub to shade the roots of your clematis.(5)

footnotes:
1. Hear them stalking
2. The ultimate in vanity
3. Their money tips her scales again
4. Halls of justice painted green
5. Soon you will please their appetite
6. Rolls of red tape seal your lips
7. Pulling your strings
8. Exploiting their supremacy
9. Hidden deep animosity
10. Inquisition sinking you

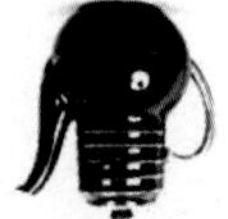

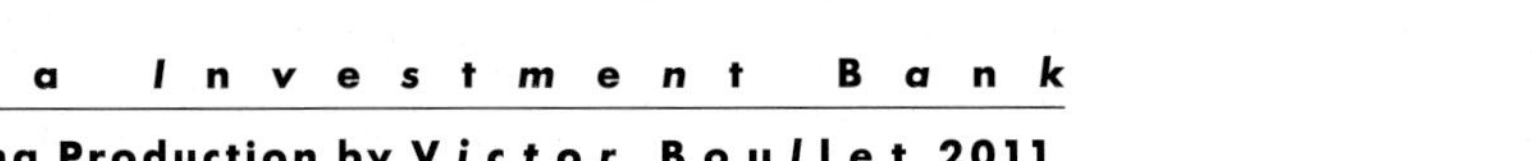

Hyena Investment Bank

A Zhejiang Production by Victor Boullet 2011

Commissioned & funded by Anna Franck Inc

Please call 1-800-ask-a-hyena – www.hyenainvestmentbank.com

Global Nepotism

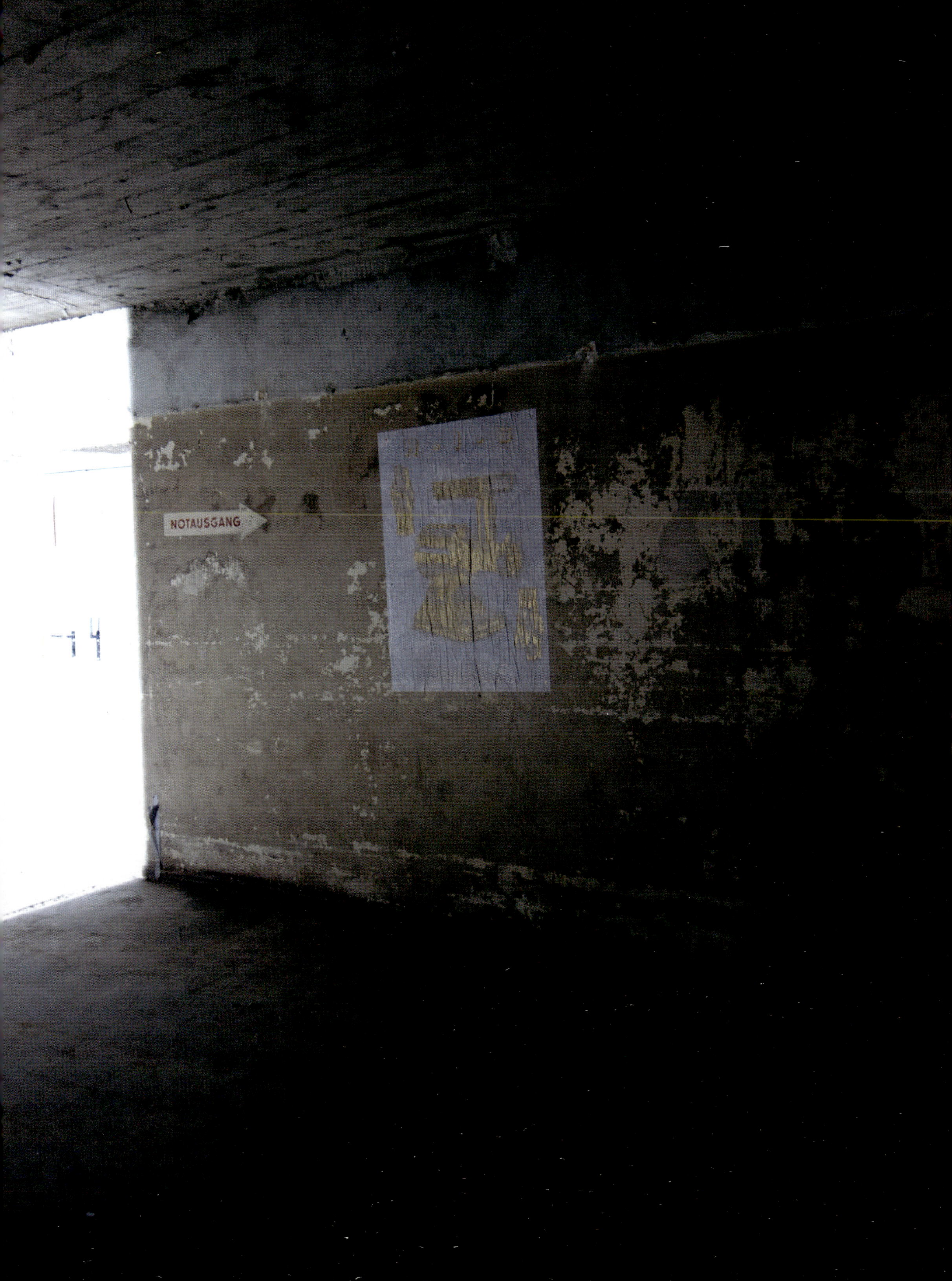
NOTAUSGANG

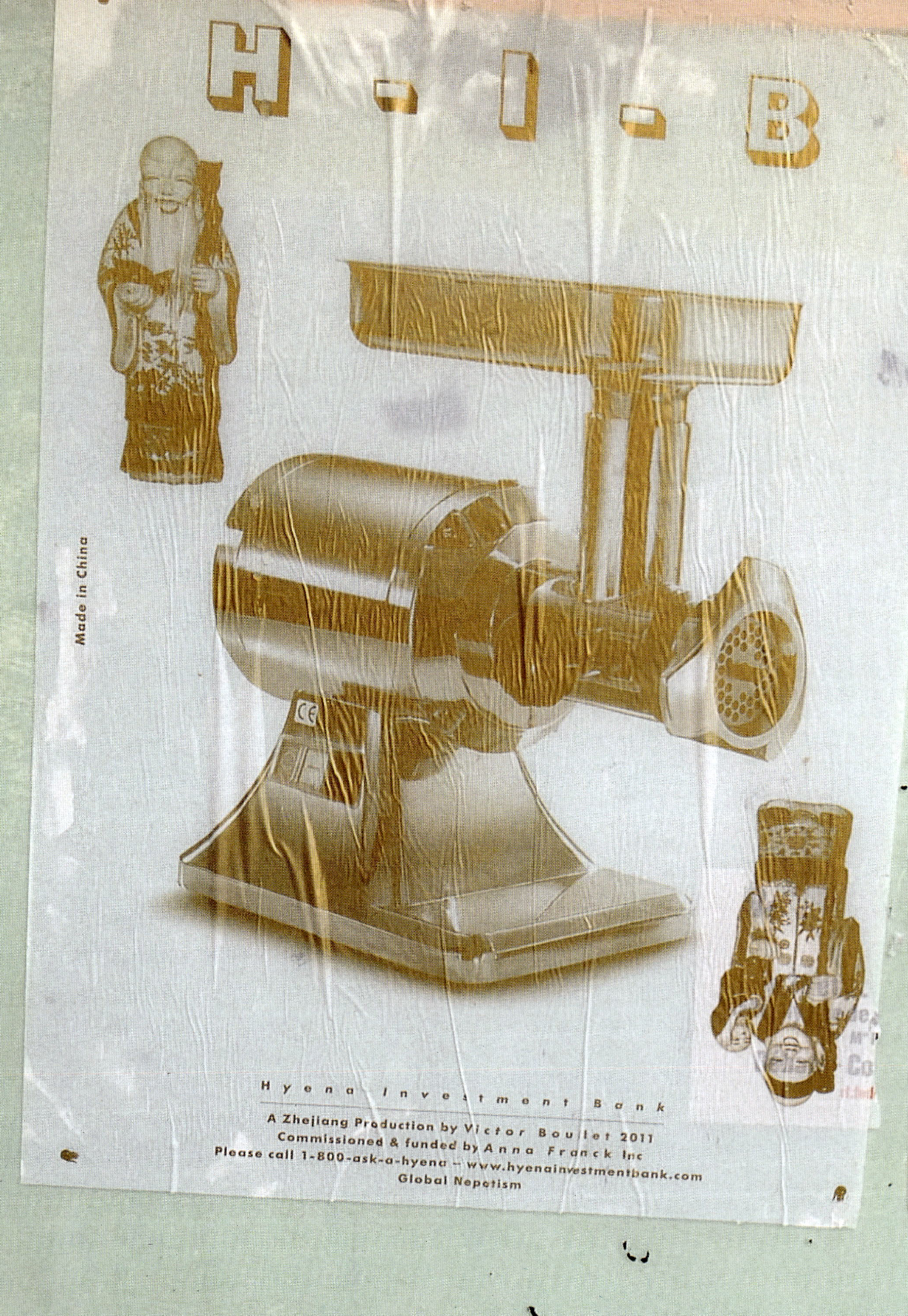
H - I - B
Made in China
Hyena Investment Bank
A Zhejiang Production by Victor Boulet 2011
Commissioned & funded by Anna Franck Inc
Please call 1-800-ask-a-hyena -- www.hyenainvestmentbank.com
Global Nepotism

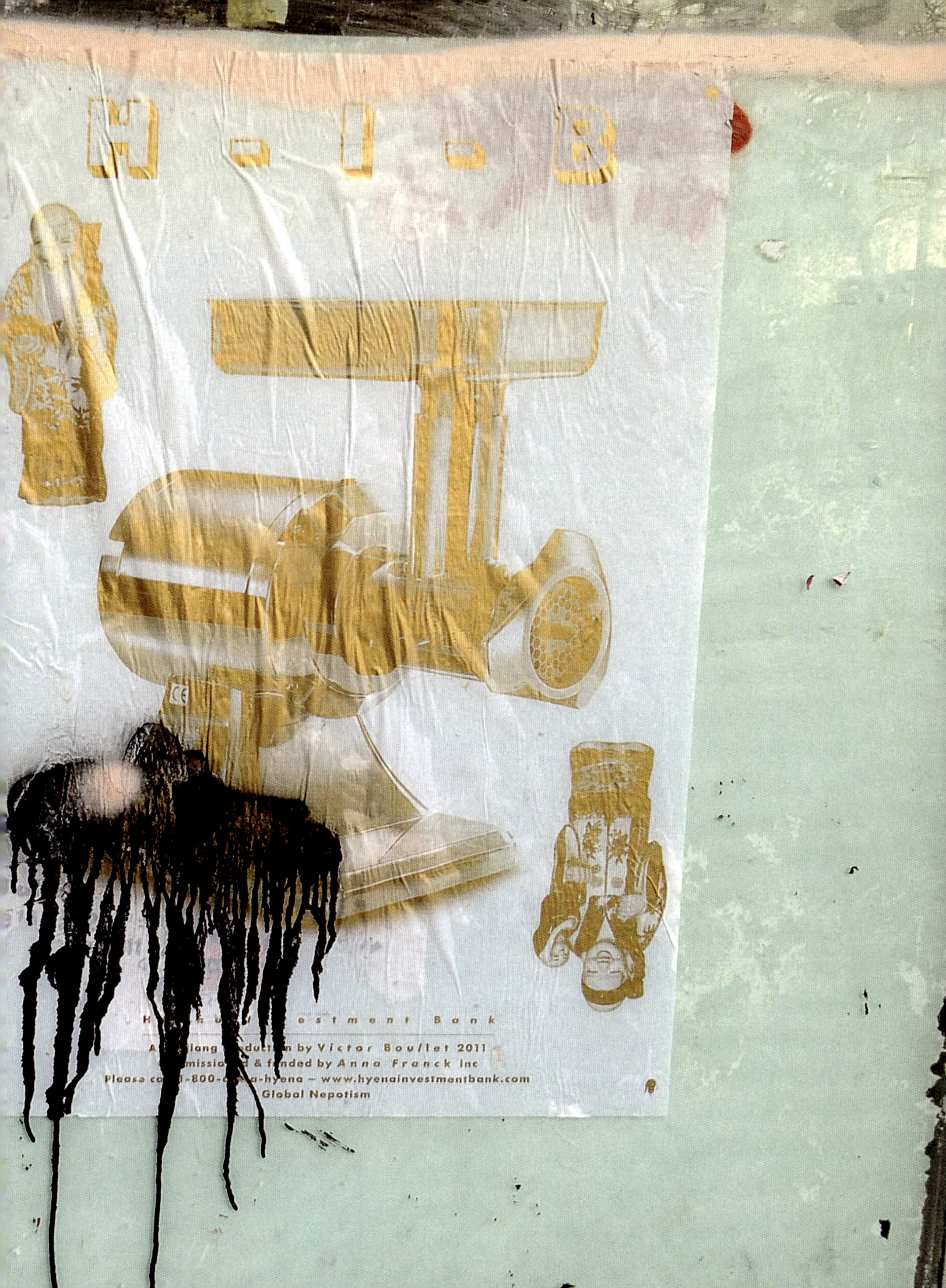
H - I - B
Bank
by Victor Boullet 2011
by Anna Franck Inc
www.hyenainvestmentbank.com
Global Nepotism

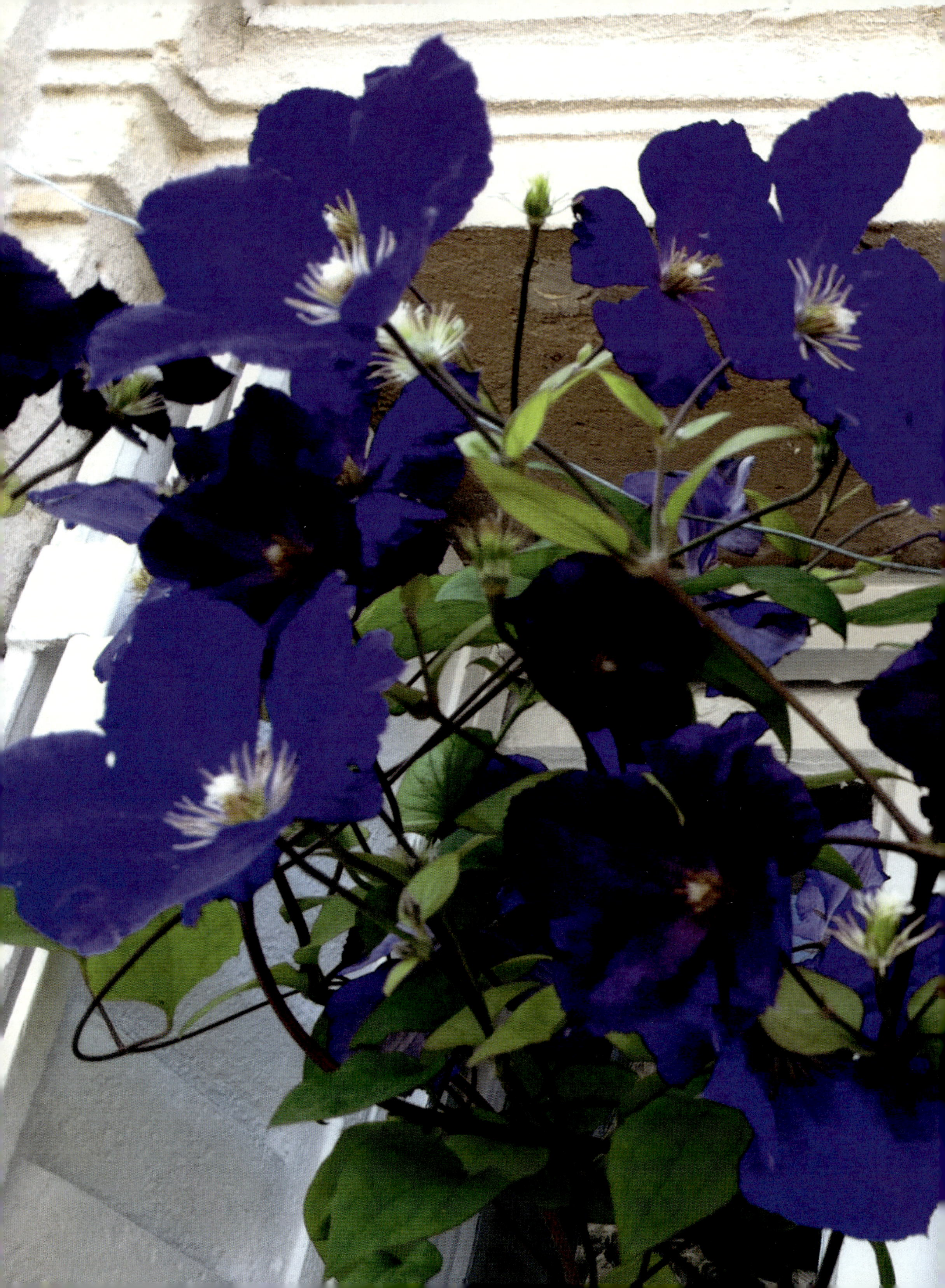

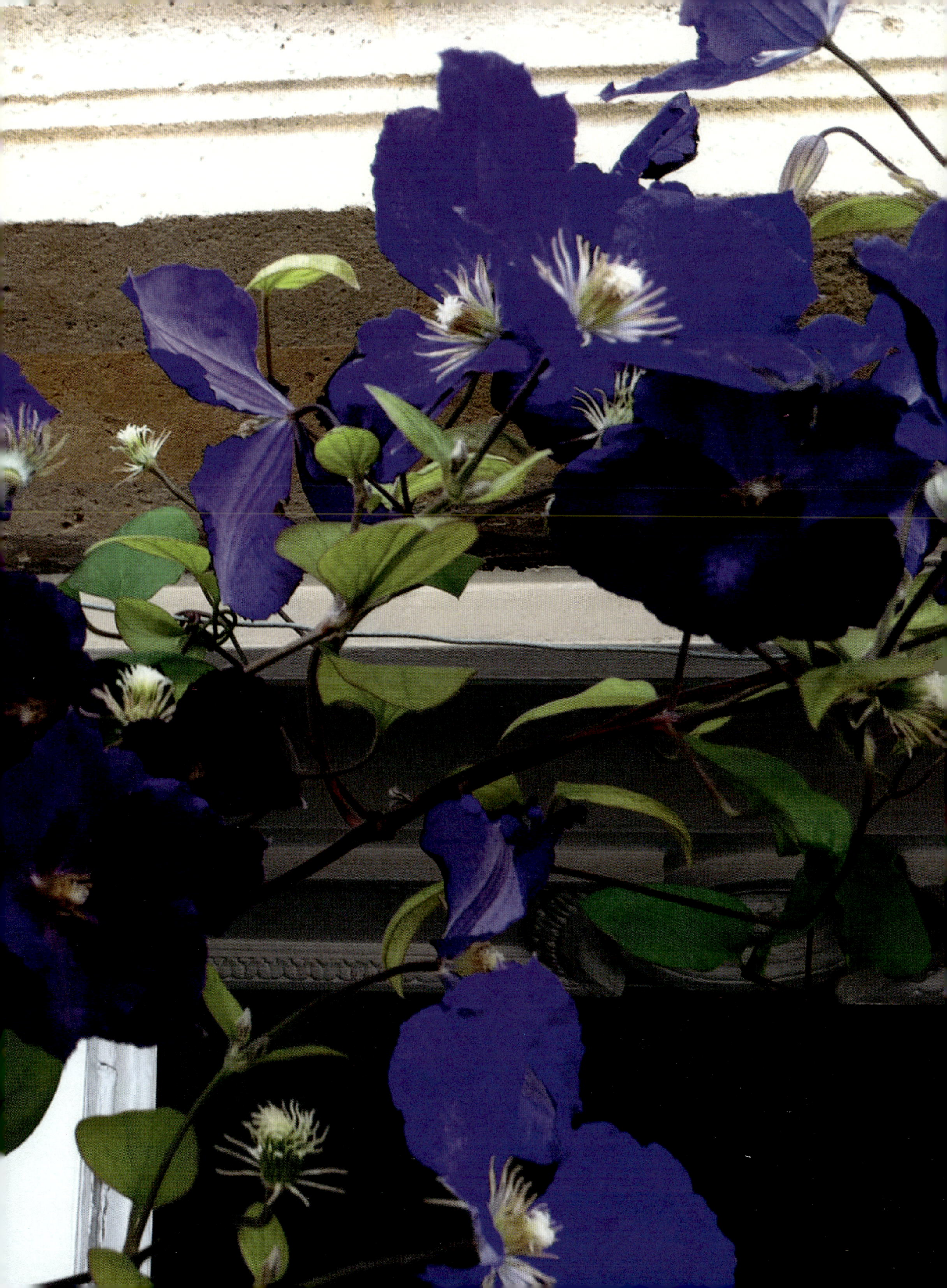

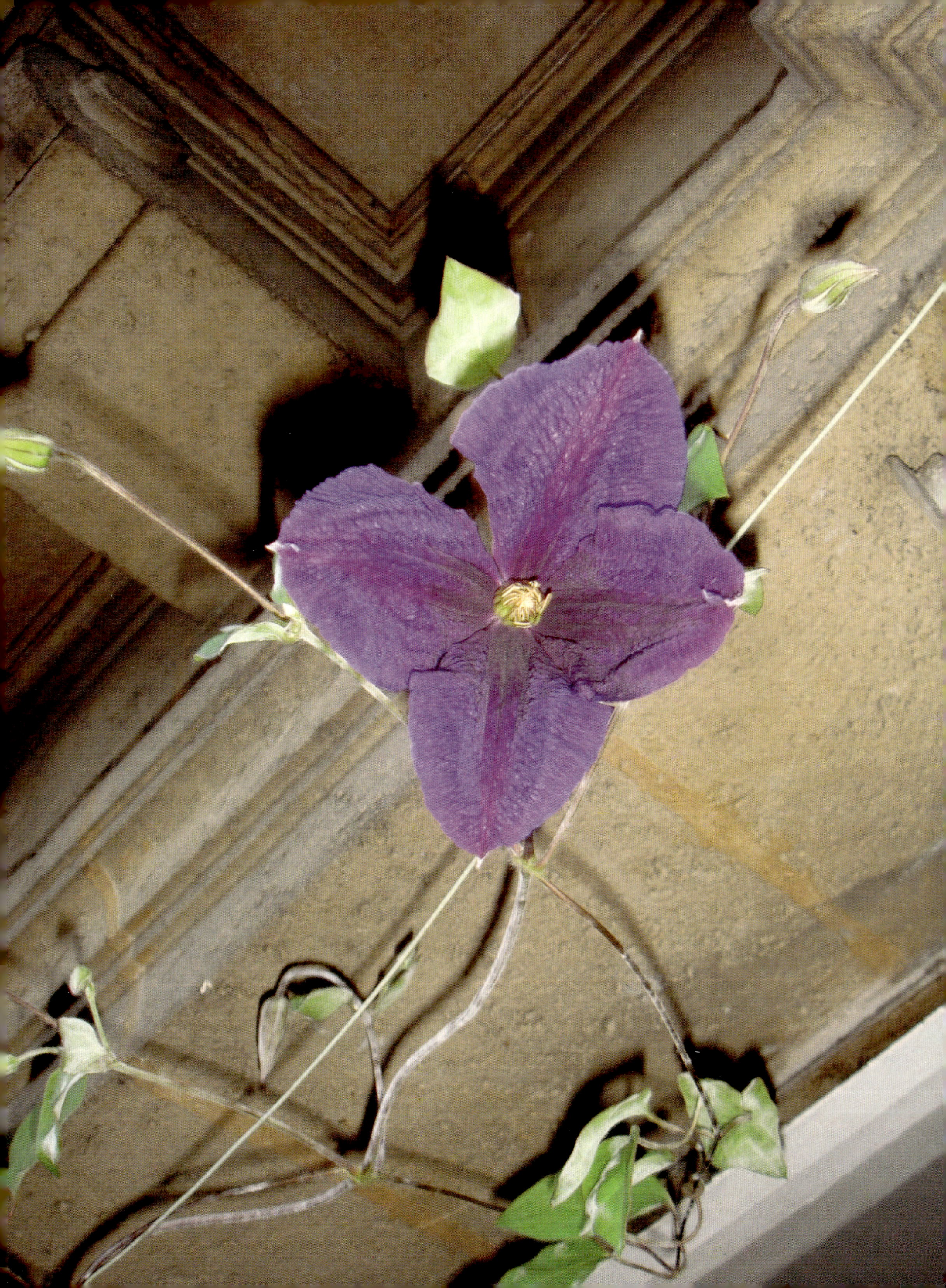

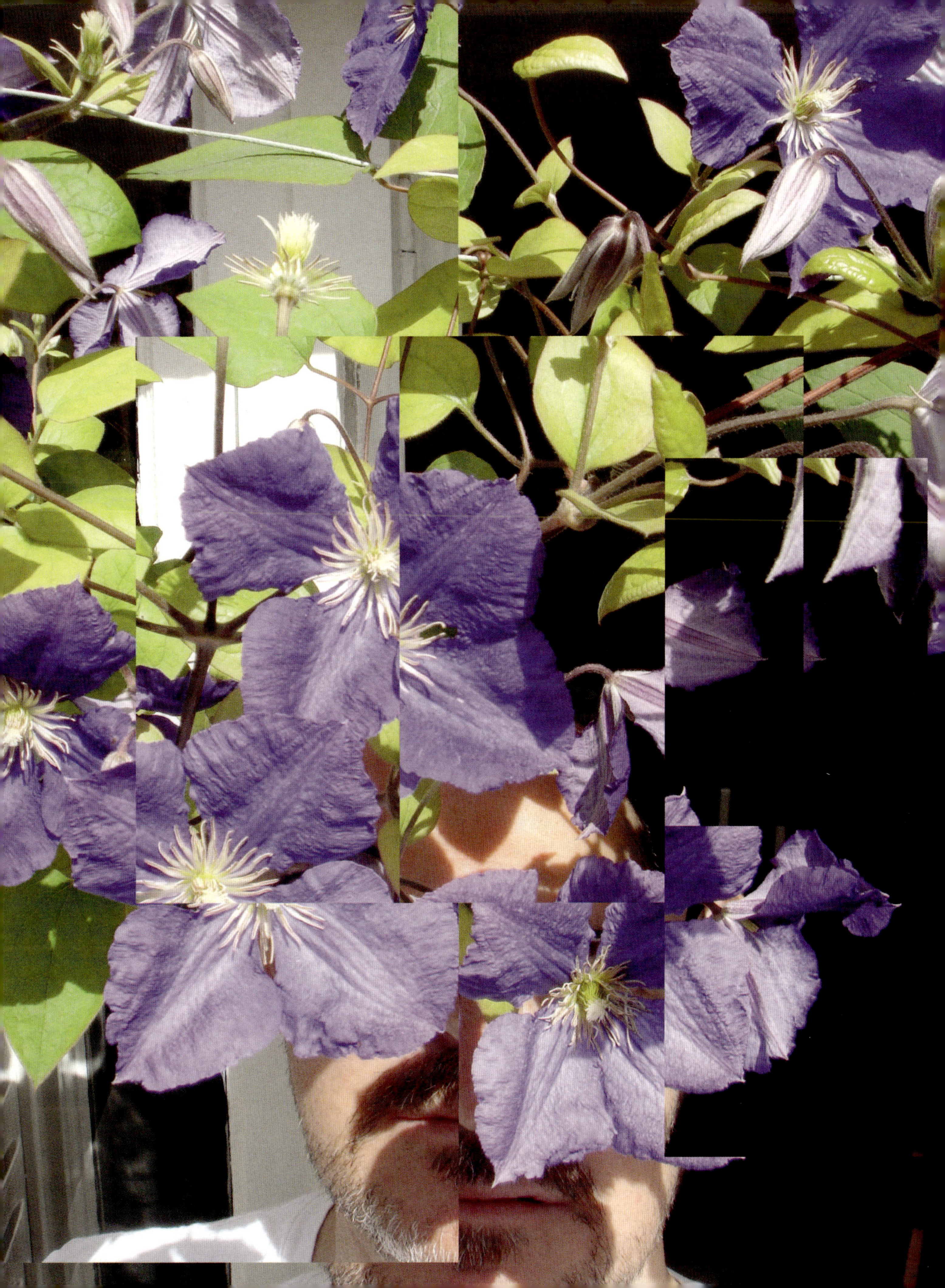

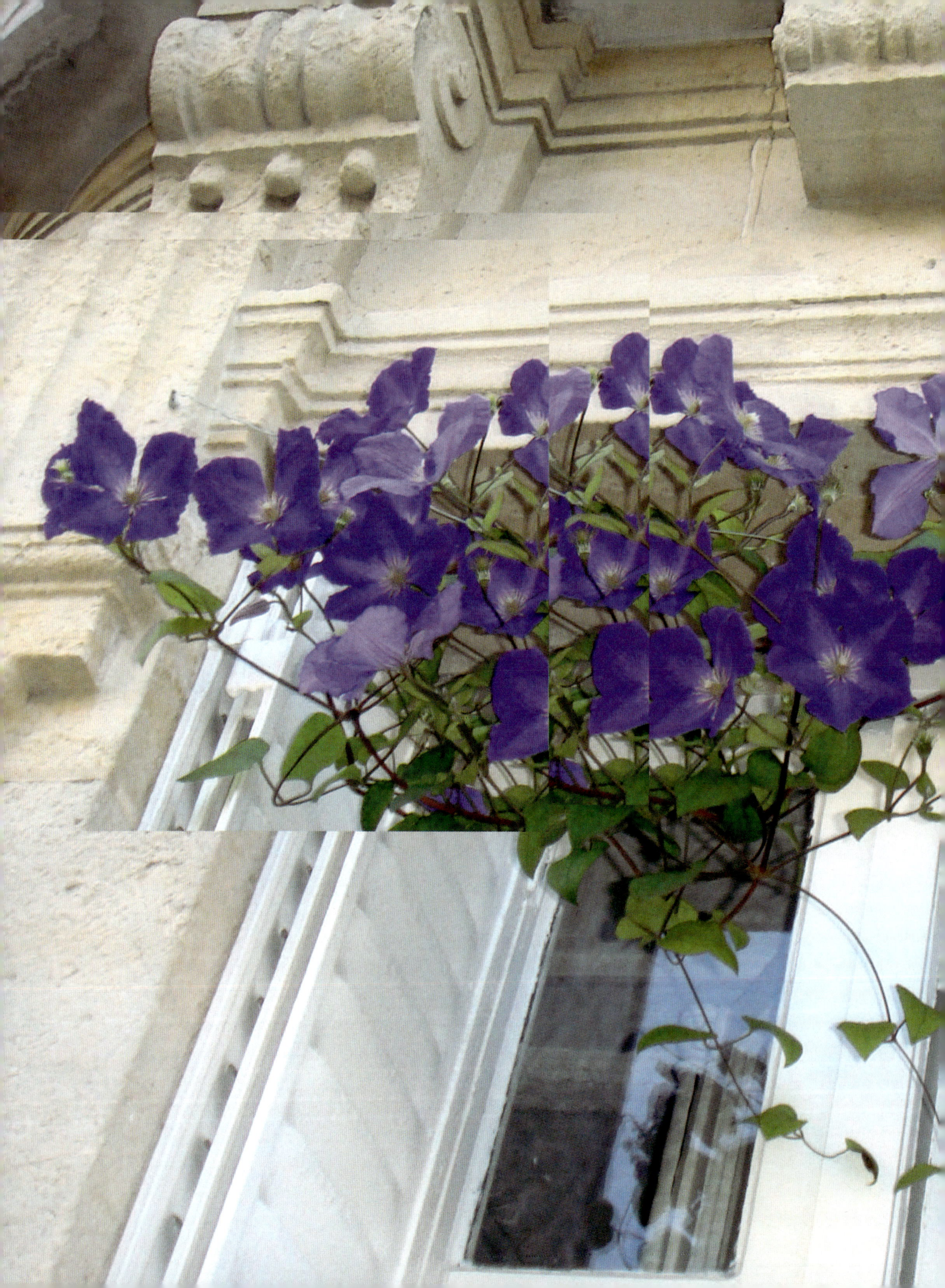

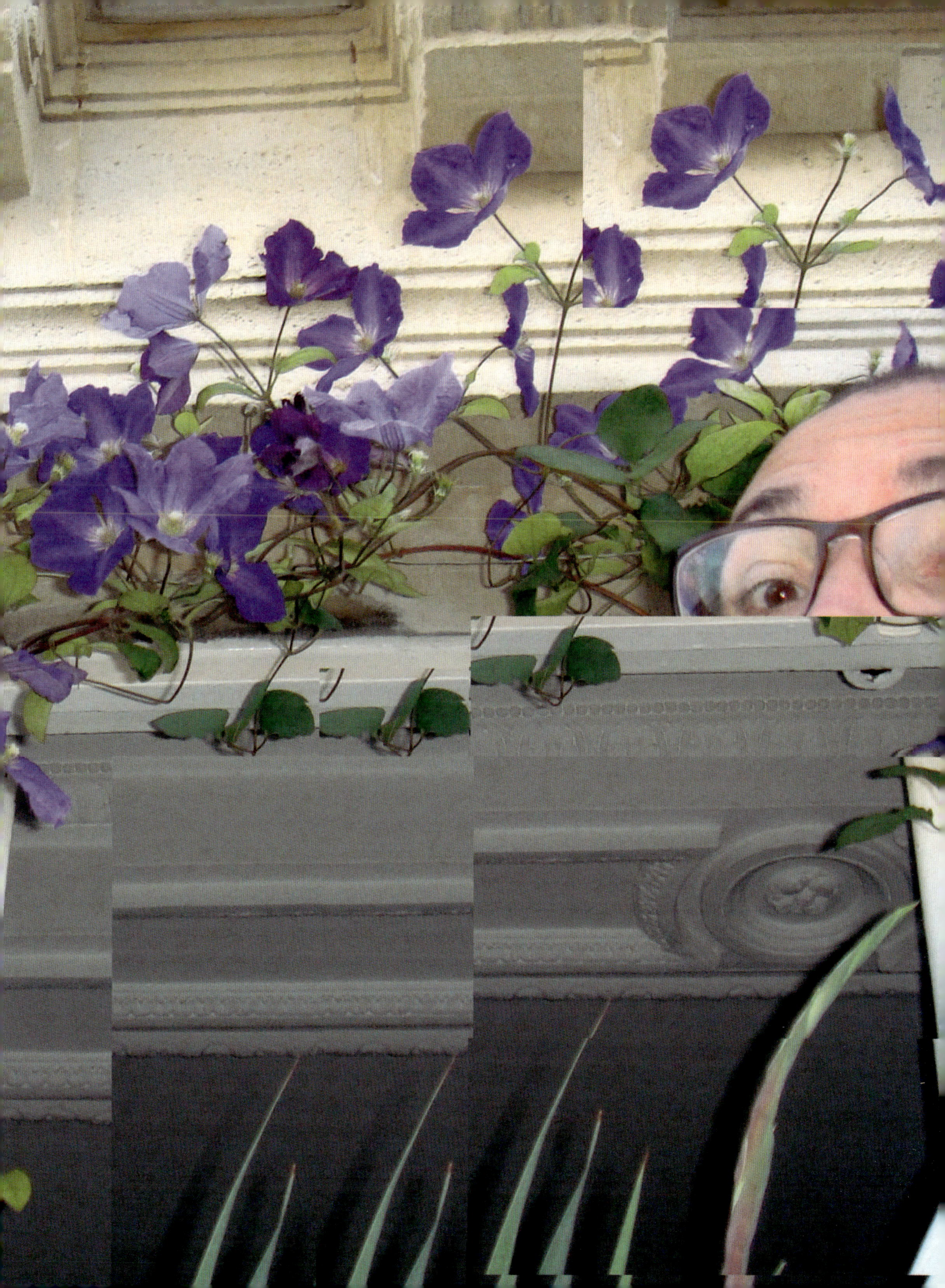

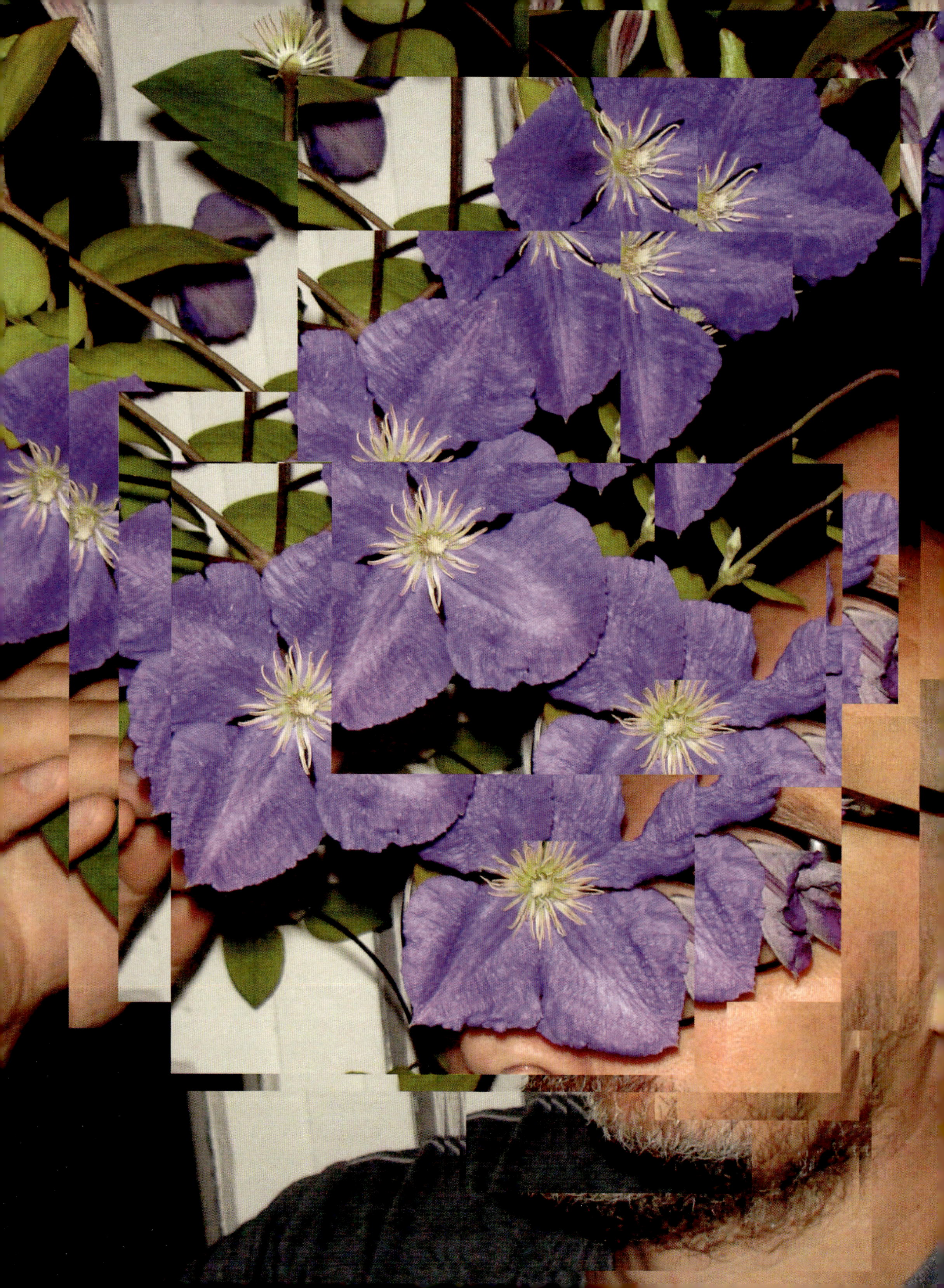

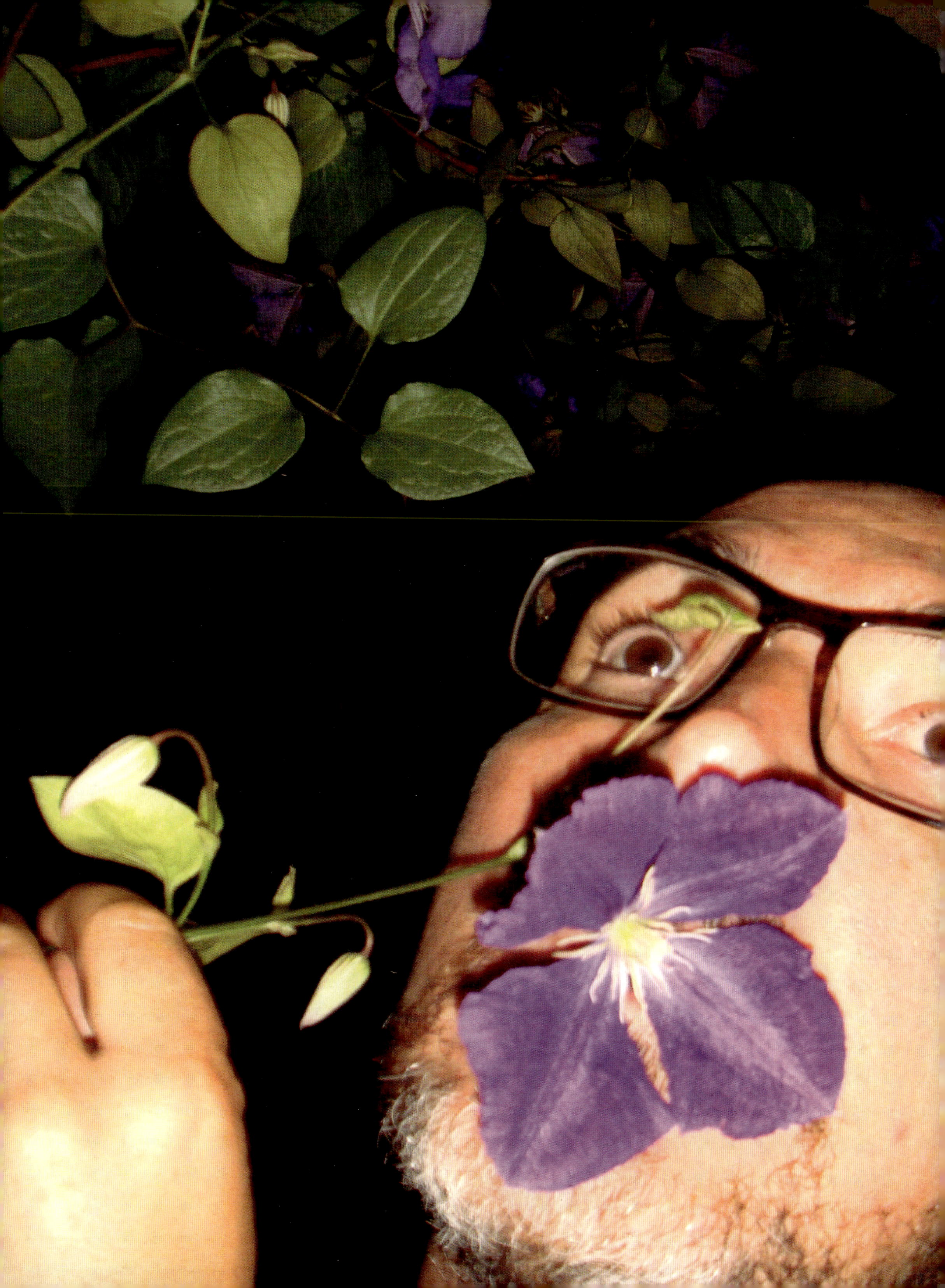

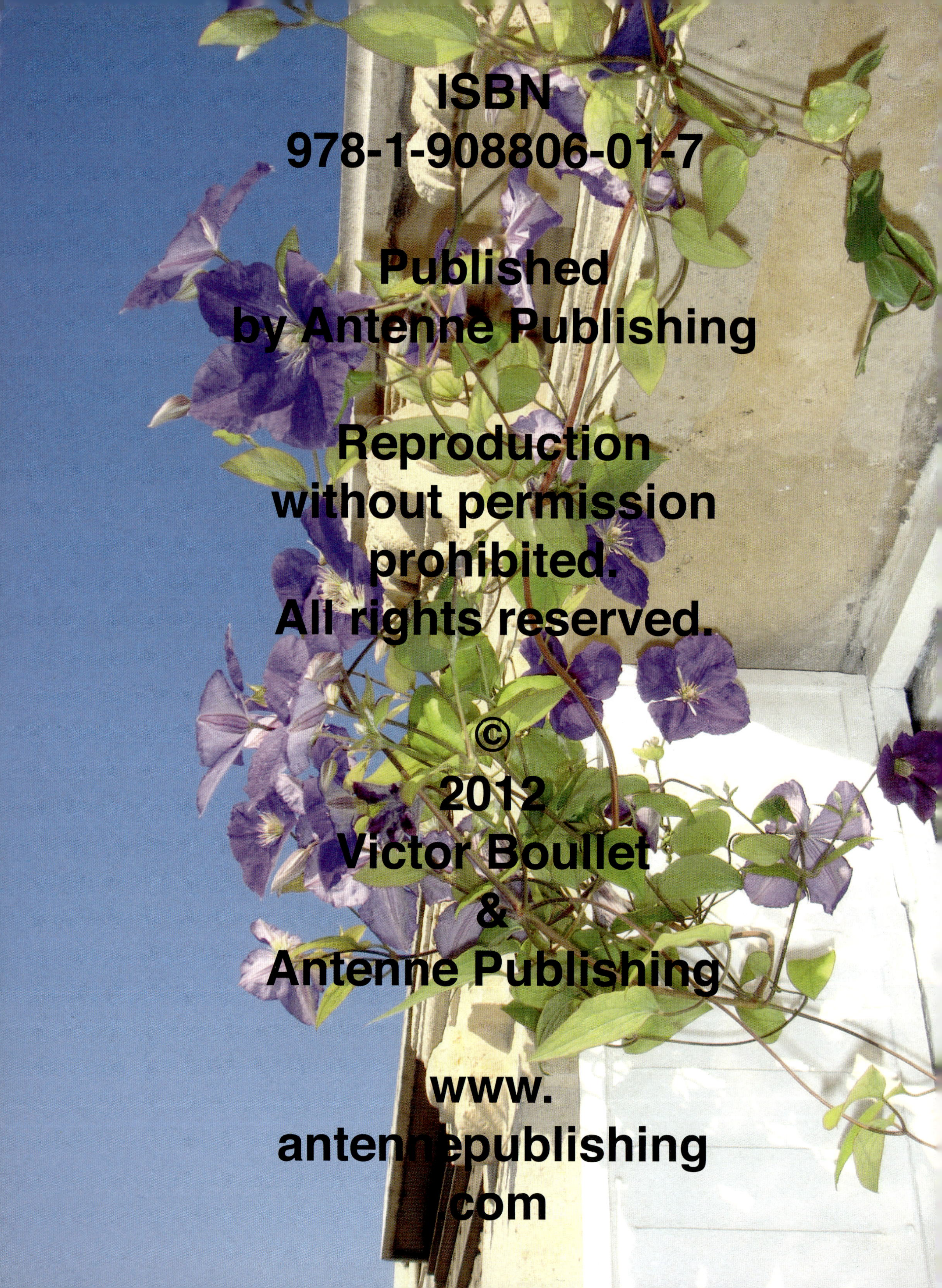

ISBN
978-1-908806-01-7

Published
by Antenne Publishing

www.
antennepublishing
com